Psychology Revivals

Gerr

CW01095245

Originally published in 1941, the blurb read: "The aim of this work is to state and understand the psychological dynamics of the present conflict. The author is a medical psychologist who has had unusual opportunities for studying German mentality. He characterizes the condition of Germany as one of dæmonic possession and Hitler as the primitive medicine-man who gained a magical ascendency by playing the role of medium to the German unconscious. He analyses the fundamental instability of the collective German psychology and relates this to the dæmonic outbreak. The ambiguous personality of the Führer is seen as the indispensable symbol of a deeply divided nation striving for unity. Whereas the pagan-Christian conflict in the soul of Christendom is urging individual consciousness to a new statement of human values, it has produced in the soul of Germany a state of collective intoxication which is the negation of individuality.

This book is the first serious attempt to depict the invisible underground causes of the European catastrophe and to state the issue in terms of epochal transition. It was German violence which started the conflagration, but the fires of anti-Christian revolt have long been smouldering in the general unconscious. Material of a varied kind, gathered from German myth and legend and from a number of contemporary witnesses has been pieced together into a comprehensive psychological survey, embracing both the personal and the impersonal aspects of the German scene. Hitler is discussed as personality, as symbol, and as a disease. The influence of the Wagnerian German myth upon Hitler's inflammable imagination is discussed and the basic ideas of Hitlerism are traced to their source.

This is the attempt of psychology to elucidate the irrational and unintelligible elements in the present chaos."

Germany Possessed

H.G. Baynes

Routledge
Taylor & Francis Group

LONDON AND NEW YORK

First published in 1941
by Jonathan Cape

This edition first published in 2016 by Routledge
2 Park Square, Milton Park, Abingdon, Oxon OX14 4RN

and by Routledge
711 Third Avenue, New York, NY 10017

Routledge is an imprint of the Taylor & Francis Group, an informa business

© 1941 H.G. Baynes

All rights reserved. No part of this book may be reprinted or reproduced or utilised in any form or by any electronic, mechanical, or other means, now known or hereafter invented, including photocopying and recording, or in any information storage or retrieval system, without permission in writing from the publishers.

Publisher's Note
The publisher has gone to great lengths to ensure the quality of this reprint but points out that some imperfections in the original copies may be apparent.

Disclaimer
The publisher has made every effort to trace copyright holders and welcomes correspondence from those they have been unable to contact.

A Library of Congress record exists under LCCN: a 41004313

ISBN: 978-1-138-69452-1 (hbk)
ISBN: 978-1-315-51697-4 (ebk)
ISBN: 978-1-138-69938-0 (pbk)

GERMANY
POSSESSED

by

H. G. BAYNES

With an introduction by
HERMANN RAUSCHNING

JONATHAN CAPE
THIRTY BEDFORD SQUARE
LONDON

FIRST PUBLISHED 1941

JONATHAN CAPE LTD.   30 BEDFORD SQUARE, LONDON
AND 91 WELLINGTON STREET WEST, TORONTO

PRINTED IN GREAT BRITAIN IN THE CITY OF OXFORD
AT THE ALDEN PRESS
PAPER MADE BY JOHN DICKINSON & CO. LTD.
BOUND BY A. W. BAIN & CO. LTD.

CONTENTS

5

CONTENTS

CONTENTS

CONTENTS

prophecy — Dynamic aspect of German unconscious
personified by Wotan myth — Wotan's monologue with
Brunhild — Hitler's identification with Siegfried —
Correspondence between Hitler's personal myth and
Wagner's version of racial myth — Hitler's horoscope —
Preponderance of perverted feminine elements in
Hitler's nature — Cruelty as a virtue — Hitler's ideal of
the *Herrenmensch* — The present struggle, a crisis of
transition — Hitler's psychological tie with his mother —
Mediumistic intuition discussed

CONTENTS

dependent upon acceptance of repressed shadow-
side — Dependence of Ideal upon scapegoat — Task
of psychological maturity — Masculine conception of
Deity, and cult of the Earth-mother — Nazi views on
rôle of woman — Over-valuation of masculine characteristics — Unconscious disciplined in relation to
woman — Meaning of reversed swastika — The Wandering Jew — Assimilation of essential quality of the
vanquished by the victor

ILLUSTRATIONS

INTRODUCTION

THE chief hindrance to a full understanding of the National Socialist phenomenon is the temptation to interpret the movement from a single angle. Some only see in Hitler the Nationalist, the agent of a reactionary movement, the protector of the propertied and old governing classes. Others see in him the leader, not of a social revolution, but of a wild revolution of destruction, supported by asocial elements. National Socialism has, to be sure, its political, its social and its economic causes. It is as much a consequence of the world economic crisis as of the Treaty of Versailles; it is an expression of German nationalism as well as the final result of Prussian militarism. But even all these factors cannot give an adequate understanding of the complex phenomenon. National Socialism has assimilated all these tendencies, and they have certainly intensified its explosive possibilities; yet although it has exploited them it is not identical with them. It is something more and springs from greater depths.

Perhaps we shall come nearer to its source if, in our survey of its general historical development, we consider National Socialism as the result of a complete ideological bewilderment, and its dynamism as a *Salto Mortale* towards affirmation of life, or movement for its own sake, or stark will to power. But even such a comprehensive approach would not provide us with a final understanding of National Socialism. It is true that, in the period after the war, the German people experienced a terrible upheaval and collapse. Every support was suddenly withdrawn, social, political, religious and moral. The nation was confronted with chaos, and was powerless to discover fresh elements of order within itself, while those recommended from without were already outworn or threadbare. But all these things do not sufficiently explain why the German people had to fall under the domination of such a movement as National Socialism. What changes were taking place in both the conscious and the unconscious? Were new social layers, different racial characters, emerging? Was the German type changing? Was there in process a mutation in the biological sense? Or were these phenomena of universal significance and Germany only a specific expression of a general situation into which Europe had fallen through the industrial revolution? Perhaps they should be viewed as an anticipation of the dissolution or self-destruction of civilization which must also eventually attack other industrialized nations.

Only a psychological analysis can provide an answer to this; an analysis of Hitler and the German people. Where else could we find the key to what is actually happening, and of the changes which begin to pervade our collective civilization? National Socialism must be regarded as both a symptom and motivating force of the profound crisis in our civilization. Only through recognizing that Germany is possessed, and through understanding the causes of this possession, will the perplexing causes of the war become clear.

This is the theme of the present work. Not only is it an essential complement to the literature on National Socialism, but it gives us the key to a real understanding. To characterize Germany and its Führer as possessed may strike one at first glance as a literary conceit. But in this work we have an experienced psychologist and doctor giving a deep analysis of the whole far-reaching problem of possession. The wealth of observation and penetrating clarity of judgment cannot, moreover, leave the politician wholly indifferent. For the author shows how the danger of self-destruction in Germany does not arise merely from the revolutionary dynamism of National Socialism, but also from the lack of effective opposition of conservative forces. This gives us a criterion which, through correcting and enlarging our former judgments, opens up an entirely new perspective. The author demonstrates the results which must ensue when, instead of thesis and antithesis standing freely opposed, one becomes forcibly suppressed by the other. They show, in a peculiarly effective way, the need for the healing mechanism of democracy, a boon which no other institution can provide. In this analysis the German partiality for organization assumes a symptomatic aspect indicating an underlying inferiority of instinct. The politician will readily agree with this illuminating criticism. Over-elaborate organization certainly constitutes a German weakness, a weakness that has hitherto been wrongly regarded as a strength. In the same way, German fanaticism is merely the over-compensation of a characteristic German defect arising from a dissociation between the planning intellect and the neglected instinct.

These are only a few examples. The results of such investigations are all the more valuable to the politician, inasmuch as analysis leads to diagnosis, and diagnosis to therapy. In this collaboration the doctor can indicate to the politician the possibilities of healing, not merely of the German possession, but also of the deeper affliction of our time. For behind the Hitler phenomenon and a possessed Germany lies something infinitely more far-reaching. The question arises whether Hitler is not himself the expression of the shadow-side of our whole civilization. Is not National Socialism, with its immediate success, a symptom of the great crisis of civilization — a crisis so deep and shattering that we are forced of necessity either to bring about a new synthesis of consciousness and instinct, or else to go under in a frightful clash of cosmic violence?

In no sense is Hitler the expression of conscious political and spiritual currents of Europe, neither is he of Germany. He is the symbol of the dark side of our civilizing experiment. He represents the flight from the tormenting tasks of civilization, the grotesque and dæmonic contradiction which runs through our life. Is there not in progress a new evolutionary phase of human development? On the one hand, there is a profusion of new possibilities for mankind; but on the other, there is a most disquieting decline of the spiritual *niveau*. Terrain long since conquered by human consciousness is lapsing back again into the realm of the unconscious. Like a terrifying menace, National Socialism here expresses a general feature of our time which aborts and embitters human achievement. Can man overcome this dangerous phase?

These are crucial questions. The Hitler phenomenon reveals the problem of accepting and assimilating the shadow-side of our civilization. We stand in the phase of transition between one world-epoch and the next. Humanity is undergoing a spiritual migration as General Smuts has called it. Right in our path lies the problem of spiritual maturity. Before we can solve this problem, we must, so the author tells us, regain those primitive warrior virtues inherent in the old conception of *amor fati*. From these there issues a deeply renewing effect, but an effect which entails the conclusion that nations less spiritually imperilled than Germany must be frightened out of their sense of security and self-confidence before they can hear the call to maturity.

Germany, on the other hand, who is living out her worst qualities in National Socialism, will (by analogy with therapeutic experience) thereby gain the possibility of healing. In her suicidal possession Germany thus accomplishes, though unwittingly, the greatest contribution to a new world; inasmuch as the struggle against National Socialism assumes thereby the value of a general healing of the crisis of civilization. Military weapons are clearly not enough to settle this issue. The essence of this war is the spiritual and psychological issue, not merely in order to counter Hitler's subtle methods of destruction; but because in the last resort, a possessed nation can be conquered only by itself, by a break-up from within. This investigation, therefore, opens up a wide and fruitful vista wherein a new human attitude begins to emerge, made strong and deep, and matured through conflict.

H. RAUSCHNING

London
May 30th, 1941

PREFACE

In psychological matters misunderstanding can be averted if, at the outset, one's angle of approach can be frankly stated. Let me explain at once, therefore, that I have called my book *Germany Possessed* because I see Germany enfolded in a terrible dream, with Hitler, the medicine man of the German unconscious, bent on realizing this power-dream in concrete form. From this standpoint, Germany appears like a colossal somnambulist carrying out machine-like activities and overcoming every obstacle, as though compelled by an unconscious will. As an organism, therefore, Germany is behaving like a man possessed. Hitler's complete belief in himself and his mission is reinforced by the magician's logic, that what he has actually achieved would be inconceivable without divine or magical support. The impossible has indeed happened. The little Austrian outcast has surpassed even the dream of the Holy Roman Empire.

Thus we are forced to accept the fact that we are living in a world-dream, in which the forces engaged have the authentic mythological character. This work is an attempt to interpret the dream. It is important that Germany's dream-state should be recognized, because an enlightened handling of German psychology is indispensable for a wise establishment of a new world-order.

So long as Germany is enfolded in her myth of the Superior Nordic Race, the effect upon the German people is very similar to a state of intoxication. It is a collective madness, a state which is essentially alien to her normal civilized mentality.

Before Germany can be brought back again into the European family she must be cured of her intoxication. We have watched her paranoidal delusion develop its fated course: the violent snapping of co-operative relationship with the Western Christian Powers at Geneva, the development of the idea of encirclement, the increasing atmosphere of hostility and suspicion, breaking out into envenomed hatred against one immediate neighbour after another, the long-prepared and secret preparations and, finally, the characteristic murderous outbreak. But since the

15

concept of paranoia belongs to psychiatry, it can be fittingly applied only to the individual case. It is better, then, to speak of Germany's state as a mythological madness which affects people from the unconscious 'like unto a great wind'. Accordingly, I have made use of Wotan as an explanatory hypothesis.

Fanatics, sleep-walkers, or hypnotized persons are not accessible to reason or argument, because their consciousness is limited to the dream-state. They are, therefore, protected from the ordinary stresses of adaptation by a serene unconsciousness of everything beyond the limited system which possesses them. They are able to act effectively within this system, because they do not realize what they are doing. Germany is living an evil dream that has been disturbing the peace of the world in one way or another for more than half a century. The dream has its root in early Teuton paganism. Therefore it had to be lived savagely. One day she will awake and see what the dream made her do. That will be her hell.

Because Germany is possessed by an archaic mythological state we must also envisage the situation in terms of primitive psychology. Hitler is the great medicine man who, before he makes a raid upon any of his weaker neighbours, performs magic in order to ensure that he has 'stronger medicine' than the enemy. The enormous prestige of the medicine man in primitive communities rests primarily upon his professional capacity to enlist the aid of spiritual powers (ancestor spirits) in times of need. The nations of Europe have obviously been bewildered by Hitler's primitive, amoral methods. His apparent belief in his own 'divine' gifts lends him an arrogant air of certainty which has had a paralysing effect upon suggestible minds. His loudly heralded programme of victory hypnotized both his own people and the nations he planned to conquer. He has used every kind of primitive trick to bemuse and confound judgment, and his technique has succeeded only because psychological knowledge is still regarded as irrelevant to the conduct of affairs. Consequently, the historian of the future will be forced to conclude that European statesmanship was for a time completely fooled by a man with the irrational mentality and methods of a primitive magician.

Hitler is not a product of the public school code. He has

not been shaped by civilized principles. He is neither a Christian nor a gentleman. His education is small and leaky, and he relies upon no dynastic tradition. His story is that of an outcast who came back and seized the machinery of power at the right moment.

This, in brief, is the standpoint of this work. I do not claim more for this viewpoint than that it is indispensable for the understanding of many strange features of the present situation. But it might also be contended that, in no aspect of our war equipment were we more unprepared than in the region of psychological strategy. Fortunately, however, the enemy is precluded by the pathological limitations of his outlook from understanding the motives of a people differing essentially from his own. It is therefore possible for us to enlighten our native sagacity by a psychological examination of our quasi-primitive foe, while at the same time learning how to take advantage of our enemy's vulnerable spot. So deeply has Hitler injected fear into every cranny of our ordered and pacific life, that he may be said to symbolize the problem of insecurity in everybody's unconscious.

I am grateful to Dr. Rauschning, a distinguished representative of German conservatism, for his foreword to my book. As a symbol of post-war relatedness, this collaboration of spirit seems already to belong to the new order. I am also much beholden to him for his invaluable published comments upon Nazi Germany and for his observations on Hitler's character and behaviour.

I owe a debt of gratitude to Mr. Rex Littleboy, to Miss Ina Jephson and to my wife for their heroic labours in the arduous work of revision. I have also to make acknowledgment to Messrs. Thornton Butterworth Ltd. for permission to quote extensively from Dr. Rauschning's *Hitler Speaks*, and to Messrs. William Heinemann Ltd. in respect to the same auther's *Germany's Revolution of Destruction*. I am indebted to Messrs. Jarrolds Ltd. for permission to quote passages and to reproduce the portrait of Hitler from Ludecke's *I Knew Hitler*, to Messrs. Constable & Co. Ltd. for the passages from Konrad Heiden's *Hitler: A Biography*, to Messrs. James Nisbet & Co. Ltd. for the citations from Wickham Steed's *Hitler, Whence and Whither?*, to Messrs.

PREFACE

Kegan Paul & Co. Ltd. for those from *Richard Wagner's Prose Writings*, and from Oesterreich's *Possession Demoniacal and Other*, to Messrs. Luzac & Co. for permission to quote from Dr. Campbell Thompson's *The Epic of Gilgamish*, and to Messrs. Baillière, Tindall & Cox for allowing me to reproduce a schizophrenic drawing and two quotations from my work *Mythology of the Soul*.

H. G. Baynes

Reed House
West Byfleet

GERMANY POSSESSED

CHAPTER I

ADOLF HITLER
PERSONAL AND DÆMONIC

I

WITH the individual problem, psychology is needed when a man comes to the end of his tether. In other fields psychology comes into its own when other means prove inadequate. Political science, economics, diplomacy, and that cynical state-opportunism known as *Realpolitik*, have all made an attempt to explain the grim confusion of the present state of affairs. But certain questions in the minds of calm, sensible people remain unanswered, and it is these insistent, residual questions which psychology must be called upon to answer:

1. How, for instance, did Adolf Hitler, a fundamentally illegitimate personality, unsupported by dynastic tradition, adequate education, or political inheritance, come to be dictator of modern Germany?
2. How is it possible for the German to be, on the one hand, obedient, domesticated, law-abiding and reasonable and, on the other, capable of wholesale and even sadistic cruelty?
3. Can we regard the Hitler phenomenon as purely German, or could a similar catastrophe overtake the British people?

Questions such as these, which are only too liable to be answered with prejudiced heat, demand just that detached consideration of the mind proper to psychological thinking. Because it is fitted to ask questions which were hitherto unanswerable, psychology has already expanded the scope of the human mind. Psychological medicine, including psycho-analysis, has grown in response to the question: 'Why is this person sick?' In like manner, medical science began with the question: 'What manner of sickness is this?' and reaped an abundant harvest by observing the various pathological processes which its question eventually disclosed.

The average mind is soon discouraged from asking questions to which no intelligible answer is available. The mind of the

21

true philosopher or scientific investigator, however, reveals itself in the tenacity with which it points a rapier-like question at the heart of nature, holding the mind steadfast to its quest, until an answer has been given. But since the answers to our questions lie in the darkest regions of the soul, our scientific quest must attune itself to Kant's humane definition of understanding: 'the realization of a thing to the measure which is sufficient for our purpose'.

When Freud observed how his hysterical patients persisted in telling him their dreams, and how talking about them seemed to improve matters, he asked the question: 'What do dreams actually signify?' This led him to inquire into the kind of mental process which produced the dream, and from this followed the discovery of the so-called unconscious mind. Thus a whole aspect of nature was revealed, which had previously been carefully camouflaged by such face-saving conceptions as accident, coincidence, fate, Providence, acts of God, and so forth. Darwin's conceptions and the growth of natural science had enormously extended the possibility of insight, so that the scientific mind of the West was beginning to be ripe for this discovery towards the end of last century.

At about the same time, and independently of Freud, Jung was observing certain irregularities in word-association tests carried out with patients as a routine procedure at the state mental hospital in Zürich. At the places indicated by these irregular reactions he looked, as it were, through the crack and asked himself the question: 'Why does this person have difficulty at this particular word?' In this way he came upon the buried complex, when he immediately recognized that same factor of repression which Freud had already described in his work with hysterical patients.

Since those days a great deal has been discovered about the unconscious. We now know that it is not unconscious in the sense that it lacks consciousness, but that its contents exist in a state of relative dissociation from ordinary waking consciousness. What we call consciousness is simply the habitual standpoint of our waking mind, just as the land, as opposed to the sea, is the normal base to which we feel we belong.

We cannot attempt to understand Hitler as a phenomenon

without some understanding of the nature of the unconscious, inasmuch as his psychology, being that of a medium, is related more to potential conditions in the unconscious than to the actual world of reality. It is as though he were equipped not only to perceive the hidden forces or tendencies of the unconscious, but also to be conditioned by them, as the wire is conditioned by the electric current which it conducts. But we must be careful what we say about mediums in general, because the portrait varies a great deal according to the degree of consciousness of the individual concerned. There are many intuitive people who can become mediumistic in regard to the unconscious situation, yet who never fall into the hysterical, possessed state which is generally characteristic of the primitive type of medium. This primitive type is, of course, that of the *shaman* or medicine man, whose prodigious prestige among his savage tribesmen rests upon his capacity for surrendering himself to, and becoming possessed by, the unconscious. The shamanistic frenzy, the wild state attained by the dervish in the dervish dance, the hysterical transports of religious revivalists and similarly induced conditions of fanatical excitement, the oratorical intoxication of the demagogue, the orgiastic frenzy of the Dionysian worshipper of antiquity — all these are forms in which the state of being possessed by the unconscious is deliberately cultivated on magico-religious grounds. Throughout antiquity and amongst practically all primitive races, this capacity for being possessed and transported by the unconscious endows the individual in question with *mana* or magical prestige. Such prestige has always rested upon exactly the same grounds as that of Hitler's in modern Germany; the individual possessed is believed to voice the will of heaven. Among savage peoples this usually means the voice of the ancestor spirits. The state of possession, therefore, is the means by which the spirit of the great, all-wise ancestor is enabled to break through from the spirit world and control events in the real.[1]

A mind accustomed to think of the unconscious in the orthodox Freudian sense, as a depository of personal refuse which accumulates from infancy onwards, may be confused, at first, by this

[1] It is probable that the ἱερόςγάμος of the antique mysteries, like the sacred coitus in the Shakti worship of India, was conceived as an act of religious piety whereby the goddess was enabled to come into the realm of the flesh, and realize herself.

conception of the unconscious as an ancestral heirloom. A conservative fish that has spent its whole existence within the confines of a small pool in a mountain stream will naturally conceive the universe in terms of the contents of its pool, unless or until it ventures down the stream and experiences the depths and terrors of the world beyond. In a word, the personal unconscious is the first and immediate psychic envelope in which we are contained. But the impersonal, or racial unconscious is the timeless psychical matrix which contains everyone, and by virtue of which the whole historical past is present as the living background of each individual psychology. The savage mind ignores the small fish, the little personal dreams that flit about the dimly lit channels of his subconscious world. But the impressive commanding dream, the 'doctor dream', immediately seizes hold of his mind. He takes it to the headman, who at once calls a palaver to discuss what it is saying.

Since earliest time the immense importance given to dreams and dream interpretation, to divination and augury, has been related to the absolute significance universally attached to revelation. This is due to the world-wide primitive belief that dreams and visions are directly communicated by wise ancestral spirits. In primitive life culture is a stream flowing from the ancestors to posterity; not through universities, museums, and libraries, but through tradition and custom and that ancestral voice which sometimes pierces the thin veil of sleep. I have known cases in which a shaman has been commanded to take up his cultural vocation by an ancestral spirit which appeared to him in a dream or vision. This image teaches him the things he has to know, and even speaks through his mouth during the shaman trance.

To sum up, when mediumship is defined as a function of the unconscious, we refer not merely to the superficial levels of the personal unconscious, but more especially to that generalized tribal, racial, or ancestral background of the mind which Jung has called the collective unconscious.

2

Upon this general psychological background it is now possible to indicate the main source of Hitler's power and to sketch in some relevant personal features.

It is not easy to get at the truth of Hitler's origins and early life. The official account is meagre and obviously arranged. Moreover, as in every totalitarian régime where only an expedient rendering of facts is forthcoming, a whole swarm of unofficial 'inside' sources of information press their own especial claim for credence. On the whole, Konrad Heiden's biography of Hitler is accepted as being the most reliable.

According to this account, Hitler was born on April 20th, 1889, at Braunau in Austria.[1] His father, who was the illegitimate son of a miller called Hiedler, was known for the greater part of his life by the name of Alois Schicklgruber; Schicklgruber being the name of his unmarried mother. Hitler's father was large and was said to resemble Marshal Hindenburg; a factor which may have had important consequences in the Führer's subsequent attitude to the aged president. Schicklgruber was first a shoemaker's apprentice and later a customs official.

Adolf Hitler was born of Schicklgruber's third marriage with a young woman, Klara Poelzl, and it was about this time that Schicklgruber changed his interesting and curious name to Hitler. Possibly he disliked his name. But it is psychologically significant that, in making the change, he reverted to the matrilineal pattern of kinship. For Hitler was the name of Klara Poelzl's mother. Thus Hitler's father performed an unconscious act of submission to the matrilineal principle. According to this principle, the main channel from the ancestors to posterity flows through the mother and, therefore, all familial responsibility, all possessions, and the general cultural heritage, including the name, are passed on through· her. The father is little more than a permanent guest in the mother's house. Hitler's father may also have been attracted to this name because of its similarity with that of his own putative father, Johann Hiedler the miller.

Another account which has wide currency, especially in Austria, is that Hitler's father was a wealthy Viennese Jew and that Schicklgruber, a mean and ungentle petty official, was attracted to Klara Poelzl more by the handsome 'consideration' which she brought with her as a dowry than by any kindling of the heart.

[1] Since part of the main argument of this study relies upon the fact that Hitler is a natural medium, it is certainly an interesting coincidence that the Schneider brothers, both notorious mediums, were also natives of Braunau. I make no attempt to explain this fact.

This account also has it that Schicklgruber treated his wife very badly and that Adolf came to hate him, not only for the mean way in which he would bring up the circumstances of his birth but also for his physically brutal treatment of his mother. Terrible quarrels between the parents resulted. It is easy to see how the idea of rescuing his young mother from the tyranny of this aged alien who masqueraded as his father could have developed in the son's mind.

In submitting this account of Hitler's personal myth by the side of the orthodox version I make no special claim for its factual truth. I give it because it supplies psychological verisimilitude for the main outline of Hitler's psychology. The other account does not. Even if the facts are proved to be different, this account will still retain its psychological validity as a myth, inasmuch as it certainly corresponds with the essential psychological situation. The spirit of resentment and venomous hatred which shows so plainly in *Mein Kampf*, and is the dynamic mainspring of his whole career, must surely have had its root in Hitler's personal history. We also know on his own testimony that, at a very early age, he decided to become an artist, in direct opposition to Schicklgruber's intention to make him pass his state examinations and enter the Austrian customs service. This desire to be an artist appeared at too early an age to have originated from his independent experience of himself and his powers. It has much more the character of a mother's secret wish for her son and, in so far as it led to a direct revolt against Schicklgruber's plan for him, it would seem to confirm the idea that the mother exploited the boy in the secret struggle of wills between the parents. Hitler could easily have acquired his feminine taste for intrigue in this early atmosphere of manœuvring for position.

More illuminating still is the insight, furnished by this myth, into Hitler's insane anti-Semitism and his passionate hatred of Austria. On this latter score Dr. Rauschning's[1] personal testimony reveals that Hitler's attitude towards Austria was regarded as insane even by his own generals. He records how in 1934 he approached General Blomberg with the idea of persuading the

[1] Dr. Rauschning is a former President of the Danzig Senate. As a member of the East Prussian land-owning class he joined the Nazi party in 1931 and was chosen by Hitler to bring the Free City into line. Irreconcilable difference of view as to Nazi methods led to his resignation.

Führer to accept mediation 'on the lines of securing Austrian consent to a common foreign policy with Germany ... General Blomberg gave me this unforgettable reply ... "I have a sort of Jester's freedom to say anything I like to the Führer. But I shall never dream of saying anything to him about Austria, and I strongly advise you to steer clear of the matter. It is being decided by the Führer alone. *It is a point on which he is not quite sane.*" '[1]

Now, according to this second account, which came to me directly from Austrian sources, it is said that after Hitler's parents had died, and while he was living in Vienna, a penniless outcast without education or apprenticeship to a craft, he tried to get some support from his wealthy father. He was turned away empty-handed. A scene is described in which his fellow-outcasts followed him to the great house and sat outside waiting for him to come out, either to participate in the father's bounty, or to pour ridicule on their fellow-outcast's discomfiture. When it is found that the twin roots of Hitler's hatred, his one consuming passion, can be traced back to his rejection by his two fathers, the one an Austrian official, the other a Jew, his intense resentment against his fatherland and his anti-Semitism become almost intelligible.

Hitler, we know, spent five years in a brooding, possessive, idle dependence upon his mother after Schicklgruber's death. The underground forces which seem to have moulded his psychology in those early years were, on the one hand, the bitter hatred of his young mother for the narrow-minded and brutal father, and, on the other, a correspondingly intimate and passionate bond between mother and son. Here we find the emotional groundwork of Hitler's fanatical psychology; his bitter revolutionary feeling against everything the father stood for, the world of safe, conservative respectability and the whole established order of society, as well as his need to be surrounded and supported by women, who invariably adopted a maternally protective or flattering rôle in relation to him. His effeminate partiality for *Milchspeise*, cream-buns and all kinds of 'soft' foods and drinks, not to mention sentimental attitude in matters of musical and artistic taste — all these factors would favour the hypothesis of a strong emotional identity with a young mother whose passionateness had turned against

[1] HERMANN RAUSCHNING, *Germany's Revolution of Destruction*, p. 153.

the father, and fell accordingly in enervating showers upon the son.

At this point I should like to clear away possible misunderstanding by explaining the significance of the myth, when it is employed, as above, as the most feasible hypothesis. In making use of this unauthorized version of Hitler's origin, for example, there is no intention of discrediting our subject by making him the illegitimate offspring of a Jew. If this account is not eventually confirmed by history, it would not affect the psychological fact that this myth of Hitler's origin was required and produced by the popular mind. A myth is never a mere record of historical events. Rather is it an emotional explanation of impressive occurrences. When Jung refers to Wotan, for instance, as offering the best possible hypothesis with which to account for the present German intoxication, he takes the mythical figure as personifying an actual state of possession which, from time to time through the centuries, has overcome the Germanic peoples. Wotan is not something which a poet has arbitrarily contrived; he is the repeated experience of a dæmonic spiritual factor which, as we know to our cost, is liable to have the overwhelming effect of a cosmic disaster. The character of Wotan in the myth is, therefore, derived immediately from experience. If the experience had been different the figure of Wotan would also be different.

Adolf Hitler has already become, to a certain extent, a mythological figure, in so far as he has attracted to himself from the German racial unconscious a profusion of mythological characters, which we shall presently discuss. Furthermore, it is in his mythological capacity, and not as a person, that he is likely to have historical significance. [1]

The desire to establish the historicity of the actual life of Jesus is, at bottom, an intellectual response to the current tendency to value cold fact as belonging to a higher order than emotional verities. From the moment the actual man Jesus became identified with, and enfolded by, the mythical Messiah, the human personality became transfigured and took on the mythic lineaments of divinity. The intellectual attempt to discredit this process of transfiguration because of a scientific infatuation with cold fact

[1] Recently, for instance, the *Voelkischer Beobachter*, having first mysticized Hitler as an immanent, watchful spirit, says 'when his name is sounded, history is swallowed up; for he has gathered all German history in himself. He is the soul of Germany made flesh.'

28

is responsible for a very great deal of our essential stupidity in regard to psychological realities.

Already the historical truth about Hitler's origin has become inaccessible. The official version, as given in niggardly doses in *Mein Kampf* and in authorized Nazi biographies, is psychologically incredible. Whatever fateful elements combined to produce this criminal genius they were surely not mixed within the uncracked crucible of Austrian *petit bourgeois* respectability. It is unfortunately impossible to authenticate the version I have given, though I know my source of information to be essentially trustworthy. We simply have to admit that the logic of psychical determinism requires an irregular familial pattern in Hitler's case. The split between the constructive and destructive elements in Hitler's nature points to an environmental complement, such as that provided by the radical incompatibility between a loved mother and a hated father. His passionate refusal to accept his putative father's ideas for his education, career, or way of life is also in favour of the Viennese version. When his real father, the Jew, also rejected him, he turned against Austria, his own fatherland, and eventually destroyed it with insane hatred. The familial pattern is also seen in the way his resentment against the land he had rejected nourished his fanatical devotion to Germany. Then again his intuitive flair for the essentials of big issues is hardly a quality that would arise spontaneously from an intact Schicklgruber background. His taste for lavish interior decoration, for handsome furniture and rare things, and, above all, his amazing political opportunism, all point to the Jewish in preference to the Schicklgruber parentage.

All the weight of internal, psychological evidence lies, therefore, in favour of the account given above, and on these grounds I find it reasonable to make use of it in this study. It is, in fact, the only account I know of which is able to carry the staggering contradiction of Hitler's moral make-up without foundering under the dead weight of improbability.

Hitler's hatred of Austria and the Jews is bound up with the picture just presented. The reported repudiation by his real father when friendless in Vienna would, if true, have reinforced the hatred which already shrouded the paternal image. The father is the possessor, the dragon, that guards and possesses the treasure which, in the primordial modality of the myth, always refers to the mother. The mother is the treasure, hard to attain and ringed around by the incest-dread, personified by the father-dragon. Applying this primordial pattern, we see the infant Adolf precluded from possession of the mother by the Schicklgruber dragon, and rejected and cast into the outer darkness by the real father who was a Jew. By far the greater portion of the wealth and power of Austria was, at that time, in the hands of Jews, and they were also guilty of an unfeeling ostentation of wealth and luxury while half Vienna was starving. One can understand, therefore, how the mind of the boy saw the Jews as the worldly possessors who lay coiled about the wealth of his motherland. Thus the revolutionary spirit of resentment and destruction was aroused and, expanding in the limitless atmosphere of the unconscious myth, eventually filled his whole world. The effect of the mythic pattern would be to identify the German nation with the mother, and the two possessing nations, England and France, with the two fathers of his personal myth. The passion of resentment which arose from his rejection by the Academy School of Art and other places in Vienna was also reinforced from his own personal myth. In the mind of the child the world outside the confines of the home is traditionally bound up with the authority of the father. This being so, the degree in which the growing youth feels committed to the world and its claims is intimately dependent upon the child's original acceptance by the father. Moreover, the child who was not accepted by the father is lamed by a bitter sense of deprivation. He will always be liable to try and 'get his own back' on the world. There can be very little doubt that Hitler's hatred and resentment developed from this original vacuum in his childhood experience.

With all this passionate turmoil in the unconscious it is not surprising that Adolf Hitler found immediate release when he discovered Wagner's *Ring*. His longing for the mother found expression in the sister-bride, Sieglinde, rescued from the brutish husband Hunding by her lover-brother Siegmund. Still more rapturously could he identify himself with Siegfried, the fearless son of the outcast Sieglinde, the killer of the possessing father-dragon; the hero who gained the treasure and rescued the sleeping Brunhild, favourite daughter of Wotan, from the circle of fire.

According to the terms of the racial myth, Brunhild would be identified with the pagan spirit of Germany which had lain dormant since Wotan departed, now to be reawakened by the man fearless enough to grasp Nothung, the heroic sword. The reader will recall how this sword was thrust by Wotan into the living roof-tree of the house, whence it could be drawn only by the man fitted for the heroic deed. Siegfried reforged the blade which had been broken in Siegmund's clash with the god. Furthermore, Nothung is clearly the sword of revolution, because Siegfried's possession of the sword leads up to and, in a sense, synchronizes with the collapse of Walhalla, the home of the former gods.

3

Such are the grounds which make it hard to believe that Hitler's precipitous psychology could have sprung from the parcelled security of a petty official's household; whereas a Jewish strain in his make-up would certainly help to explain his uncanny shrewdness and his political flair. His illegitimate birth too would account for the uncontained, rebellious character of his whole mental action. Inasmuch as no limiting social framework sheltered and contained his childhood in an established form, it is in a sense logical that no restraining scruples have since deterred him from his Icarus-like dream of power. This type of outcast genius reveals, in nearly every case, if not actual illegitimacy, a pattern of changeling psychology that results from a fatal emotional deadlock in the parental relationship.

Thus, in choosing the most probable account of Hitler's origins, it is safer to be guided by the deep logic which controls psychological reality, than by the many specious attempts either to blacken or to whitewash the most hated and adored figure in Europe.

But although the biological facts are obscure there are certain biographical details which are beyond question. At the age of 18 he travelled to Vienna with a portfolio of ambitious drawings, on the strength of which he planned to begin his career as an artist. His drawings were rejected by the Academy School of Art. He was told that they 'proved unmistakably that he was not suited to be an artist'. Undaunted, he put his helm over a few points and steered his genius towards architecture. About this time his mother died and he was left friendless, penniless and with practically no education. Unwanted and undisciplined he soon drifted into the flood-water of casual labour and semi-vagrancy which abounded in pre-war Vienna. For three years he lived in a hostel, taking irregular meals at a soup-kitchen and finding occasional employment as a street-cleaner or house-painter.

The hostel in which Hitler lived housed the dregs, the human-rat population of Vienna. At times he was reduced to begging in the streets. Both among his fellow-outcasts in the hostel, and at the hands of wealthy passers-by — of whom one in every five was a Jew — Hitler doubtless found abundant cause to nourish his hatred of the Jews.

Not long before the outbreak of the war he left Vienna for Munich, where he maintained himself in various occupations allied to the building trade. With this background of misery and poverty we can understand how the war came to him as his one chance of deliverance. He writes in *Mein Kampf*:

> To myself the outbreak of war came as a redemption from the vexatious experiences of my youth. Even to this day, I am not ashamed to say that, in a transport of enthusiasm, I sank down upon my knees and thanked heaven out of the fullness of my heart for the favour of having been permitted to live in such a time (p. 145.)

Obscurity again conceals the precise form in which Hitler allowed his martial qualities to appear. It is even doubtful whether he ever reached the front line, though he received the Iron Cross, first class, and other distinctions for bravery. At one time he was orderly to a regimental staff. Then he served as mess-waiter in the officers' mess and, again, as a dispatch-runner. He was not popular among his fellow-soldiers: they could not stand his obsequiousness towards officers or men of higher rank. This attitude is still ludicrously manifest in the photograph of Hitler shaking hands with Hindenburg on receiving the office of Chancellor. In another picture we observe the embarrassed diffidence of the corporal, wearing a frock-coat and balancing a top-hat on his knees, sitting beside the great Field-Marshal in uniform. There is an indication in his expression of the despised inferior, as though the illegitimate, outcast Jew could not quite believe what had happened to him.

32

ADOLF HITLER, PERSONAL AND DÆMONIC

The fact that, with all his latent ambition, Hitler never rose above the rank of corporal is, to my mind, significant. Hitler has been presented to us as an unscrupulous gangster politician lusting for power. If this were the whole truth, the fact that he never got beyond the rank of corporal during four years of active service is quite unintelligible and psychologically contradictory.

Actually there is no excess of the crude male in Hitler's make-up. His longing for action and his cult of brutality derive from a constant struggle to overcompensate his habitual subjectivity and effeminacy. From the field of direct action, where sheer physical mettle is demanded, Hitler has always fled, and at times, incontinently. Outwardly he overplays the part of the overbearing male with jack-boots and whip, but within he has to wrestle with womanish fears. Like an amateur actor, fearful of being inaudible and invisible, he shouts and screams and gesticulates. But beneath this façade the outcast in him still wonders what it all means.

After the war he put his knowledge of the habits of the human rat to good purpose by becoming an *agent provocateur*, a spy in the pay of the military authorities who were determined to root out Communist agitation among the discharged soldiers in Munich. But Hitler went further than his employer intended. With Jewish shrewdness he sensed the possibility of winning the discontented unemployed, thereby gaining power over the revolutionary movement instead of suppressing it. He persuaded Ernst Röhm,[1] the officer under whom he worked, that his plan was feasible, and before long he had found his political feet with the discovery of his rhetorical powers. But it was not until he discovered the German Workers' Party that he became a full-fledged platform orator.

By the end of 1922, Hitler was a political force to be reckoned with. He developed simple effective formulas which, though only distantly connected with fact, produced an almost audible emotional vibration among his audience. He shouted the glorious news to his audience that they had not been defeated as they imagined. They had been stabbed in the back by Jews and Bolsheviks in the very moment of victory. Every one of his formulas was calculated to make his listeners feel that they had been

---

[1] This man became Hitler's trusted friend, a position which he paid for with his life on June 30th, 1934.

wronged and betrayed and that now they must stop at nothing to regain their rights. He would dash from one crowded meeting to the next in a great car, assuring an eager public that Germany had not really lost the war and that a great future was in store for them. He was not taken very seriously, but everyone came to his meetings to listen to the good news and to watch his amazing performance on the platform.

It is fortunately not essential to our purpose to follow Hitler's political development. This aspect of his life has been flood-lit from the beginning. Little of interest can be deduced about the man from his public utterances, which have the character of a performance staged solely for political effect.

4

Although in one sense Hitler is a phenomenon which dominates the world, as a human being he is almost non-existent. One searches the pages of *Mein Kampf* in vain for any expression of native personal feeling. An expressionless face works, effeminate white hands gesticulate, but nothing real is said. A stream of political emotions, intermingled with eddying torrents of resentment and hatred, beats against a paranoidal distortion of European history. For the German mind the book is doubtless a significant political tract, but for the world beyond it reads like the ultimatum of a lunatic.

Fortunately, however, we have an eye-witness who watched Hitler and his entourage with a trained and disciplined eye. Dr. Rauschning's book, *Hitler Speaks*, gives us what we failed to find in *Mein Kampf*, a portrait of the man himself. Here we get a picture of a man possessed and driven by the unconscious, a political orator who has cultivated his mediumistic powers for the purpose of intoxicating the mass-mind. We also see him, a prey to his own primitive magic, suffering lonely hours of terror.

And so we come to the dæmonic aspect of Hitler's psychology. The first citations from Dr. Rauschning's book depict the side of Hitler's nature that is turned away from men and human reality, and is in league with what the primitives call the spirit-world.

He loves solitary walks. The mountain forests intoxicate him. These walks are his divine service, his prayers. He watches the passing clouds, listens to the moisture dropping from the pines. *He hears voices.* I have met him when in this mood. He recognizes nobody then; he wants to be alone. There are times when he flies from human society.[1]

Amid the ecstasy of his speeches, or in his solitary walks in the mountains, he feels that he does possess this quality. (That of being the supreme magician.) But in the many vacant hours of lethargy he feels humiliated and weak. At such times he is irritated and unable to do or decide anything.[2]

Dr. Rauschning gives also memory impressions of talks in which Hitler unburdened himself of his inmost thoughts and ideas. On one of these occasions Hitler said:

In the subconscious the work goes on. It matures, sometimes it dies. Unless I have the inner incorruptible conviction: *this is the solution,* I do nothing. Not even if the whole party tried to drive me to action. I will not act; I will wait, no matter what happens. But if the voice speaks, then I know the time has come to act.[3]

Here we begin to get a glimpse of the shamanistic character of Hitler's power. His turning from the concrete to the spirit world[4] must not be judged as neurotic refusal — although in the second citation the neuropathic evidence is clear — since it is equally evident that traffic with the unconscious is Hitler's *métier*, his indispensable spiritual resource.

The following accounts of shamanism, by scientifically trained observers, present a parallel picture of the way in which possession by the spirits is cultivated in primitive societies for much the same magical ends. Although containing many points of difference, they none the less provide an indispensable clue for a deeper understanding of Hitler's psychology:

He who is to become a shaman begins to rage like a raving madman. He suddenly utters incoherent words, falls unconscious, runs through the forests, lives on the bark of trees, throws himself into fire and water, lays hold on weapons and wounds himself, in such wise that his family is obliged to keep

[1] Hermann Rauschning, *Hitler Speaks* (Thornton Butterworth Ltd.), p. 255.
[2] ibid., p. 219.　　[3] ibid., p. 181.
[4] The primitive spirit-world is for us the unconscious.

watch on him. By these signs it is recognized that he will become a shaman. An old shaman is then summoned to whom has been entrusted knowledge of the dwelling-places of such spirits as live in the air and under the earth. He teaches his pupil the various kinds of spirits and how they are invoked. Amongst the Yakuts the consecration of a shaman is accompanied by certain ceremonies: the old shaman leads his pupil up a high mountain or into the open fields, clothes him in shaman's robes, provides him with the tambourine and drumstick, places on his right nine pure youths, on his left nine pure maidens, then gives him his own robe and placing himself behind the new shaman makes him repeat certain words. *Before all else he commands that the candidate abjure God and all that is dear to him inasmuch as he promises to devote his whole life to the demon who will fulfil his requests.*[1]

This abjuring of God, in order to become wholly given up to the possessing demon, provides us with an answer to much that has defied explanation in Hitler's psychology. Indeed, the sentence I have italicized, with minor alterations, would supply all that is needed for his epitaph.

Another description of shamanism amongst the Altai given by Radloff is as follows:

The future shaman receives no preliminary instruction or teaching from his father, and does not prepare himself for the profession; the shamanistic power falls upon him suddenly, as a sickness grips the whole man. The individual, destined by the power of the ancestors to become a shaman, suddenly feels in his limbs a langour and lassitude which manifest themselves in violent trembling. He is seized with violent and unnatural yawning, feels a heavy weight upon his chest, is suddenly moved to utter inarticulate cries, is shaken by feverish shiverings, his eyes roll rapidly, he dashes forward and whirls round like one possessed until he collapses in sweat and rolls on the ground a prey to epileptic convulsions. His limbs are numbed, he seizes everything he can lay hands on to swallow it involuntarily . . . After a little while what he has swallowed comes out again dry and unchanged . . . All

[1] V. M. MIKHAILOWSKY. See *Transactions of the Russian Royal Society of Natural History, Anthropology and Ethnography*, 1892. English translation in *The Journal of the Anthropological Institute of Great Britain and Ireland*, vol. XXIV (1895), p. 85. (Quoted by T. K. OESTERREICH in *Possession Demoniacal and Other* (Kegan Paul, Trench, Trubner and Co.), p. 301.

these sufferings grow continuously worse until the individual, thus tormented, at length seizes the drum and begins to shamanize. Then, and then only, is nature appeased, the power of the ancestors has passed into him and he can now do no other, he must shamanize. If the man designed to be a shaman opposes the will of the predecessors and refuses to shamanize, he exposes himself to terrible afflictions which either end in the victim losing all his mental powers, becoming imbecile and dull, or else going raving mad and generally, after a short time, doing himself an injury, or dying in a fit.[1]

Rauschning's description of Hitler rolling on the floor, foaming at the mouth and uttering hoarse cries, not to mention his own confession of being carried along by an irresistible force, provides a pathological picture which accords in psychological essentials with the above account. In a subsequent citation from Dr. Rauschning we even find the psychic bodyguard of 'pure' youths.

Mikhailowsky emphasizes the pathological character of those who become shamans. They have, in fact, to go through a preparation of several years, constituting a thorough neuropathic training. Here are some details concerning the Buriat shamans:

The dead ancestors who were shamans customarily choose amongst their living descendants a boy who shall inherit their power. This child is recognized by several signs: he is often pensive, a lover of solitude, he has prophetic visions and is occasionally subject to fits during which he remains conscious. The Buriats believe that the child's soul is then amongst the spirits who teach him ... If he is to become a white shaman he goes to the abode of the spirits of the west, a black shaman to the spirits of the east. In the palaces of the gods the soul learns under the guidance of the dead shamans all the secrets of the shamanistic art; it impresses upon its memory the names of the gods, their abode, the forms with which they should be worshipped and the names of the spirits subject to the great gods. After undergoing trials the spirit returns to the body. Every year the mental tendencies are accentuated; the young man begins to have fits of ecstasy, dreams and swoons become more frequent. He sees spirits, leads a restless life, goes from village to village and tries to shamanize. In solitude he gives himself up whole-heartedly

[1] W. RADLOFF, *Aus Sibirien*. Lose Blätter aus dem Tagebuche eines reisenden Linguisten, vol. II (Leipzig, 1884), pp. 16 ff.

to shamanistic practices in no matter what place, forest or hillside, beside a blazing fire. He invokes the gods in a strange voice, shamanizes, and often falls senseless. His friends follow him at a certain distance and watch him to see that he takes no harm.[1]

With these first-hand descriptions we have an invaluable touchstone with which to test the principal hypothesis of this work, namely, that Hitler is a medium whose power over the German people rests upon the same primitive foundation as that of the shaman. When Hitler dramatizes his neuropathic tendencies, it is an instinctive performance done to impress the suggestible mass-psyche. At the primitive collective level — the level to which Germany has regressed — the man who has been singled out by the spirits to shamanize is immediately accepted as a man of unusual spiritual power.

I use the word spiritual here in the primitive sense, i.e. having to do with spirits. We can be almost certain that the original conception of the spirit, or of spiritual powers, was based upon the primordial experience of possession. The word comes from the Latin *spiritus*, breath; *spirare*, to breathe. The German word *Geist* and English 'ghost' both carry the meanings, soul or spirit as well as breath or blast. From ancient times *Geist* or *gast* (Old English) have had the meaning of a supernatural being. This primitive form also meant fury, anger; in a word, the state of possession by a spirit. The early Teutonic god Woden or Wotan is, for example, a wind or sky-deity. He is the *furor teutonicus*, which, of course, means nothing more nor less than a spiritual infection or intoxication. Thus, in its dynamic aspect, spirit means something very different from its ideal connotation. When, for instance, we speak of the guiding spirit or Holy Spirit, we no longer think of the primitive experience of possession from which these concepts have arisen; yet it cannot be denied that the only way in which man can actually experience the power of the spirit is through the seizure of his mind as by a *force majeure*. Whenever, therefore, we speak of spirit or god, we are referring ultimately to an object of immediate psychical experience, although something that cannot be concretely proved or rationally understood.

[1] loc. cit., p. 87.

38

When dealing with psychical factors it is irrelevant to apply to them criteria which are proper to a totally different 'sphere of reality. When we are told that a man hears voices, or has seen a spirit, or has been bewitched, it is useless to rationalize these things away as 'imaginary' or 'unreal'. If these things mean more than mere idle fantasy, they are definite facts of psychical experience which have to do with the existence of a mental complex which, at certain times, can exercise an overruling force. Because of the fact that personification is native to the unconscious or primordial psyche, either in the form of dream, fantasy, or hallucination, people habitually think of 'spirits' as personalities, albeit somewhat vague and tenuous.

No one could assert that Hitler is insane merely on the ground that he hears voices[1] and sees spirits. As we have just seen, these are not uncommon experiences on the primitive level. The question of sanity or insanity rests rather upon the subject's attitude to the experience, in other words, his degree of insight. Insanity is always a matter of behaviour. It is a mistake to assume that it rests on the nature of the experience. Anyone may experience the archaic contents of the unconscious and be temporarily carried away by violent, primitive affect, or even experience hallucinations. Yet relatively few people are driven insane by such experiences. They are able to ride the storm and assimilate the irrational event. Some, lacking the necessary elasticity of mind, may be lamed by the primeval affect which possessed them. Others are caught by the unconscious complex, like a swimmer caught by a whirlpool. They are fascinated by the archaic content which seems to galvanize them with primitive energy. They begin to feel as though they had been exalted for some hidden purpose, or inspired by the breath of God. These are usually the doomed ones. For when one loses the measure of one's common human stature and becomes identified with deity, sanity has already departed.

When we read between the lines of the apparently incomprehensible utterances of the insane we constantly come upon this basic theme: *I am God.* The belief may hide behind a variety

[1] There is, for example, the historical case of Joan of Arc. Although it must have been self-evident to a great number of Englishmen of her day that Joan was just a crazy peasant girl, the most conservative institution in the world has long since accounted her celestially sane and blessed.

of disguises such as: 'God moved me to say this', 'God spoke to me', 'God told me to do it'; or it is the hidden motive of certain kinds of exalted or irrational behaviour, even though the idea of divine instigation may be vehemently denied.

The mystery cults of antiquity were rooted in the central mystical identification of the worshipper with the god. The mystery of the Communion in the Christian religion also rests upon this same foundation. It is no mere coincidence that the central core of the religious mystery and the central delusion of the insane should be identical. Though, in fact, only the apparent content of the experience is identical: the attitude with which one receives and apprehends an experience being the essential integrating factor of the total event. In the religious mystery-initiation the experience is carefully prepared for, and is held strictly relative to the religious rite of which the experience of divinity is the climax. Whereas in the delusion of the insane, there are no preparatory steps, no directing elders to assist one's understanding of the event, and no means of keeping the experience within the safeguarding relative framework.

The archaic content of the unconscious tends to claim an all-or-none absolutism. The state of insanity is immediately bound up with this absoluteness of the autonomous complex. As a relative truth held within the co-ordinated complex of experience the mystical event can be the star which guides a man to his individual truth. But as a totalitarian voice claiming absolute sway, such a spirit becomes a ruthless, destroying power.

In the presence of a totalitarian spirit, such as the one that rules Germany, we cannot, I think, find a better criterion than that given by Jung at the end of an essay on *Spirit and Life*:

> The fullness of life requires more than just an ego; it demands spirit, that is, an independent, overruling complex which is apparently alone capable of calling into living expression all those mental possibilities which the ego-consciousness cannot reach.
>
> But just as there is a passion that strives for blind unrestricted life, so there is also a passion that yearns to bring the whole of life as a sacrifice to the spirit, just because of its creative superiority. This passion makes of the spirit a malignant growth that senselessly destroys human life.

Life is a test of the truth of the spirit. Spirit that drags a man away from all possibility of life, seeking fulfilment only in itself, is a false spirit — the guilt resting also in the man, since he can choose whether he gives himself up to the spirit or not.

Life and spirit are two powers or necessities, between which man is placed. Spirit gives meaning to his life, and the possibility of the greatest development. But life is essential to spirit, since its truth is nothing if it cannot live.[1]

Germany at the present time presents a deadly conflict between these two powers. On the one hand, we discern the reckless collective spirit of totalitarianism; on the other, the individual human being in all his complex relatedness. In the following quotation from Dr. Rauschning we catch a glimpse of the way spirit can become directly hostile to the living being.

It would be well if every ideological pretension were subjected to the test: is it favourable or unfavourable to the living being? Hitler, for instance, is reported to have said:

There will be no licence, no free space, in which the individual belongs to himself. This is Socialism — not such trifles as the private possession of the means of production. Of what importance is that if I range men firmly within a discipline they cannot escape? Let them then own land or factories as much as they please. The decisive factor is that the State, through the party, is supreme over them, regardless of whether they are owners or workers. All that, you see, is inessential. Our Socialism goes far deeper. It does not alter external conditions; no, it establishes the relation of the individual to the State, the national community. It does this with the help of one party, or perhaps I should say, of one order.[2]

In the above citation Hitler shows a diabolical shrewdness. He knows that if the essence of a man has yielded to the Nazi spirit, what remains is not significant. He recognizes that the great mass of human beings, even though they respond to the idea of freedom, live the greater part of their lives in a collective state when they prefer to be contained, led and passively herded.

[1] C. G. JUNG, *Contributions to Analytical Psychology* (Kegan Paul & Co., London, 1928).
[2] *Hitler Speaks*, p. 190.

At bottom, they will not face the responsibility of being free. This is the ultimate basis of Machiavellian cynicism. You can do what you like with the mass-animal, so long as you give it a containing herd-slogan.

It is indeed tragic that the spirit of constructive socialism in England has been almost wholly occupied with surface problems of material distribution, and the so-called hard facts of economics; while Hitler, the master of destructive socialism, is guided by a diabolical genius to the spiritual core of the whole problem of freedom. Socialism needs to learn that it is more important for a man to feel responsible for his freedom than to be contained in a political party or union.

As we study Dr. Rauschning's observations we are impressed by the fact that Hitler speaks of mankind only as a mass-animal. Just as we can ransack the pages of *Mein Kampf* for any individual trait of its author, so we may search in vain throughout Hitler's utterances for any positive reference to the individual human being and his unique destiny. That this elimination of the individual is part of Hitler's deliberate policy is proved by the following:

> At a mass meeting, thought is eliminated. And because this is the state of mind I require, because it secures to me the best sounding-board for my speeches, I order everyone to attend the meetings, where they become part of the mass whether they like it or not, intellectuals and *bourgeois* as well as workers.[1]

When we consider that the essence of the Christian enfranchisement was that the soul of the slave was as good as the soul of Caesar in the eyes of God, and remembering that the great nations of antiquity, prior to the liberating message of Christ, were slave states, we must see that the spiritual freedom contained in His idea of the kingdom of heaven, was a royal, indestructible inheritance offered to each individual being. The democratic freedom for which we are now fighting is rooted directly in this noblest gift of God to man. Now let us listen to the message of Hitler:

> To the Christian doctrine of the infinite significance of the individual human soul and of personal responsibility, I

[1] loc. cit., p. 209.

42

oppose with icy clarity the saving doctrine of the nothingness and insignificance of the individual human being, and of his continued existence in the visible immortality of the nation.[1]

These words represent, in my view, the inner core of Hitler's destructive influence in the world to-day. If he has to utter his saving doctrine with icy clarity, this can only mean that something warm and living and human has to be killed. He even tells us in so many words that this something is the individual human soul to which Christ gave a royal significance. In order to live in Hitler's universe man's soul has to be saved from the burden of the responsibility of consciousness, the one specifically human attribute. And the way to achieve this end is to dissolve the moral individual in the amoral mass.

It is significant that both Hitler and his Italian prototype, Machiavelli, combine a pathological one-sidedness with insufficient culture. The following account of Machiavelli in the *Encyclopaedia Britannica* could almost as well have been written of Hitler:

> Concentrating his attention on the one necessity for organizing a powerful coherent nation, Machiavelli forgot that men are more than political beings. He neglected religion, or regarded it as part of the state machinery. He judged private virtue to be the basis of all healthy national existence; but in the realm of politics he subordinated morals to political expediency. He held that the people, as distinguished from the nobles and the clergy, were the pith and fibre of nations; yet this same people had to become wax in the hands of the politician — their commerce and their comforts, the arts which give a dignity to life, and the pleasures which make life liveable, neglected — their very liberty subordinated to one tyrannical conception. To this point the segregation of politics from every other factor which goes to constitute humanity had brought him; and this makes us feel his world a wilderness.

Hitler's world would have to be described in even harsher terms. Yet it is not enough for our purpose to declare the whole Nazi *Weltanschauung* insane; because, frenzied or not, we have to discover why the Nazi spirit is so bent upon extinguishing

[1] loc. cit., p. 222.

43

individual consciousness, and forcing it down to the level of the sheepfold.

Individuality and collectivity are a basal pair of opposites. They are mutually so antagonistic that only an integrated individuality is able to hold them in balanced opposition. A philosophy built exclusively around either end of this essential dichotomy tends to be ruthless and fanatical.

5

That this dualism is fundamental in our biological inheritance is shown in the two main primitive forms of puberty initiation. In one the youth is encouraged to perform some feat of individual bravery as seen amongst the Achumawi Indians, the Eskimo, or the Masai in East Africa. Amongst the Achumawi, for example, the lad wins the favour of his *tinihowi* (a kind of externalized soul, probably ancestral in origin, projected in the form of a little animal) by plunging into a solitary crater-lake in the mountains at the going down of the sun. He is told that he is going to die, but that if his *tinihowi* approves of him it will rescue him. His whole success as a warrior, runner, hunter, or medicine man is dependent upon the relation he keeps and cultivates with his *tinihowi*. But he must never bring it back to the village, nor must he ever speak of it to anyone. It is a purely individual concern.

In contrast to this, there is the collective type of initiation in which the youths are herded together and are subjected to needlessly cruel ordeals. Sometimes they even die under the torture. The object of the initiation is to wrench them away from their home and the state of childish dependence upon the parents, while, at the same time, initiating them into the tribal or military organization which, from then onwards, claims their absolute submission. The former type of initiation is calculated to bring out individual quality and mettle; the latter, collective obedience and docility. The former type is found principally among the indigenous, food-gathering peoples who have clung to the piety of the original human state, living in small communities in a kind of natural communism. The latter type is expressive of the collectivized society. It tends to repress individuality and the spontaneous human reaction, in favour of a militaristic hierarchy of power. We must regard these as opposing tendencies, rather than types; inasmuch as most forms of puberty initiation contain elements of both. But since one element is usually in the ascendant it is possible to distinguish human societies according to this vital criterion. Wherever, for example, the individual tendency is uppermost, slavery is non-existent; while among collectivized peoples it is almost impossible to suppress it.

Tracing this biological dichotomy still further down in the natural order we see the solitary animals, like the great carnivora and birds of prey, at war with the gregarious creatures. We observe the fact that many of the latter, when migrating, follow the pattern of the leader and the herd. When the herd has reached the feeding or breeding ground, it tends to break up into small units, in order that the individual principle can come into play.

Observing the behaviour of migrating animals we note another significant feature. A definite deterioration of character accompanies the migratory phase. In its individual habitat the creature is vigilant, adapted and instinctively secure. In its migratory, collective phase it is reckless, often suicidal, and manifests in general a regressive type of reaction. The relatively solitary lemming of the Norwegian uplands and the migrating horde of lemmings swimming out into the western sea to drown, are two very different creatures. The human animal is subject to a similar psychological modification when he becomes merged in a vast human tide which uproots him from his adapted mode of life.

Modern man, whether Gallic, Teutonic, Anglo-Saxon or Slav, has a complex psychology embracing many individual and collective elements of primitive nature. Notwithstanding the widest range of racial variety, an historical tendency exists for nations to follow either the individualistic or collectivistic tradition, and to adapt their political life accordingly. Individual freedom has been won and passionately defended by the Anglo-Saxon and Celtic peoples, and any attempt to stampede them into a Hitlerian compound would be destroyed by scorn and ridicule. The relatively individualist form of culture would also appear to have more stability, inasmuch as all the great states which have succumbed to totalitarian tyranny since the Great War were first confounded by revolution.

The fanatical collectivism of Hitler's Germany must inevitably have a profound effect upon individual German psychology. One result to be anticipated is a compensatory swing-over to the side of individuality. This movement across to the other side will take place all the more readily because the one-sided collectivist attitude has resulted in a kind of mass-insanity. The present supremacy of mass-mentality can be illustrated from Hitler's own psychology. In the following citations from Dr. Rauschning's record one is struck, for example, by the fact that Hitler is quite unable to adapt to the individual aspects of a problem, whereas when he is seduced by his collective dream his mind expands as though flooded with prophetic visions. Dr. Rauschning writes:

> He quickly became impatient if the details of a problem were brought to him. What is known as the mastery of material was quite unimportant to him.[1]

> One thing is certain — Hitler has the spirit of a prophet. He is not content to be a mere politician.[2]

Hitler says:

> Can there be anything greater and more all-comprehending? Those who see in National Socialism nothing more than a political movement know scarcely anything of it. It is more even than a religion; it is the will to create mankind anew.[3]

Again, according to Dr. Rauschning,

> There were stages of which he must not allow even himself to speak. Even this, he said, he intended to make public only when he was no longer living. Then there would be something really great, an overwhelming revelation. In order completely to fulfil his mission he must die a martyr's death.
> Yes, he repeated, in the hour of supreme peril I must sacrifice myself for the people.[4]

[1] loc. cit., p. 183.   [2] loc. cit., p. 241.
[3] loc. cit., p. 242.   [4] loc. cit., p. 247.

It is apparently impossible to focus Hitler's ultimate objective in the speech of ordinary men. He himself is inclined to foam at the mouth when the immensity of his vision seizes him. It is this visionary Hitler who says:

> But the day will come when we shall make a pact with these new men in England, France, America. We shall make it when they fall into line with the vast process of the reordering of the world and voluntarily play their part in it. There will not be much left then of the clichés of nationalism, and precious little among us Germans. Instead there will be an understanding between the various elements of the one good ruling race.[1]

We must not examine a visionary's utterances too narrowly, nor is it possible ever to hold Hitler to anything he has said. But, none the less, this last statement throws a rather unexpected light upon the idea of a purely German hegemony. Clearly at the back of Hitler's mind there is the dream of a federation of ruling-world powers with Germany, alias Hitler, as the master architect. It would not, of course, be a federation of equal, sovereign states, but an amalgamation of ruling peoples erected upon a National Socialistic plinth. Everything, apparently, is defensible that is done in the service of this vast dream. History and pre-history must be rewritten in order to prepare the people for their national and supernational destiny:

> The one and only thing that matters to us, and the thing these people [i.e. the scientists] are paid for by the State, is to have ideas of history that strengthen our people in their necessary national pride ... In all this troublesome business we are only interested in one thing — to project into the dim and distant past the picture of our nation as we envisage it for the future ... Prehistory is the doctrine of the eminence of the Germans at the dawn of civilization.[2]

Dr. Rauschning believes that Hitler's anti-Semitism is simply another aspect of this all-embracing fantasy. He also seems to be informed of the more plausible account of Hitler's parentage when he writes:

> Explanations of this [his anti-Semitism] may be sought in his personal experience, and, incidentally, it may be that under

[1] loc. cit., p. 230.   [2] loc. cit., p. 225.

Nüremberg racial legislation Hitler himself is not entitled to
be classed as 'Aryan'; but the intensity of his anti-Semitism
can be explained only by his inflation of the Jew into a
mythical prototype of humanity. . . .
Israel, the historic people of the spiritual God, cannot but be
the irreconcilable enemy of the new, the German Chosen
People. The one god excludes the other. At the back of
Hitler's anti-Semitism there is revealed an actual war of the
gods.[1]

It is not immediately apparent what the author means by
Hitler's 'inflation of the Jew into a mythical prototype of
humanity' unless he is referring to the tragic figure of Ahasuerus
the Wandering Jew. But in my view Hitler's personal history of
rejection by his Jewish father is nearer the mark. Hitler's
fanaticism is the very breath of the deity he serves. Hatred and
resentment are, as we know, hunchback qualities and Hitler's
unassuageable brutality is the measure of a crooked Thersites
mind. The sadism of such a nature invariably seeks a victim
upon which it can wreak its abysmal resentment against life.
But, quite apart from the personal cause of his spleen, the Jews
are the classical victim. They also represent the detached kind of
consciousness which Hitler is determined to annihilate, since it
is the one thing which could expose and criticize the primitive
mass-suggestion upon which his own position rests. The Jews
are also international in precisely the wrong way for the realization
of his great dream; inasmuch as the existing order of society is
intimately bound up with, and supported by, the system of
international business, finance, and general relatedness which has
been cultivated in large measure by the Jews. We know, too,
that Hitler's sadistic hatred was fed on garbage of the worst kind.
Dr. Rauschning tells us that:

> Hitler was simply on thorns to see each new issue of the
> *Stürmer*. It was the one periodical that he always read with
> pleasure from the first page to the last.[2]

It would be fatally easy to lose patience with our subject, and
to accept Hitler's obvious morbidity as a sufficient explanation of
the Nazi intoxication. We cannot do this, however, since this
particular madman is still accepted as a heaven-inspired leader

[1] loc. cit., p. 232.   [2] loc. cit., p. 234.

by a multitude of our fellow-men and is, moreover, utterly resolved to make his crazy dream come true. All our common-sense conclusions based upon so-called normal premises are beside the mark in judging the case of Hitler. The vital question is no longer whether or not Hitler is insane, but rather towards what goal is insanity driving him. Madmen are dangerous because they are possessed and believe themselves inspired. They can also command a subhuman cunning in the execution of their fantasies. To see the whole picture in perspective, therefore, we must also pay attention to the inferiority in Hitler's psychology from which the grandiose fantasies have developed as a compensatory overgrowth.

We have already put our finger upon the factors of rejection, illegitimacy, and Jewish blood, all of which would be capable of engendering their own peculiar virus of inferiority. The retentive eye of Dr. Rauschning now adds another pathological item to the picture. He writes:

> Everything about him is 'spasm', to use a favourite word of his. Nothing about him is natural. His professed love of children and animals is a mere pose . . . He can spend whole days lazing and dozing. He hates to have to read with concentration. [1]

Many observers have noted this apathetic inertia in Hitler's character. We recall how he idled away five years clinging in neurotic helplessness to his mother before necessity prised him away. The same basic factor reveals itself in Hitler's precarious and unreliable attention. A pronounced defect in attention is one of the classical symptoms of psychotic and psycho-neurotic disorders. It is, therefore, frequently associated with a history of idle dependence and an inability to hold a position. Other familiar traits with a neuropathic character are self-pity and a constant demand for scapegoats.

> In the past he used to complain for weeks at a time, blaming the ingratitude of his followers, or the unkindness of fate, for his inactivity. He was fond of posing as a martyr and dwelling on the idea of premature death. At such times he would seem to be giving up. He was then full of compassion, but only for himself. [2]

[1] loc. cit., p. 254.   [2] loc. cit., p. 256.

GERMANY POSSESSED

Everyone who has had personal dealings with Hitler complains of the exasperating uncertainty of his attention. Ludecke, for instance, who knew Hitler well in the early days of the Nazi movement, writes:

> Even on ordinary days in those times it was almost impossible to keep Hitler concentrated on one point. His quick mind would run away with the talk, or his attention would be distracted by the sudden discovery of a newspaper, and he would stop to read it avidly, or he would interrupt your carefully prepared report with a long speech as though you were an audience.[1]

Dr. Rauschning records a similar impression:

> Never was a real conversation with Hitler possible. Either he would listen in silence, or he would 'speechify' and not allow one to speak. Or he would walk restlessly up and down, interrupt constantly and jump from one subject to another as if unable to concentrate.[2]

In his manic periods, when psychic tension seeks release in shamanistic frenzies, Hitler's defect in attention makes normal intercourse impossible. A frenzied 'racing' of the mental process produces a flight of ideas and usually culminates in a characteristic hysterical fit. His fury rises suddenly to gale-velocity. Dr. Rauschning writes:

> It was interesting to watch Hitler talk himself into a fury, and to note how necessary to his eloquence were shouting and a feverish *tempo*. A quiet conversation with him was impossible. Either he was silent or he took complete charge of the discussion.[3]

Dr. Rauschning describes one of Hitler's paroxysms when someone had dared to expostulate with him about some brutal deed of his S.S. guards. He writes:

> The occasion was my first experience of Hitler's paroxysms of rage and abuse. He behaved like a combination of a spoilt child and an hysterical woman. He scolded in high, shrill tones, stamped his feet, and banged his fist on tables and walls. He foamed at the mouth, panting and stammering in uncontrolled fury: 'I won't have it! Get rid of them all!

[1] K. G. W. LUDECKE, *I Knew Hitler* (Jarrolds Ltd., London), p. 63.
[2] *Hitler Speaks*, p. 250.   [3] loc. cit., p. 68.

50

Traitors!' He was an alarming sight, his hair dishevelled, his eyes fixed and his face distorted and purple. I feared that he would collapse or have an apoplectic fit.
Suddenly it was all over. He walked up and down the room, clearing his throat, and brushing his hair back. He looked round apprehensively and suspiciously with searching glances at us. I had the impression that he wanted to see if anyone was laughing. [1]

Perhaps it should be explained that the storm of indignation, described above, was not Hitler's reaction to the filthy brutalities of which complaints had reached him, but was levelled at those who had 'made a fuss' about such trivial matters.

This emotionality of Hitler's has certain interesting features. Hatred is undoubtedly Hitler's possessing dæmon; but because it draws its poisonous energy from his early experiences, it is never a pure reaction to its present ostensible cause. His emotional outbursts seem, therefore, to be worked up, as though his dæmon were reluctant to perform. Dr. Rauschning's record is as follows:

Almost anything might suddenly inflame his wrath and his hatred. He seemed always to feel the need of something to hate. [2]

He also observes:

The convulsive artificiality of his character is especially noticeable in such intimate circles; particularly notable is his lack of any sense of humour. Hitler's laugh is hardly more than an expression of scorn and contempt. There is no relaxation about it. His pleasures have no repose. [3]

On the one hand, therefore, we get the impression of convulsive, uncontrolled emotionality, and, on the other, a curious lack of any individual expression, as though we had to do with a mask, or a man whose personal psychology had been obliterated. On this point we have first-hand testimony from no less an authority than Professor Jung of Zürich. The following excerpt is taken from the report of an interview given by Professor Jung to Mr. H. R. Knickerbocker, the well-known American correspondent.

I saw the Duce and the Führer together in Berlin the time Mussolini paid his formal visit. I had the good luck to be placed only a few yards away from them and could study them

[1] loc. cit., p. 89.   [2] loc. cit., p. 91.   [3] loc. cit., p. 68,

well ... In comparison with Mussolini, Hitler made upon me the impression of a sort of scaffolding of wood covered with cloth, an automaton with a mask, like a robot, or a mask of a robot. During the whole performance he never laughed; it was as though he were in a bad humour, sulking. He showed no human sign. His expression was that of an inhumanly single-minded purposiveness *with no sense of humour.* He seemed as if he might perhaps be hiding inside like an appendix, and deliberately so hiding in order not to disturb the mechanism. [1]

6

The conception of Hitler which now begins to take shape is that of a man whose native personality has been pushed into the background by his collective mediumistic function. This is brought out in the following. Hitler says:

Ultimately we National Socialists stand alone, as the only ones who know the secret of these gigantic changes and, therefore, as those chosen to set their seal on the coming age. [2]

At the end of his book Dr. Rauschning gives a picture of Hitler being carried helplessly along like a straw swept over a weir:

He used himself to be the one to push on; now everything has begun to take charge. He is being carried away. He is only able with difficulty to keep his feet. And suddenly all the problems are pressing at once! He no longer has any freedom of decision. These deadly problems have acquired a will of their own. They are dragging him the way he does not want to go. Must he now carry out the things he has passionately fought against? Is he not being carried along, step by step, in the opposite direction to the one he meant to take? [3]

This picture of the Führer being caught, as it were, by his shamanistic function and dragged towards his fate by the unconscious forces he had planned to lead, is of a different complexion from that of the ambitious demagogue of the caricaturists. In the American interview Jung is reported as saying:

[1] Published in *The Cosmopolitan*, January 1939.
[2] *Hitler Speaks*, p. 130.   [3] loc. cit., p. 286.

I should say that ambition plays a very minor rôle in Hitler. I don't think Hitler has personal ambition beyond that of the average man.

Herr Ludecke says:

I was impressed by his obvious indifference to his personal appearance.[1]

Nor can I be certain his aim included, at that time, a personal ambition for power.[2]

It is difficult to believe that any man could find himself in the position which Hitler occupies to-day without the motive of ambition playing a major rôle. What Jung almost certainly means is that Hitler is to be regarded as a phenomenon of nature, a man born with a certain fateful aptitude which attracted him towards the historical power-dream in the German unconscious at the moment when this latent force was beginning to stir like a dragon under the earth. All witnesses are agreed that Hitler, the man, was never sufficiently ambitious to master any craft which could bring him wealth, position, or even a bare livelihood. Nor, as we have seen, did ambition help him towards promotion in the army. He seems, indeed, always to have evaded any lesson or task which might involve a normal measure of self-discipline. Dr. Rauschning tells us:

A decision one way or the other was not to be had from him. This was not the first time that, when difficulties arose, he simply pushed aside everything he had just planned and lost all interest in the pile of wreckage that remained behind. He ignored all difficulties that threatened to be troublesome to him and refused to be reminded of them.[3]

This is the all-too-familiar picture of neurotic impatience, not that of the ambitious rival of Napoleon. And yet, accepting this clear evidence of Hitler's incompetence in the face of real difficulties, how are we to explain the amazing feats of organization and improvisation actually accomplished during his régime? And how are we to account for the fact that men of first-rate ability like Herr Schacht and Herr Thyssen gave Hitler their full support under the conviction that he was a genius? This is indeed a

[1] *I Knew Hitler*, p. 25.   [2] ibid., p. 84.   [3] *Hitler Speaks*, p. 184.

53

remarkable fact. Hitler did not strike them as merely an eloquent political demagogue with one or two bold ideas. Eagles are not caught with bird-lime. What assuredly impressed these men of affairs was not so much Hitler's ideas as a certain ruthless tenacity of will that would carry a project through by hook or by crook, and an uncanny flair for timing his stroke.

In order to achieve this impersonal intensity of will the ego must first be consumed or displaced by a more powerful psychic factor which, *ex hypothesi*, must possess a supra-personal nature. For all his sadistic cruelty and neurotic inferiority there is surely some quality of greatness in Hitler's make-up which fitted him to become the vessel of German ambition. This is what the men who backed him must have sensed. The flame that burned behind those eyes did not flicker with the personal timidities, doubts, and expectations of ordinary people. His passion of hatred gave Hitler an aloofness to all genial pleasures and forbade participation in essential human joys. His fanatical intensity of will is, therefore, the measure of his identification with the dæmon he serves. The astonishing dynamic impression he leaves upon so many keen observers is surely the effect of the all-embracing complex which makes use of him quite ruthlessly for its own purpose. Using Jung's invaluable touchstone we see in Hitler's own psychology that same annihilation of the living being by a rapacious spirit as we see throughout Hitler's Germany.

To understand Hitler properly we must at least credit him with one basic quality of greatness: he was able to stand being rejected, outcast and starved of all that makes life tolerable for a young man, without becoming crushed and hopeless. His personal suffering kindled a flame of impersonal hatred, and out of this hatred grew his mythological devotion to the idea of the greater Germany. He could not live his personal life; for nowhere was he accepted in the days when acceptance would have meant everything. He felt himself 'despised and rejected of men', but he did not allow this feeling to become his epitaph.

To people who have never experienced what it is to be cast out of paradise, this aspect of Hitler's fate may seem unimportant. But, in fact, no other factor leaves such an indelible mark on the mind as this early experience of rejection. To the child-soul acceptance is heaven, and rejection is hell. The expanding ring of acceptance, beginning with the parents and ending in the mystical experience of divine love, is the essential condition of human happiness. Hence the anticipation of acceptance is an inherent longing of the soul. It is rare indeed to find a man in whom the early frustration of this longing has not sown a bitter harvest of cynicism and resentment.

The revolutionary agitator arose out of the ashes of deprived youth, and with a passion of destruction Hitler plunged into the political whirlpool, resolved to compensate his own instinctual frustration in the fulfilment of the great Germanic dream.

Germany was ripe for revolution during those bitter years of the French occupation of the Ruhr, and it first gained its hold among the unemployed, and the unadaptable, those, in fact, who had never given their allegiance to the existing order. National Socialism offered, not a paradise, but something tangible and real to all the undernourished, frustrated masses of the post-war period. Dr. Rauschning says:

> For all those who have been unsuccessful in the battle of life, National Socialism is the great worker of magic. And Hitler himself is the first of these. Thus he has become the master-enchanter and high priest of the religious mysteries of Nazidom. [1]

7

Experience of the depths of the human soul teaches us that the man who aspires to be the magician must first renounce the path of love. It also teaches us that the man who is cruel to others has first been cruel to his own instincts. Reading between the lines of *Mein Kampf* with this experience to guide us, we can discern the human frustration out of which the magician grew. This view is supported by the following observations of Dr. Rauschning, which explain why Hitler's personal psychology has remained so elusively in the background. He writes:

> Most loathsome of all is the reeking miasma of furtive unnatural sexuality that fills and fouls the whole atmosphere round him, like an evil emanation. Nothing in this environment is straightforward. Surreptitious relationships, sub-

[1] loc. cit., p. 219.

stitutes, and symbols, false sentiments and secret lusts —
nothing in this man's surroundings is natural and genuine,
nothing has the openness of a natural instinct. [1]

With this vital information in our hands the following picture of the
sadistic, inhuman side of Hitler's character follows logically enough:

All the more astonishing are the explosions of his 'determined
will', his sudden activity. Then he neither tires nor hungers;
he lives with a morbid energy that enables him to do almost
miraculous things. (Cf. primitive state of possession.)
Everything is done then, in his own words, 'with determination', 'without tolerating' (whatever obstacle might be in
question), 'fanatically'. But everything about him is jerky
and abrupt. He is entirely without balance. And in this
respect he shows not the slightest improvement as he grows
older. He has no natural greatness, even in the vastest of his
new and vast rooms.

Hitler used to like to be seen with a riding whip in his hand;
he has given up this habit. But the qualities it revealed
remain — contemptuousness, arrogance, brutality, vanity.
Hitler has never mounted a horse; but the tall riding boots
and the riding whip bore witness to his resentment at past
years of submission to his officers . . . He is full of resentments.
A chance word, an association of ideas, may arouse them at
any time. . . .

But Germany's Führer is not only vain and as sensitive as a
mimosa; he is brutal and vindictive. He is entirely without
generosity. He lives in a world of insincerity, deceiving and
self-deceiving. But hatred is like wine to him; it intoxicates
him. One must have heard his tirades of denunciation to
realize how he can revel in hate.

Brutal and vindictive, he is also sentimental — a familiar
mixture. He loved his canaries, and could cry when one of
them sickened and died. But he would have men, against
whom he had a grudge, tortured to death in the most horrible way. He eats incredible quantities of sweetmeats and
whipped cream; and he has the instinct of the sadist, finding
sexual excitement in inflicting torture on others. In Roman
history he gloats over such a figure as Sulla, with his proscrip-
tions and mass executions. Once he recommended to me as
instructive reading a banal novel of which Sulla was the
hero. [2]

[1] loc. cit., p. 257.   [2] loc. cit., pp. 256-57.

It is essential that this aspect of Dr. Rauschning's account should not be omitted, for, without it, Hitler's psychology is not intelligible as a whole. This pitiful being, with his all-too-masculine dramatizations of power, excluded nature from his personal life, preferring a rotten, perverted substitute in its place. The overacted emotional scenes are symptomatic of this intellectualized substitute for sexuality. His instinct is accordingly cold and erratic. There is no real kinship with his kind. For the same reason he is altogether too touchy and effeminate to hold a man's friendship. The picture of Hitler's childhood, with its exclusive emotional dependence upon the mother, and corresponding alienation from the father, rises vividly to mind when we read:

> It is to women's encouragement that he owes his self-assurance. It is absurd that he, of all men, should always be surrounded by a crowd of women, most of them rather overblown — that women, indeed, launched him on his career.
> Hitler was discovered by women, society ladies who pushed him forward, when still a young man, after the Great War. It was the wives of some great industrialists, before their husbands, who gave him financial support, surreptitiously supplying him with money and, in the inflation period, with valuables. It was in the company of a clique of educated women that the paid propagandist developed into a political prophet . . . it was they who pampered him and ministered to his conceit with extravagant advance laurels. Women's gushing adulation, carried to the pitch of pseudo-religious ecstasy, provided the indispensable stimulus that could rouse him from his lethargy. It is curiously reminiscent of the feminine adoration lavished on the arid and unattractive Robespierre . . . In the struggle for power it was the women's vote that brought Hitler to triumph. In the mass meetings in every town the front rows were always filled with elderly women of a certain type, married and single. . . .
> Hitler, as I see him, is a personality so exclusively wrapped up in himself that he is incapable of genuine devotion. And thus the more or less morbid women who swarm round him and pay him homage, women with more than a touch of hysteria, are a deliberately selected company.[1]

The suspicion that Hitler is emotionally immature or retarded

[1] loc. cit., pp. 258-59.

is confirmed by his predilection for the exaggerated and pretentious in art and literature, and by his intense dislike of the introverted and contemplative. Possessed by the dynamism of an
overmastering complex, Hitler feels action to be the only reality
fit for men. He is reported to have said, for instance:

> We approach the realities of the world only in strong emotion
> and in action. I have no love for Goethe. But I am ready to
> overlook much in him for the sake of one phrase — 'In the
> beginning was action'. Only the man who acts becomes
> conscious of the real world. Men misuse their intelligence.
> It is not the seat of a special dignity of mankind, but merely
> an instrument in the struggle for life. Man is here to act.
> Only as a being in action does he fulfil his natural vocation.
> Contemplative natures, retrospective like all intellectuals,
> are dead persons who miss the meaning of life.[1]

Yet Hitler has been taken for a mystic. One is relieved to know
that Hitler has no love for Goethe. For had he loved the greatest
of Germans we should have had to reconsider our conception of
Hitler's genius.

Those of my readers who are acquainted with Jung's psychological conceptions will recognize in the features I have underlined
the condition known as anima-possession. For those unacquainted
with Jung's works, it must be explained that the unconscious of a
man tends to spontaneous personification as a feminine figure.
Man's soul is naturally feminine, as woman's soul is naturally
masculine. These personifications appear empirically in dream
and fantasy material, as also in romantic literature. Heathcliff,
the demon-lover of *Wuthering Heights* who, in the end, undermines
the heroine's loyalty to home and husband, by calling to the
vagrant, undomesticated primordial part of her soul, is an excellent example. Rider Haggard's Ayesha, She-who-must-be-
obeyed; W. H. Hudson's Rima in *Green Mansions*; Leonardo da
Vinci's Mona Lisa — these are a few classical examples of the
animus and anima in art and literature. When a man is possessed
by the unconscious in such a way that he is impelled, driven,
intoxicated by archaic moods and affects, we speak of him as
anima-possessed. It is also characteristic of the anima-possessed
subject to become inflated by grandiose dreams of power. Com-

[1] loc. cit., p. 221.

pare, for instance, the boundless fantasy of world dominion with which Ayesha tries to intoxicate Leo. In romantic literature the anima is usually the last survivor of an ancient culture, is frequently of royal birth, and exercises an uncanny power over elemental forces. Sometimes, as in the case of Kundry's relation to Parsifal, the anima is transformed from a wild, unbridled enchantress into a ministering function.

Hitler is an illiterate man with great natural gifts for eloquence and mediumship. Thus, he was naturally attracted to the possibility of becoming the prophet of the crude semi-mystical tendencies fermenting in the German unconscious. No woman with the latent capacity for playing the anima-rôle to a budding prophet could resist such an opportunity. His dynamic illiteracy, his tumultuous moods and roaring eloquence, and his crude, unstable character, were sure to arouse soaring fantasies of feminine power. Women of the pioneering type rarely fall in love with the finished product. They want a half-formed soul, nebulous and plastic, corresponding to their own formative emotional urge; an untilled field ready for enthusiastic exploitation.

Hitler, as he was and still is, would never have been accepted on equal terms by his fellows in the world of men. However useful the function of mediumship may be, and however patiently one might, for scientific purposes, tolerate the hysterical, effeminate moods that so often go with it, the basic fact remains, men with 'temperament' are not loved or admired by their fellow-men. It is, therefore, quite excluded that a man with Hitler's nature could obtain an important or responsible position in the practical world of affairs. What, then, happened to Germany that it became possible for this perverted, neuropathic individual to grasp supreme power? This profoundly interesting question merits a chapter to itself. But before leaving the morbid aspect of Hitler's psychology, I must include a description of a scene given by one of Hitler's psychic bodyguard. In this scene Hitler is obviously haunted by a terrifying ghost. Dr. Rauschning records it as follows:

He often wakes up in the middle of the night and wanders restlessly to and fro. Then he must have light everywhere. Lately he has sent at these times for young men who have to keep him company during his hours of anguish. At times

these conditions must have become dreadful. A man in the
closest daily association with him gave me this account.
Hitler wakes at night with convulsive shrieks. He shouts for
help. He sits on the edge of his bed, as if unable to stir.
He shakes with fear, making the whole bed vibrate. He
shouts confused, totally unintelligible phrases. He gasps as
if imagining himself to be suffocating.

My informant described to me in full detail a remarkable
scene. Hitler stood swaying in his room looking wildly
about him. 'He! He! He's been here!' he gasped. His lips
were blue. Sweat streamed down his face. Suddenly he
began to reel off figures, and odd words and broken phrases,
entirely devoid of sense. It sounded horrible. He used
strangely composed and entirely un-German word-forma-
tions. Then he stood quite still, only his lips moving. He
was massaged and offered something to drink. Then he
suddenly broke out:

'There, there! In the corner! Who's that?'

He stamped and shrieked in the familiar way. He was shown
that there was nothing out of the ordinary in the room
and at last he gradually grew calm.[1]

No wonder that Hitler had to discover that: 'conscience is a
Jewish invention'.[2]

The secret of Hitler's maniacal extraversion, with its inhuman
insistence on movement, marching, action at all costs, is now in
our hands. When extraverted activity becomes compulsive it
must be regarded as a neurotic means of escape. But escape from
what? The above scene supplies a clue. Hitler has worse things
than murder on his mind. He has to drive himself, and everyone
else, into furious activity, because he cannot stand the company
of his own thoughts. When he chose Berchtesgaden for his home,
he chose a place, intended from the beginning of time, for introverted peace. Hitler has transformed it into a place of swarming
industry and activity. The mountains have no peace night or day.
There is a ceaseless human onslaught of rock-blasting, road-
making, building, demolition, and general military fuss. This is
the place Hitler chose for seclusion.

We meet this ambiguity at every turn in Hitler's psychology.
The longing for seclusion is, as we shall see, one of the major

[1] loc. cit., p. 251.　　　[2] loc. cit., p. 220.

threads in his horoscope. Yet, although he has spent a fortune in building his utterly secluded Eagle's Eyrie on the summit of the Obersalzberg, he is eternally excluded from its enjoyment. He is proud to show this place and to receive his distinguished diplomatic visitors there. But even there among the mountain peaks he cannot escape from his own thoughts, while soldiers in machine-gun nests guard the approaches. No sooner is he there, but he is driven by pursuing ghosts to a fresh bout of ambitious scheming. Behind Hitler's fanatical extraversion, therefore, we discern a soul in torment.

8

All I have so far attempted is to select those traits and peculiarities of our subject which immediately catch a doctor's eye, knowing that this pathologically toned portrait must necessarily suffer from a certain bias. Though no deep understanding of Hitler as a contemporary phenomenon can be reached without taking psycho-pathology into account, yet we cannot explain the creator of the Third Reich in purely medical terms. These selected features have only to be placed in position for the portrait to speak for itself. But in the following chapters we must deal with factors in the general contemporary condition which, because they corresponded with certain essential features of Hitler's psychology, he was able to seize and manipulate.

CHAPTER II

WOTAN, GOD AND DÆMON

I

WE must now investigate the peculiar upheaval which rendered the whole of Germany a more or less willing accomplice to Hitler's predatory ideas. I have neither space nor competence to deal with the historical background of the present German tragedy; but some mention of historical factors is essential for our understanding of the Hitler-phenomenon. When Smuts, for example, speaks of the present condition as a 'spiritual migration of mankind', we need to inquire from what historical aspect of our modern world mankind is migrating, and towards what goal.

An invaluable clue to the nature of the migration is afforded by Jung, who, as far back as 1918, made a remarkable prediction concerning the catastrophic potentialities in the German unconscious; a prophecy which is now being realized in full. He wrote:

> Christianity had the effect of dividing German paganism into an upper and a lower portion, and — by dint of repressing this dark under side — it succeeded in domesticating the bright upper portion and adapting it to civilized requirements. But the excluded lower portion still awaits deliverance and a second domestication. In the meantime, through association with other relics of antiquity in the collective unconscious, it inevitably brings about a peculiar and increasing activation of the collective unconscious. The more the absolute authority of the Christian *Weltanschauung* loses its hold, the more audibly can we hear the pacing to and fro of the 'blond beasts' in their subterranean dungeon, threatening us with an outburst which is bound to have devastating consequences.[1]

An even more extraordinary foreshadowing of events was made

[1] C. G. Jung, from a contribution to *Schweizerland*, IV Jahrgang, No. 9, p. 470, Juniheft, 1918.

by the German poet Heine, in 1835. Reviewing contemporary
revolutionary tendencies in German philosophy, he saw that if
these idealist forces ever became transmuted into action, terrible
results must follow. Having first discussed the grim possibilities if
the transcendental idealists in the ranks of Kant and Fichte broke
loose into active revolution, he says:

> But most of all to be feared would be the philosophers of
> nature were they actively to mingle in a German revolution,
> and to identify themselves with the work of destruction . . .
> The Philosopher of Nature will be terrible in this, that he has
> allied himself with the primitive powers of nature, that he
> can conjure up the dæmoniac forces of old German pan-
> theism; and having done so, there is aroused in him that
> ancient German eagerness for battle which combats not for
> the sake of destroying, not even for the sake of victory, but
> merely for the sake of combat itself.
> Christianity — and this is its fairest merit — subdued to a
> certain extent the brutal warrior ardour of the Germans,
> but it could not entirely quench it; and when the cross, that
> restraining talisman, falls to pieces, then will break forth
> again the ferocity of the old combatants, the frantic Berserker
> rage whereof Northern poets have said and sung — the
> talisman has become rotten, and the day will come when it
> will pitifully crumble to dust. The old stone gods will then
> arise from the forgotten ruins and wipe from their eyes the dust
> of centuries, and Thor with his giant hammer will arise
> again, and he will shatter the Gothic cathedrals.
> When you hear the trampling of feet and the clashing of
> arms, ye neighbours children, ye French, be on your guard . . .
> Smile not at my counsel, at the counsel of a dreamer, who
> warns you against Kantians, Fichteans, Philosophers of
> Nature. Smile not at the phantasy of one who foresees in the
> region of reality the same outburst of revolution that has
> taken place in the region of intellect. German thunder is of
> true German character. It is not very nimble, it rumbles
> along somewhat slowly. But come it will, and when you
> hear a crashing as never before has been heard in the world's
> history, then know at last the German thunderbolt has
> fallen. At this commotion *the eagles will drop dead from the
> skies* and the lions in the farthest wastes of Africa will bite
> their tails and creep into the royal lairs. There will be played

in Germany a drama compared to which the French revolution will seem but an innocent idyll. At present it is true that everything is tolerably quiet; and though here and there few men can create a little stir, don't imagine these are the real actors in the piece. They are only little curs chasing one another round the empty arena, barking and snapping at one another, till the appointed hour when the troop of gladiators appears to fight for life and death.

And the hour will come. As on the steps of an amphitheatre, the nations will group themselves around Germany to witness the terrible combat. I counsel you, ye French, keep very quiet, and, above all, don't applaud. We might readily misunderstand such applause, and, in our rude fashion, somewhat roughly put you to silence. For, if formerly in our servile, listless mood we could oftentimes overpower you, much easier were it for us to do so *in the arrogance of our new-born enthusiasm.* You yourselves know what, in such a case, men can do; and you are no longer in such a case. Take heed, then! I mean it well with you. Therefore it is I tell you the bitter truth. You have more to fear from a free Germany than from the entire Holy Alliance with all its Croats and Cossacks. . . .

As you are, despite your present romantic tendency, a born classical people, you know Olympus. Amongst the joyous gods and goddesses quaffing and feasting of nectar and ambrosia, you may behold one goddess, who, amidst such gaiety and pastime, wears ever a coat of mail, the helm on her head and the spear in the hand.

She is the goddess of Wisdom. [1]

When Hitler is blamed as the author and originator of the present cataclysm, it is salutary to read this testimony of a German seer written more than a century ago. We do not see what Fate is preparing in the dim background of the world stage. But these two historical witnesses seem to lift the veil, so that our eyes reach beyond to the distant perspective where we behold the shadowy outline of titanic forms. These are the forms I see behind Hitler's shamanistic leadership.

Without discussing the revolutionary development in German philosophy associated with the names of Kant, Fichte, Schopen-

[1] Extract from HEINE's 'Religion and Philosophy in Germany', printed in *The New Statesman and Nation* for June 22nd, 1940.

hauer, Hegel, von Hartmann and Nietzsche, the conception of a vast and fateful dynamism, conceived now as impersonal will, now as ethical teleology, or again as the unconscious, can be traced in a more or less steady crescendo throughout the great period of German philosophy. Thus the dynamism of the German unconscious has inspired German thinking as it has impelled German policy. It is not possible, however, to do more in the present work than allude to certain facts and causes which might account, to some extent, for the present volcanic upheaval.

Commenting upon Jung's prophecy in my work *Mythology of the Soul*, I wrote:

> The basis of Jung's prognosis rests upon the principle that nothing dies until it is lived out. Many things have been superseded in the millennial rush of European civilization. They may have disappeared from view, but everything that has been swallowed is not necessarily done with. Vital affects which have their roots in the primordial psyche are never extinguished. They bide their time and reappear at the psychological moment.
> The French Revolution, the terror in Russia, in Germany, in Spain, show what can happen to civilized nations when Christian forms decay and the archaic underworld breaks through. As the authority of the Church wanes the repressed pagan antithesis must surely come to the surface. The demoralization and disillusionment which followed the War were undoubtedly intensified by the dawning realization that our boasted civilization was not as Christian as we had believed.[1]

A page or two later the same theme is continued as follows:

> Abundant signs make it clear that the unlived pagan unconscious has broken through the Christian crust, and that this volcanic disturbance, as predicted by Jung, has shaken the whole world, setting in motion a great spiritual migration that is essentially hostile to the historical Christian values. That Central European psychology is harking back to the Middle Ages can hardly be questioned. Not only is the atavistic momentum manifest in the persecution of the Jews and in the frank revival of pagan mythology and religion,

---

[1] H. G. BAYNES, *Mythology of the Soul*. (Baillière, Tindall & Cox), pp. 864-65.

but we are invited to regard the Rome-Berlin axis as a modern attempt to repeat the power-fantasy of the Holy Roman Empire, albeit on a new ideological footing. [1]

The emergence of pagan psychology at a crisis in German history was, in any case, a highly probable event, as anyone with a knowledge of German folk-tales could have foreseen. In the quotation from Jung reference has already been made to the manner in which the barbaric psychology of the early Germans was forced into the Christian mould, and we have seen how Jung based his forecast of an anti-Christian upheaval upon a probable re-activation of this surviving paganism below the civilized crust. The following legends, which have been selected from a wealth of similar tales all over Germany, show that Jung's prognosis was supported by abundant mythological evidence. This repressed pagan psychology acted like an underground magnet upon German development, eventually bringing about an unwilled backward movement into German archaism. Had this backward movement been recognized as an historical necessity and been directed by wise statesmanship, it is conceivable that this dissociated element in the racial psyche could have been assimilated by a reborn Germany.

Many of these legends are concerned with warlike heroes of the past whose death translates them to a temporary sleep in rocks, caves or mountains, until the hour strikes when they shall rise again. Pagan deities, like Holda and Venus, are sequestered in mountains. Wodan and King Charles dwell in the Odenberg. Folk-tales tell how living men have gained entrance into such mountains. Tannhäuser, for instance, sojourned for years at the court of Venus. Another legend tells how a blacksmith was looking in the undergrowth on the Odenberg for a hawthorn with which to make his hammer-helve, when suddenly he saw a gap he had never noticed before in the face of the cliff; he stepped in, and stood in a new world of wonders. Strong men were bowling balls of iron. They challenged him to play, but he declined. The iron balls, he said, were too heavy for his hand. The men were not offended; they told him to choose what present he would have. He begged for one of their balls, took it home, and put it among his stock of iron. Afterwards, wanting to work it, he made it red hot,

[1] loc. cit., p. 866.

but it burst into pieces on the anvil and every piece was sheer gold.[1]

Through experience with dream-analysis we recognize at once a familiar idiom of the unconscious in this 'stepping across the line' or 'through the looking glass' into another world where wonderful things happen. The 'other world' always refers to that sphere of psychic potential where the imaged contents represent the fluid form of possibilities. Dormant or nascent forms await the advent of the heroic will which can transform them into the actual. The miracle of the conscious will resides in its power of raising an emergent possibility out of the stream of mechanical causation, transforming it from the wreathing mist-forms of the unconscious into something inescapably real. The *motif* of the forging of the sword (symbolizing the will) from the fragments saved from his father's broken blade, marks the beginning of Siegfried's career as a hero. His father, Siegmund, also extracted the magical sword from the tree where it lay embedded as a latent potential till the hero came to transform it into the effective deed.

The blacksmith sees strong men bowling balls of iron. These strong men are the heroes of the past. But iron balls are not part of the heroic equipment. They are probably cannon balls or thunderbolts,[2] that is to say, symbols of a dynamic potential that is, humanly speaking, overwhelming. This accounts for the fact that the blacksmith finds them too heavy for him. The smith is, of course, Wayland the Smith, whose story is told in one of the oldest songs of the Edda. We also find allusions to this figure in the Anglo-Saxon *Beowulf* and *Deor's Lament*. There are abundant local traditions of the wonderful smith in Westphalia. In the light of what was said above concerning the heroic function which forges the actual from the unconscious potential, it is understandable that the practical will should be symbolized as a smith who does wonders. Daedalus is the classical figure of the wonder-working smith, and his reputation as the cunning inventor who, in order to escape from Crete, made wings for himself and his son Icarus, with which to fly the Aegean, shows that the smith is not

[1] STALLYBRASS, *Grimm's Teutonic Mythology* (G. Bell & Sons), vol. III, p. 953.
[2] The skittle playing sounds like rolling thunder. They say in North Germany, when it thunders: 'The angels are playing at bowls.'

67

merely an artificer. He is also the discoverer of unconscious possibilities; hence his quasi-divine reputation. For what is there in
man more clear in its affirmation of the creative 'grain of the sun'
than this very capacity to bring off the thing he intends, therewith
converting the possible into the actual?

The myth then explains how the crude balls of iron can be
converted into gold. Dynamic potentiality is commonly figured in
dream-language as something round or spherical, suggesting a
vital process in a contained or embryonic state. The crux, therefore, lies in the smith's choice. This again is the prerogative of the
will. But freedom of the will would be an empty mockery without
the disposable energy which alone could make it effective. Hence
the idea of freedom is closely associated with the symbolism of
energy or value. Yet, in order to choose reasonably, a superior
awareness or recognition of possible value must be presupposed.
Freedom and efficacy of the will are, therefore, dangerous gifts
without the saving light of consciousness.

In choosing one of the iron balls the smith enacts, as it were, the
law of human creation, for a man must first become aware of its
possibility before he can create any new thing. This consciousness
of potential value is akin to the alchemical power of converting
base metal into gold. But it is not the consciousness which stops
at the mere act of recognition; it is consciousness combined with
the transforming heat of creative passion. It is because the smith
makes it red hot with his own fire that the ball changes into gold.
Jung has shown[1] how the age-old quest of alchemy was also concerned with this same creative work of converting the unconscious
psychical potential into spiritual gold through the process of
individuation.

In the Mecklenberg legend of the tipsy peasant, which we shall
discuss presently, we have another example of the common substance that is changed into gold as soon as the subject performs the
task commanded him by the representative of the unconscious.
It is demonstrably true that any man who understands and is
willing to carry out such indications of the unconscious will
observe this symbolical transformation.

The bursting of the ball into pieces suggests the idea of energy,
contained under pressure, being suddenly released. This is the

[1] C. G. JUNG, *The Integration of the Personality* (Kegan Paul & Co.).

moment of manifestation, or emergence, when the energy-process changes from the state of latency into activity.

Another familiar *motif* in German legend is that of the king waiting in an underground cavern until his beard has grown three times round the table, when it is said he will issue forth with all his army. It is told, for example, how a certain king disappeared with his army a long time ago in the Guckenberg, near Fränkisch-gemünden. But when his beard has grown three times round the table at which he sits, he will come out again with all his men. Once a poor boy who went about the neighbourhood selling rolls met an old man on the mountain and complained that he could not sell much. 'I will show thee a place', said the man, 'where thou canst bring thy rolls every day, but thou must tell no man thereof.' He then led the boy into the mountain, where there was plenty of life and bustle, and a lot of people buying and selling. The king himself sat at a table and his beard had grown twice round it. The lad now brought his rolls there every day, and was paid in ancient coin, which at last the people in the village would not take. They pressed him to tell how he came by it, and he confessed all that had taken place. Next day, when he wished to go into the mountain, he could not so much as see it, let alone find the entrance.

The beard belongs to the archetype of aged wisdom. In this idea of encircling the table three times an epochal turn of events is suggested, along with the idea of eternal recurrence. In the recurring cycle of events a time is due to come when this ancient principle shall re-emerge as a ruling power. As a latent or dormant potential, the figure reminds one of the dormant Shakti, the symbol of primordial energy in the *Kundalīnī tantra*. She is conceived as coiled three and a half times around the *lingam* at the base of the spine. This conception of a threefold coil has, therefore, to do with latent energy, like the iron balls or thunderbolts of the former legend.

The poor boy who cannot sell his rolls but listens instead to the voice of the spirits is, of course, the medium. Hitler was just such a case himself. He regularly failed to sell his rolls, but learned instead how to tune in to the racial unconscious. Here again we come across the populated, busy 'other world' up in the mountains where the banished pagan spirit-world is to be found, in the heart and bosom of Nature. This bustling underworld might be regarded as compensatory to the rather empty consciousness of the medium. Those who are fatally allured by the unconscious make as a rule only fitful efforts at conscious discipline and adaptation.[1] But in the same degree as the conscious life is impoverished, there is compensatory activity in the unconscious.

The transaction of the legendary money in exchange for the fresh rolls is an example of the law of reciprocity which also governs relations between the conscious and the unconscious. The fresh rolls are, of course, a symbol of conscious valuation and attention; in a word, nourishment. It is as though the time, interest, patience and understanding one can bring to this shadowy 'world of the spirits' were the very stuff of life to the unconscious. When one pays serious attention to dreams the unconscious thrives and blossoms like earth that is tilled. The ancient coin represents historical value lying buried or latent in the unconscious which can now be exchanged for present interest (the rolls). But the legend also contains a warning. The lad speaks of his traffic to others and the magic suddenly disappears. This tacit pact of secrecy is reminiscent of Lohengrin's injunction to Elsa, or of Cupid's understanding with Psyche, that she must never try to look on his face. The need for great discretion in regard to one's dealings with the unconscious — which, as experience shows, is very real — probably derives from the fact that the amount of energy available for the shadow-world, being, at the best, rather limited, is easily dispersed. Hence, it is essential that dissipation of energy through indiscriminate chatter be avoided. Moreover, the nature of unconscious activity is queer and irrational. Conservative communities tend to be unsympathetic and suspicious towards anyone who has dealings with the underworld. Accordingly, it behoves those who have the care of sensitive plants not to expose them unnecessarily to harsh winds.

The significance of this legend lies in the implied warning that what is a royal boon for individual understanding, may prove to be a dangerous illusion for mankind in general. So long as the lad keeps his secret in its own place it is like manna in the

---

[1] J. M. BARRIE's *Mary Rose* offers an excellent study of a psychology that was caught by the unconscious and lamed for ordinary adaptation. She too wandered across into the 'other world'.

desert. His kinship with the pagan gods and heroes would mean a mediumistic awareness of the depths within, and a feeling of support and sanction. But as soon as he speaks of it to others outside the experience, his sensitive individual discovery is spoiled.

As Jung suggests in his paper 'Wotan', it was conceivable that the experience of the German god could have been taken in an introverted way and the individual German might have found renewal of life through a genuine acceptance of the experience. The issue would depend, as always, upon how the experience was understood. In point of fact, the issue was never really in doubt because from the beginning, the raging collective aspect of Wotan was in the ascendant in Germany's pagan experience. The possibility of doing honour to a god, or of mediating a saving truth to thirsty souls, is not visible to those afflicted with the Himmler blindness.

This idea of discovering and honouring the early gods or heroes is to be found in many local legends. In Westphalia, for instance, between Lübbecke and Holzhausen, above Mehnen village on the Weser, stands a hill called Die Babilonie, in which Wedekind (Weking) sits enchanted, waiting till his time shall come. Favoured ones who find the entrance are dismissed with gifts.[1]

Again, in the old mountain castle of Geroldseck, Siegfried and other heroes are supposed to dwell. They too will reappear and come to the help of the German people in its time of utmost need.[2] A Thuringian legend tells of the sleeping Frederick Barbarossa:[3]

He sits at a round stone table under the Kyffhäuser, resting his head on his hand, and nodding with blinking eyes. His beard grows round the table; it has already made the circuit twice and when it has grown round the *third time* the king will awake. On coming out he will hang his shield on a withered tree, which will then break into leaf, and a better time will dawn. Yet some have seen him awake. A shepherd, having piped a lay that pleased him well, Frederick asked him: 'Fly the ravens round the mountain still?' The shepherd said 'Yes. Then must I sleep another hundred years.' The

[1] STALLYBRASS: *Grimm's Teutonic Mythology* (G. Bell & Sons), vol. III, p. 953.
[2] loc. cit., vol. III, p. 955.
[3] To be correct this name should refer to the Emperor Frederick I, who was crowned Emperor at Rome in 1155. But the legend, at least in its earlier form, is believed to refer to his grandson Frederick II (1194-1250) who was the last of the Emperors of the great Roman combine. His immediate successors failed to hold the empire together. Thus it is reasonable to depict the dream of German world dominion as going into the unconscious with Frederick II.

shepherd was led into the king's armoury and presented with the stand of a handbasin, which the goldsmith found to be sheer gold.[1]

According to another version, when the ravens stop flying round the mountain the moment will have come for Barbarossa to awaken and establish a new Roman Empire.

Following our methods of dream-interpretation, we infer that this legendary figure represents a surviving dream of power which lies dormant in the racial unconscious, awaiting the historical moment of emergence when it will resume its earlier possession of the German mind. The ravens, as we have seen, are the special messengers of Wotan; hence their presence in this connection identifies Barbarossa mythologically with Wotan. Like Noah's dove, they symbolize an intuitive process whereby a slender instinctual liaison is maintained between the unconscious ancestral potency and the main stream of conscious life.

In other legends, Frederick sits in a cave in the rock near Kaiserslautern, or at Trifels by Anweiler, or in the Unterberg near Salzburg. The same story of the beard growing round the table is related of Charles the Great or Charles V. When the beard has reached the last corner of the table for the third time, the end of the world begins. A bloody battle is fought on the Walserfeld, anti-Christ appears, the angel-trumpets sound and the Last of Days has dawned. The Walserfeld has a withered tree which has been cut down three times, but its root has always sprouted and grown again. When next it begins to leaf the fight is imminent, and will begin when the tree bears fruit.

> Then shall Frederick hang his shield on the tree, all men shall flock to it and make such a slaughter that the blood will run into the warriors' shoes and the wicked men shall be slain by the righteous.[2]

The foreshadowing of an eventual world conflict between the Christian conscious and the pagan unconscious is alluded to in the following passage:

> Frederick Redbeard in the Kyffhäuser and Unterberg, Charles Longbeard in the Unterberg and Odenberg, Holda in the Horselberg, all express one mythic idea, but with a

[1] loc. cit., pp. 955-56.   [2] loc. cit., p. 956.

different story tacked to it in every case. Charles fights a stupendous battle and is then gathered up in the Odenberg, whence he will issue one day to new war and victory. Frederick is coming out of the Unterberg to fight such a battle. In the 13th-15th centuries the people associated with it the recovery of the Holy Sepulchre. The Heroes of Odenberg and Kyffhäuser have no such purpose set before them. The older programme is that upon their awakening comes the great world battle, and the Day of Judgment dawns. Of this the mention of anti-Christ leaves no doubt. Here we see the connection with the myth of the world's destruction. The suspended shield may signify the approaching Judge. Even the sign of the tree turning green again looks to me more heathen than Christian.[1]

In the following Low Saxon legend, the repressed pagan element is symbolized by the ash-tree (associated with Wotan) which springs out of the unconscious and is protected by a mysterious black horseman:

> An ash, it is believed, will one day grow up in the church-yard of Nortorf in the middle of Holstein. No one has seen anything of it yet, but every year a small shoot comes up unnoticed above the ground, and every New Year's night a white horseman on a white horse comes to cut the young shoot off. At the same time appears a black horseman on a black horse to hinder him. After a long fight, the black rider is put to flight and the white one cuts the shoot. But some day he will not be able to overcome the black one, the ash-tree will grow up, and when it is tall enough for a horse to be tied under it, the king with mighty hosts will come and a terribly long battle will be fought. During that time his horse will stand under the tree, and after that he will be more powerful than ever.[2]

In this legend the German forefathers seem to have peered ahead and seen the day, which was sure to come, when the white horseman of Christianity would not be able to overcome the black one, and when Wotan's ash-tree would spring again. This is the same conclusion as that reached by Jung, that the 'blond beasts' would break loose as soon as the authority of Christian culture had weakened, and values had become fluid again.

[1] loc. cit., p. 957.   [2] loc. cit., p. 960.

2

These legends are especially significant because, as we have already shown, Adolf Hitler claims to be anti-Christ or, at all events, to represent the anti-Christian principle. We know, as Hitler must also know, that the coming of anti-Christ has been prophesied, even from early Christian times, to coincide with the end of the second Christian millennium. This prophecy was probably based upon the following astrological calculation. On account of the precession of the equinoxes, it takes approximately two thousand years for the spring-point (i.e. the beginning of the Zodiacal sign Aries) to move through a Zodiacal constellation. This two-thousand-year span, or Platonic month, represents an astrological epoch. Christ was identified with the fish, because the time of His birth approximately coincided with the entrance of the spring-point into the constellation of the Fishes. Therefore He was called *Ichthus* (the fish) and in the carved inscriptions in the Roman catacombs He was alluded to by the symbol of the fish. Because of this synchronicity, and in view of the two-thousand-year cycle, it was prophesied by the astrologers that anti-Christ would appear at the end of the second millennium. These calculations are of considerable interest. They are the fruits of man's original empirical attempt to systematize the cycloid nature of human events over very wide periods. For this purpose, human events were related to the movements of the heavenly bodies. Astrology is a kind of ancient almanac, compiled through the centuries, of deep human tides and changes viewed intuitively from the standpoint of the unconscious.

From the astrological viewpoint, therefore, the present upheaval has to do with the transition of the sun in the world's horoscope, from the sign of Pisces to that of Aquarius, which corresponds to the next turn of the spiral. For the view is held by many that, before the close of the present century, the world-horoscope will fall under the rulership of the qualities and values that are, astrologically speaking, taken to belong to Aquarius. Already, therefore, it might be possible to conceive the character of the Aquarian man as in the embryonic or formative state.

I mention these astrological considerations because we know that Hitler gives great weight to astrological forecasts. They also point to the existence of a widely accepted belief that the present disturbances are manifestations attendant upon the passing away of the Christian epoch and the birth of a new spiritual star. From the same wide historical viewpoint, we may regard the contest being waged in Europe as a recrudescence of the ancient pagan-Christian conflict, rather than as a struggle between contending national groups. Viewing democracy, not as a mere political orientation, but as the form of society which agrees best with our fundamental Christian values, we see at once that Hitler's scorn of 'the decadent democracies' is bound up with his declared anti-Christian bias.

We know that this repudiation goes deeper than a dictator's aversion from the parliamentary form of government. Hitler is perfectly aware that he stands in opposition to the central truth of the Christian revelation. Let me once again quote his words, for their importance cannot be over-emphasized:

> To the Christian doctrine of the infinite significance of the individual human soul and of personal responsibility, I oppose with icy clarity the saving doctrine of the nothingness and insignificance of the individual human being, and of his continued existence in the visible immortality of the nation.[1]

Yet although Hitler stands in stark opposition to our fundamental Christian values, he is no true pagan. Paganism would repudiate Hitler just as vigorously as Christendom is rejecting him. No cultivated people either in the past or present would willingly tolerate a ruler who regularly broke his pledged word, dishonoured treaties, abided by no human pact, and refused service either to wife, friend or god. Yet, in spite of Hitler's incompatibility with either side, it is undeniable that the present division in Europe has to do with the pagan-Christian conflict within the soul of Christendom.

Let us examine this paradox from another angle. It was predictable, as Jung has shown, that trouble would eventually come from the suppressed pagan elements in the German unconscious. How did the Germans differ in this respect from peoples farther west? To answer this we must glance back to the establishment of the Holy Roman Empire. The Teutonic barbarians

[1] *Hitler Speaks*, p. 222.

were not persuaded of the truth of Christianity: they were pitch-forked into the Christian fold straight from polydæmonism and nature-worship. Their indigenous mythology had little in common with a highly refined oriental religion which was rooted in a mystical surrender to a God of love.

It is a fatal illusion of power-psychology to believe that conquest is synonymous with conversion, and that a super-imposed plan implemented by force is an advance upon evolution. There is a peculiar irony in the fact that the very people which suffered most from the totalitarian ruthlessness of the Holy Roman Empire should have harked back to the same grim fallacy in their present dealings with subject peoples.

With our present knowledge we know that the inevitable result of such coercive measures is a dangerous dissociation between the repressed levels in the unconscious and the totali-tarian conscious standpoint. Symptoms of this vast repression are not lacking in the subsequent history of Christendom. The break-up of the Holy Roman Empire was followed by the witch-madness, in which it has been estimated that something like two million witches were burned in Europe during the space of a hundred years. Records of the trials of witches leave no doubt at all that the Church had to deal with a widespread renegade movement that was seeping back underground to pagan ritual and practices. The allure of the repressed antithesis was sensed as a terrible danger, seducing man's allegiance away from the authoritarian Christian fold. The rites of the witches' Sabbath, like the black Mass, were a mixture of surviving pagan ritual and a satanic caricature of the Christian Mass.

The persecution of the Jews sprang almost certainly from the same unrecognized pagan-Christian conflict, inasmuch as the Jews were the people who refused to accept the divinity of Christ. It is as though the Jewish nation were singled out by fate to play the terrible rôle of the scapegoat, upon whom the still unChristianized savagery of the Christian unconscious could be projected.

But the Wotan-worship, the preaching of Hitlerism in the churches, the whipped-up revival of Teutonic paganism and its mythology, the pitiless persecution of the Jews — all these things are symptoms of the basic disorder, just as the raised temperature, the quickened pulse, and the flushed skin are symptoms of bodily infection. The most immediate and poisonous result of the spiritual infection is revealed in the indifference of the Nazi State to the well-being of the individual.

Outrage and injustice to the individual human being is inherent in every one of the charges which the world is levelling against this great nation. It is as though it had unaccountably turned renegade from its Christian civilized tradition. The systematic cruelty of the concentration camps; the predatory filching of money, valuables, and means of livelihood from harmless citizens; the persecution of Catholics, scientists, writers, anyone indeed who had a free standpoint and who was capable of criticizing the criminal public acts of the German rulers; the invasion, wholesale robbery and slaughter of weaker nations; the suppression of the international scientific spirit in every branch of culture; the cruel shifting of whole populations from lands and homes where they had lived for generations to new and often ravaged districts — these and a thousand other pitiless violations of Christ's individual human being can be brought home to the Germany led and governed by Hitler.

But what the reflecting mind asks, and the historian of the future will have to answer, is the question: What was the evil spirit which took possession of Germany? Where did it come from and what made Germany yield herself to it? Viewing it as broadly as we can, Germany is in the grip of a terrific and cruel force, more in the nature of an earthquake, flood, or mighty whirlwind than any analysable human factor. Just as a natural disaster is indifferent to the human beings it destroys, the spirit of Nazi Germany is disdainful of everything the natural man holds most dear.[1] This spirit, which is possessing and destroying Germany,

[1] I had the opportunity of seeing an example of this dæmonic ruthlessness whilst at Berchtesgaden in the spring of 1938. It having been decided that another hospital was required, presumably for military purposes, a site was chosen which involved the demolition of five private villas. Some of these were actually occupied when the demolition work was begun. I was told that there was no question of individual compensation where the needs of the state were concerned. The road up to the hospital was driven through fences and private grounds without the least regard for the rights of property-owners. No one could explain why the Führer had chosen this particular plot of ground when open country lay at his disposal within a stone's throw. Someone offered the excuse that the villas had not been marked on the map shown to the Führer. It seemed curiously symptomatic of Hitler's psychology that, while the most grandiose building schemes were being carried through in Berlin and other cities, the homes of individual Germans were being needlessly sacrificed in Berchtesgaden.

must therefore be the object of our research. Our analysis of
Hitler in Chapter I led us to the conclusion that we have to deal
with a man possessed. It is as though, in his own person, Hitler
manifested the spiritual disorder that has seized upon the whole
nation.

3

It is our reasonable habit to explain the events of the contemporary world by reference to economic, political, or sociological
factors, and in this rational category there is little place for
possession. Still less is there place for the primitive pagan conception of God as an overwhelming dynamic force. Were it
possible to feel completely satisfied with the politico-economic
explanation of the present world situation, psychology would have
nothing relevant to add. But since this is not the case, our discussion must be largely concerned with the hypothesis that war
has broken out between peoples who serve different gods.

In a recent illuminating essay Professor Jung describes the
empirical psychological picture of contemporary Germany in
terms of a mass-possession which he calls *Wotan-redivivus* or the
furor teutonicus. For him Wotan is the hypothesis which expresses
the most significant dynamic aspect of present-day Germany.[1]
He is the god who is the 'possessor' of the German people, a fundamental and irrational quality of the German soul which remains
latent in the unconscious until the time arrives when it emerges
like a cyclone, dispersing all culture and reason, and rousing the
nation to a state of fury.

Wotan is essentially a dramatic figure and, like the other gods,
he is a personification of psychical powers existing eternally in
the unconscious.

The following citation is translated from Jung's article:

> If I am not mistaken, it was soon after Hitler's seizure of
> power that *Punch* had a cartoon representing a furious
> Berserker, wrenching himself free from his fetters . . .
> Germany is a land of spiritual catastrophe where certain
> facts of Nature make only a patched-up peace with Reason,
> the ruler of the world. The antagonist is a wind, penetrating
> into Europe upon a wide front from Thrace to Germany

[1] Jung's article was actually published in 1936.

78

from the boundless tracts of Asia, now blowing the nations together from without, like shrivelled leaves; now from within, inspiring world-shattering thoughts — an elementary Dionysos breaking through the Apollonian order. The generator of the storm is called Wotan. For closer investigation of his character we need more knowledge not only of his historical effects in mental and political disorders and revolutions, but also some mythological evidence of those primordial times before Reason had begun to explain everything in terms of man and his limited possibilities: discerning rather the deeper causes in the things of the soul, and their independent activity and power. Earliest intuition always personified these forces as gods, characterizing them carefully and comprehensively, according to their inherent nature, in the form of myths. This was the more possible because it concerned the established primordial type or image inherent in the unconscious of innumerable tribes who in turn characterized them by the traits peculiar to their behaviour. One can therefore speak of a Wotan archetype operating collectively as an independent psychical power, and through its effects weaving an image of its own nature. Wotan has his own biology, distinct from that of the individual who, from time to time, is seized by the irresistible influence of this unconscious mass-condition. On the other hand, in times of peace, the existence of the archetype is as unsuspected as a latent epilepsy. Could those Germans who were grown up in 1914 have guessed what they would be like in 1935? Yet such is the astounding effect of the wind-god 'who bloweth where he listeth', and of whom one cannot know whence he cometh or whither he goeth; who seizes upon everything that comes in his path and overthrows everything that has no inner resistance. When the wind blows, everything shakes that is inwardly or outwardly insecure.[1]

This character of Wotan as a god of wind and tempest and revolution is rather different from that of the paternal Zeus-like figure who booms melodiously from the stage in Wagner's *Ring*, though it is most probable that Hitler was first inspired by the Germanic myth through the influence of Wagner. According to Grimm[2] Wuotan (O.H.G.) is derived from *watan*, Sanscrit

[1] C. G. JUNG, 'Wotan', published in *Neue Schweizer Rundschau*, March 1936.
[2] I. S. STALLYBRASS, *Grimm's Teutonic Mythology* (G. Bell & Sons, London), vol. IV, p. 1327.

vâdanas, and is closely connected with weather, Old High German *wetar*; also *aër*, aether and wind. He is storm, *byr*, *furia*, wild hunter, spirit.

This dynamic aspect of Wotan also bears another name, Yggr, meaning terror. Yggr is represented as the rider in the air, the furious hunter. Yggdrasil is the horse of dread, the storm-courser, perhaps the rushing god himself under his dæmonic aspect. Further significant insight into the character of the god is the connection between *watan* and *wuot=wuth*, fury. Again, in the popular language of Bavaria, *wueteln* means to bestir oneself, to swarm, to grow luxuriantly, to thrive.

The ambiguous god-dæmon character of Wotan belongs to him as a primordial being. In the primordial levels of the unconscious the opposites are not yet sundered, but lie together side by side. Grimm tells us that Wuotan, the wise god who rules the world, also stirs up wars and rebellions. Thus the maker of visions and runes is also a wild, wandering, destructive dæmon. The latter aspect is closely linked up with the idea of mass-conflagration or frenzy. Thus we constantly find references to the *Wuetunges her*, later *wütende heer*, the furious host or wild hunt of medieval belief, which was led by Wuotan. It was doubtless this aspect of Wotan, degraded to a fiendish, bloodthirsty devil, which still lingers in the form of a Westphalian curse.

A Mecklenberg legend representing Wotan as this dæmonic spirit of the wild, intuitive hunt is remarkably appropriate for the present German condition. Doubtless it was such legends as this which Heine had in mind when he wrote of the 'dæmoniac forces of old German pantheism'.

> A peasant was coming home tipsy one night from town, and his road led him through a wood; there he heard the wild hunt, the uproar of the hounds, and the shout of the huntsman above him in the air. '*Midden in den weg!*'[1] the voice shouted, but he took no notice. Suddenly out of the clouds a tall man on a white horse plunged down right in front him. 'Are you a strong fellow?' said he, 'Here, catch hold of this chain, we'll see who can pull the hardest.' The peasant

---

[1] We are told that 'it is only those who keep in the middle of the road that the rough hunter will not molest, that is why he calls out to travellers: "*midden in den weg!*"'

bravely grasped the heavy chain, and up flew the wild hunter into the air. But the peasant had twisted the end of the chain round an oak that grew near, so the hunter tugged in vain. 'You must have tied your end to a tree,' said Wod coming down. 'No,' replied the peasant, 'look, I am still holding it in my hands.' 'Were you heavier than lead,' said Wod, 'up you must come with me.' As quick as lightning he leapt towards the clouds, but the peasant forestalled him as before. The dogs barked, the wagons creaked and the horses neighed overhead, while the tree groaned to its roots and seemed to twist round. Again the huntsman tried to jerk his opponent off his feet and the peasant's heart began to sink, but no, the oak held firm. 'You are strong,' said the hunter, 'many's the man I have carried away, you were the first that ever held against me three times, you shall have your reward.' The peasant was making off when from unseen heights a stag fell groaning at his feet, and there was Wod leaping off his white horse to cut up the game. 'Thou shalt have some blood and the hind quarter.' 'But my lord,' said the peasant, 'I have neither pot nor pail to put it in.' 'Pull off thy boot,' cried Wod. The man did so. 'Now walk, with blood and flesh, to wife and child.' At first the load seemed light, but presently it grew heavier and heavier, so that he could hardly carry it. With back bent and bathed in sweat, he at last reached home, and behold, the boot was filled with gold, and the hind-quarter was a leathern pouch full of silver. [1]

Such folk-tales are rooted in the primordial levels of the collective psyche. A myth is indeed the dream of a people and, like a dream, only gives up its gold when treated symbolically. Regarding the legend, therefore, as a symbolical representation of the racial psyche, Wod, or Wotan, the wild huntsman, personifies an unconditioned intuitiveness in the Teutonic psyche. It reveals itself as a kind of ideological exaltation in which an ideal objective is pursued with the savage intensity of a Berserker. [2]

Like Pegasus, the winged horse of Bellerophon, Wod's aerial

[1] STALLYBRASS, *Grimm's Teutonic Mythology*, vol. III, p. 924.
[2] Name applied to the twelve sons of the hero Berserk, grandson of the eight-handed Starkadder and Afhilde. Berserk was famed for the reckless fury with which he fought, always going into battle without armour. His twelve sons were his equals in courage (*Encycl. Brit.*). From another source we learn that the Berserker were originally men who could assume the form of bears. The name being derived from the *Sark* or shirt worn by them which was made from the skin of a bear or other animal (*Brockhaus Encycl.*).

81

horse Sleipnir is also white, a colour which usually refers to the upper spiritual element as opposed to the dark, chthonian forces of earth. Hence Sleipnir, like Pegasus, not only carries Wotan to war or to the hunt, he is also the steed on which poets rise to divine heights. The 'middle of the way' is to be interpreted as a saving bit of advice, especially needed by a people inclined to lose touch with their instinctive roots, and to become seduced by one-sided excitements. The chain means something earthy and strong. The tree is the symbol for an attitude that is firmly rooted in reality; not a fixed rule laid down by the intellect and enforced by the will, but rather an instinctual allegiance to the essential conditions of life. The intoxicated peasant thus personifies the besetting weakness as well as the latent strength of the German nature. Figures like Peer Gynt, Til Eulenspiegel, or this drunken peasant are born out of the racial unconscious as symbolical characterizations of the national genius. The latent strength of the German character is brought out in the shrewd and instantaneous cunning of the peasant when challenged by the possessing frenzy of the wild god. Though intoxicated, he is, above all, a peasant with a peasant's realism. This saving realism shows itself in two ways. First, the common-sense expressed in keeping to the 'middle of the way'. Second, his immediate recourse to the tree with its rooted strength.

The idea of the stag in Wotan's hunt seems to correspond with the Chimaera which was Bellerophon's quarry when he rode Pegasus to the hunt. Chimaera was a female monster with a lion's head, a goat's body, and the hind part of a dragon. It was a destructive, fire-breathing monster; in other words, a characteristic denizen of the primordial unconscious. It has to do with the incest-dread which transforms the maternal image into a devouring monster. The stag, from its royal bearing and branching horns, is closely associated with the unfolding or creative potentiality of the phallic energy. It is therefore of the greatest significance that the fantasy quarry must be brought to earth before its latent potentiality can become evident. This aerial stag, in association with the drunken peasant, also implies a tendency in Teutonic psychology for the sexual *libido* to be displaced upwards, producing a state of intellectual compulsion.

Assembling these associations into coherent form, we reach the conclusion that the German folk are liable to be carried off by gusts of spiritual intoxication, that their fundamental strength lies in a realistic common sense bequeathed by a shrewd peasant ancestry, and that, if they are staunch enough to withstand the tendency to collective exaltation, they could tap a boundless store of creative energy — the true gold of human effort.

It is interesting that this aspect of Wotan as the spirit of mass-intoxication is countered by an individual aspect, in which he becomes the inspiring wind of prophecy and poetry. In his intuitive, inspirational character he is conceived as overseeing all things, seated upon a chair of peculiar structure. The gift of vision seems to have resided somehow in the position or character of the chair, since everyone who sat in it received the divine privilege and was inspired by the god. This intuitive quality of vision links Wotan with Hermes and Mercury; and just as Hermes was pre-eminently the giver of good things to the Greeks, so Wotan was also the dispenser of bounty. Thus Wotan is connected with the word *wunsch* (wish) which is derived from *wunja, wonne,* meaning bliss. The wish had originally an almost magical significance and was associated with the idea of the gift of the gods.

Another name for Wotan was Omi or Oski, meaning rush, or impetus. Thus, from the age-long experience of the god, three attributes or qualities have been evolved: *wuot*=fury, *wunsch*= ideal or wish, and *omi*=impetus. The benevolent, grace-bestowing god of the poet and seer has his dæmonic counterpart in the raging storm-dæmon, who strikes terror among men, and sends a thrill through nature. Omi or Woma, this dæmonic personification of Wotan, is thus equivalent to the Hindu Indras, 'whose rush is heard in the sky at break of day, in the din of battle, and in the tramp of the furious host'. He is often depicted driving through the air at the head of his *wütende heer.*

The Norse Odin has only one eye, for when he desired to drink at Mimi's fountain, he was obliged to leave one of his eyes in payment. Mimi, of course, is the chthonian artificer, the Nordic Vulcan. We must, therefore, interpret this transaction as the need of the spiritual, intuitional sky-principle to make peace with (psychologically, give value to) the realities of earth.

Wotan's weapon is Gungnir, the wonder working spear, which he lends to heroes whose victory he wants to ensure. Siegmund received a similar gift when he found the magical sword Nothung in the tree where Wotan, with divine foreknowledge, had thrust it.[1]

Like Apollo, to whom the wolf and the raven were sacred, Wotan has two wolves which follow him in the fight and fall upon the dead. He has also two ravens which sit upon his shoulders and whisper into his ear whatever they see and hear. Their names are Huginn and Muninn, from *hugr* (*animus* or thinking) and *munr* (*mens* or mind). They are both brave and cunning and, as their names clearly imply, they personify differentiated psychological functions. We can assume, therefore, that the two wolves symbolize a corresponding pair of instinctive functions. The team of four functions represents the idea of fourfold totality, the ground-pattern, as it were, of the general psychical structure.

Finally, Wotan is the Wanderer, thus again providing a parallel with Hermes. Many are the tales of his wanderings, his wagon, his way, his retinue. The constellation of the Great Bear, some-times called Charles's Wain, bore the name of *Wuotane's wagan* in heathen times, and in some regions the Milky Way was called *Wuotane's wec*.

In a recent monograph Martin Ninck[2] has reconstructed a full-length portrait of Wotan. The feeling of the renewed power of the god is conveyed, even through the pages of an objective, scientific account. In ten chapters based upon innumerable references, the author describes Wotan as the Berserker, the Storm-god, the Wanderer, the Warrior, the Wish and Love-god, the Lord of the dead, the Lord of those slain in battle and of those who thirst for secret knowledge, the Magician, and the god of

[1] Regarding the tree as the guardian of ancestral value, we find a similar theme in our own tradition, in the promise of Drake to return with an invincible spiritual host when those coming after him should sound his drum in the moment of dire need. The presence of this latent ancestral quality lying ever ready in the un-conscious is expressed in Henry Newbolt's poem:

> Drake he was a Devon man an' ruled the Devon seas,
> (Capten, art tha sleepin' there below?)
> Rovin' tho' his death fell, he went wi' heart at ease,
> An' dreamin' arl the time o' Plymouth Hoe.
> 'Take my drum to England, hang et by the shore,
> Strike et when your powder's runnin' low;
> If the Dons sight Devon, I'll quit the port o' Heaven,
> An' drum them up the Channel as we drummed them long ago.'

[2] MARTIN NINCK, *Wotan und germanische Schicksalsglaube*, Eugen Diederichs, Jena, 1935.

Poets. In an illuminating research into the origin of the name, Ninck also shows that Wotan incorporates the driving-emotional as well as the intuitive-inspirational side of the unconscious: on the one hand, god of fury and madness; on the other, the skilled in runes and pronouncer of destiny.

In his article on Wotan Jung compares Wotan with the gods of antiquity:

> Although the Romans identified Wotan with Mercury, his individuality does not really correspond with any Roman or Greek god. He leads a roving life, like Mercury; he has the government of the dead in common with Pluto, also with Kronos. His frenzy links him with Dionysos, at all events in his mantic form.[1]

As the psychic instigator of collective momentum,

> this Germanic god represents a totality corresponding, on the primordial level, to a psychic situation in which man is unable to will differently from the god; he must, therefore, fall under his sway completely, as to a fate. With the Greeks, on the other hand, there were gods who gave their help against other gods, and the all-Father Zeus was not far from the ideal of a benevolent, enlightened despot.[2]

The totalitarian state of mind, in which it is inadmissible to entertain another viewpoint or even to see the common rights of other people, manifests this all-or-none exclusiveness of the primitive state of possession.

Jung continues:

> But Wotan gave no indications of age: as the spirit of the times turned against him he simply vanished, as was his wont, remaining invisible for more than a thousand years. This simply means that he worked anonymously and indirectly.
> Archetypes are like river-beds which the water has abandoned, but to which it returns again after an indefinitely long period. An archetype is like the course of an old river in which the waters of life, having flowed a long time, have worn a deep channel. The longer they were contained in the same bed, the more likely are they sooner or later to return to it. If the life of the individual within a certain state is regulated

[1] C. G. JUNG, 'Wotan' in *Neue Schweizer Rundschau*, March 1936.
[2] Ibid.

like a canal, then the life of that nation will resemble the course of a torrent that knows no master; no human master at all events, only one that has ever been stronger than man. The League of Nations, which should have had international authority, is, according to some, like a child needing help and protection; according to others, it is a premature birth. Thus the life of nations rolls on unchecked, unguided, unconscious, like a huge boulder that goes hurtling down a slope, and which only a tremendous obstacle could ever bring to a standstill. So political events go from one cul-de-sac to another, like a mountain torrent that finds itself caught in gorges, winding turns, or even bogs.

Wherever the mass begins to move instead of the individual, human ordering ceases, and the archetypes begin to operate. This happens also in the life of the individual when situations are encountered which he can no longer master with his accepted categories. What a so-called leader does when called upon to deal with the mass in motion we [in Switzerland] can see without ambiguity, both to the south and the north of our own country.

Christianity has been attacked on a wide front by the national god. It matters little whether this god calls itself technology and science, as in Russia; or Duce, as in Italy; or German Faith, the German Christian movement, or the State, as in Germany. 'German Christian' is, in fact, a contradiction in terms. It would, therefore, be much better if this movement went over into the camp of Hauer's German Faith movement[1] and joined those nice well-meaning people who honestly admit that they are possessed, yet give themselves endless trouble to dress up the new undeniable fact [i.e. the fact of possession], in a conciliatory, historically-adjusted garment in order to make it not quite so alarming. Thus great figures are seen in a comforting light; the great figures, for instance, of German Mysticism, such as Meister Eckhart, who was a German and also possessed. In this way it is possible to

---

[1] In a footnote Jung mentions the case of a Dr. Langmann, who bears the title *Oberkirchenrat* of the Evangelical Church, and who officiated at a funeral wearing his S.A. uniform and jack-boots. In the course of his funeral address he gave instructions to the dead hero for his journey to Hades, directing him to Walhalla, the home of the sacrificial heroes Siegfried and Baldur, who, 'through their blood-sacrifice, nourish the life of the German nation', just as Christ had done in his time. Dr. Langmann concluded his address with the following prayer: 'May God send the nations of the earth down the clanking road of arms through history. Lord, bless Thou our fight.'

avoid the offensive question: Who is the possessor? It was always 'God'. But the more Hauer gravitates from his world-wide Indogermanic circle to the Nordic one, and particularly to the Edda, and the more German does the faith that is its expression become, the clearer does it also become that the Germanic god is the actual god of the Germans.[1]

On the ground that effective religious feeling rests upon experiential knowledge rather than upon faith, Jung writes:

> I should therefore advise the German Faith movement not to be too prudish. Those who understand will not confuse them with the clumsy disciples of Wotan, who merely affect a belief. The German *Glaubensbewegung* has representatives who should, intellectually and humanly, be in a position not only to believe, but to know that the god of the Germans is Wotan and not the universal Christian God. This is no disgrace but a tragic experience. From time immemorial it has been a terrible thing to fall into the hands of the living God. Jahveh is no exception: there were once Philistines, Edomites, Ammonites and others who stood outside the Jahveh experience, and certainly found it disagreeable. The Semitic experience, called Allah, was for the whole of Christendom, and for a very long time, a most grievous thing. We, who stand outside, are liable to pass judgment on the Germans to-day as though they were responsible doers: it would perhaps be more correct to regard them also as endurers.[2]

Jung finishes his paper with the following comforting prediction:

> In order to be consistent in the application of our admittedly singular method of approach, we must conclude that Wotan is not only his restless, brutal, and stormy character; he must also be this very different ecstatic and inspirational character of his other aspect. If this conclusion turns out to be right, then National Socialism will not remain the last word, but during the next years, or perhaps decades, underground things must be expected of which at present we can only form a dim conception. The reawakening of Wotan is un-doubtedly a regression, a harking-back, and through the damming-back of the river it has broken through into its

[1] C. G. JUNG, 'Wotan' in *Neue Schweizer Rundschau*, March 1936
[2] Ibid.

former bed. But the damming-back of a current is not everlasting; it can also be a *reculer pour mieux sauter* when the water
will begin to flow over the barrier. Then it will be revealed
what Wotan 'murmured with Mimi's head'.[1]

4

I have quoted at length from this essay of Jung's, because,
besides being not easily accessible to readers in this country, it
is entirely appropriate to our theme. For it will be observed
that the character of Wotan is equivocal in a special way, and
that this double aspect of the German god corresponds with the
ambiguous nature of the Nazi spirit. The inspirational, creative
side of Wotan breathes the free air of individuality. A single
human being is inspired; he begins to dream dreams and see
visions. Thus the wise, poetic, mantic personality of Wotan is
associated with singleness and a certain spiritual readiness.
Whereas the storm-dæmon, the war-spirit, the raging, Berserker
hunter is as clearly a collective phenomenon, as the character
of 'raging host' indicates. These contradictory aspects of Wotan
correspond with the Apollonian-Dionysian antithesis of the
Greeks; with, however, this crucial distinction. In Greece, the
conflict of opposing tendencies was intensely conscious, creating
the polar distinctiveness and clarity of the Greek mind; whereas
in the German Wotan, the opposites are not yet sundered, but lie
incorporated side by side in one dæmonic figure. This lack of
differentiation of the opposites denotes a primitive psychological
level[2] which the educated pagan of antiquity would have
despised. It is well to bear this fact in mind when we glibly
speak of the Nazi philosophy as harking back to paganism. The
shocking and terrifying thing about Nazism is not so much its
insensate brutality as its complete anaesthesia to moral and ethical
values. The Wotan-possessed disciples of Hitler are clearly
incapable of knowing what is sacred and what obscene. They
are feared by all men not because they are strong and indomitable,
but because they spurn just those vital and venerable feelings

---

[1] C. G. JUNG, 'Wotan' in *Neue Schweizer Rundschau*, March 1936.
[2] In a great many primitive languages opposite qualities, such as black and white,
are denoted by the same word.

which unite the whole human race. In his ordinary civilized state no one is more sensible of moral values than the German. In his present morally dissolute condition, he is apparently numb to the very things which before touched him to the quick. This is why we are driven willy-nilly to the hypothesis of possession. Only the man who is possessed suffers so grievous a transformation of character.

Another aspect of the Wotan contradiction can be alluded to at this point, although it will be dealt with again at a later stage. Up to the end of 1934 everyone who had cultural dealings with Germany came across devoted, enthusiastic individuals for whom the new wind that was blowing through Germany was a veritable inspiration, a commanding and transforming power. At that time a real renascence was unmistakably stirring, and Hitler seemed to be voicing something that could rightly be called prophetic. In those earlier Nuremberg rallies there was a gal-vanizing enthusiasm which was sensed, and eventually shared, by thousands of young people from every country of Europe, from every part of the British Commonwealth, and from the Americas. There was an unmistakable religious feeling in those vast camps, organized shows, and victorious battalions of youth. At that time Hitler was as much a positive symbol for Germany as Lenin had been for Russia; for, like Lenin, he was himself, at that time, exalted by the bright flame of revolution. There was a numinous flame, a compelling sacrament of power which had taken possession of German youth, and Hitler responded to it.

This *numinosum* can be represented in terms of the mantic, inspirational side of Wotan. But after the criminal *volte-face* of June 1934, the whole movement took a sinister turn. The religious enthusiasm seemed to congeal and sought a more and more materialistic expression. The previous austerity was seduced into widespread corruption. The whole spirit changed. Everyone who could wield party-influence began to intrigue unscrupulously for positions of power, and to fill his pockets with money gained by the skilful use of blackmail, frequently aimed at his party comrades. The corruption spread, and the spirit of the later phase of Nazism became almost unbelievable in its insane lust for power. Ruthless German might in its crudest possible expression crushed every delicate individual growth out of existence, and the youths who went out as missionaries of the new spirit degenerated into 'Quislings' and political mercenaries. This change, gradually sensed by the sobering mind of Germany as the most terrible betrayal, has been vividly recounted by Otto Strasser[1] in his book *Hitler and I.* A similar betrayal was felt in Russia when the flame of revolution, which Lenin had kindled, was quenched by the despotic and brutal Stalin.

This second phase corresponds to the insensate, collective dynamism of the Wotan possession, and it is important to remember that the inherent contradiction between the earlier and the later phase of the Nazi movement was also to be found in the character of Wotan. It goes without saying that those contained by what Jung terms the 'Wotan experience' are quite unconscious of the real state of affairs. For them the opposites are not differentiated. The good and evil aspects of Wotan are still bound together in primordial unity, so that the only truth, for those contained by the god, is his invincible dynamism. The disadvantage of this state of primitive identification is, however, almost as great as its energic advantage. Durable morale relies upon a state of moral tension in which good and evil are sensed as opposing spiritual powers. But the primitive state of possession is essentially a state of intoxication which, by its nature, is transient. What remains when the frenzy is past?

5

The psychological view of the German phenomenon provides us, I believe, with the most reliable means for judging the catastrophe of our time. Jung advises those of us who stand outside the German experience to try to understand it from within. At scientific conferences in Germany during recent years I have seen National Socialist enthusiasts actually come to Jung asking him to tell them what was really happening to Germany, and why they had to do such unaccountable things.

In dealing with Germans in general since Hitler came to power, one has constantly been made aware of an unmistakable

[1] Strasser describes how Hitler made his choice between revolution and re-action on June 30th, 1934. 'The date,' he writes, 'on which he took up his position in opposition to the New Order, a decision which meant for him simply "the flight into war." It was out of fear of the German revolution that Hitler and the old Prussian forces of which he is the instrument sought their safety in war.' (Quoted from an article by Strasser in *The Spectator*, May 10th, 1940.)

gulf dividing those within the experience from those without. It is not merely a question of whether one has to do with a member of the Nazi party, or even a Nazi sympathizer. The sense of an unfree mind, of someone being secretly held and gripped by a dreaded power, is always present. The universal espionage naturally accounts for the reserve, but apart from this, one senses a subtle alienation of spirit. One gropes in vain for the genuine individual reaction, the essential touchstone of reality in one's dealings with a fellow-being. Instead of a frank individual expression one is given a mass-feeling, or a collective view. Throughout Germany, whether one belongs to the party or not, the terrorist atmosphere has made genuine human intercourse impossible.

But it would be incorrect to assume that this alienation of individuality belongs specifically to the new Germany of Adolf Hitler. As long ago as 1875 Paul Anton de Lagarde wrote:

> Everything depends on individuals, and Germany lacks nothing so much as the individual human being. With her worship of the State, of public opinion, of Kultur, and of success, Germany singles out for hostility the individual human being, through whom alone she can live and win honour.

Nietzsche came to much the same conclusion. In 1888 he writes:

> What the higher schools of Germany really do accomplish is this: they brutally train a vast crowd of young men, in the smallest possible amount of time, to become useful and exploitable servants of the State.

The Hegelian philosophy of Right, in which the state is idealized as the consummation of man, expresses a rather similar tendency. The attempt to shift morality from the consciousness of the individual, where alone it belongs, towards the ethical life of the family and the state, is already very clear in Hegel. He does not treat the family as a biological unit nor as the result of a contract, but as an instinctive realization of the moral life. He conceives the state as developing

> through ever wider associations until it emerges finally as the full home of the moral spirit, where intimacy of interdependence is combined with freedom of independent growth.[1]

[1] *Encyclopaedia Britannica*, Fourteenth Edition. Article of Hegelian Philosophy.

And again:

> The state is the consummation of man as finite; it is the necessary starting point whence the spirit rises to an absolute existence in the spheres of art, religion and philosophy.[1]

In this realm of absolutes good English words seem to faint under an impossible burden. But Hegel was no nationalist and, like Nietzsche (whose ideas have also been travestied by modern German developments), he would have felt outraged could he have seen for what ends his conception of the absolute state was to be employed. Like Goethe, Hegel felt no patriotic shudder at the national disaster when Napoleon overthrew the power of Prussia at Jena. He saw in Prussia, as all southern Germans do, only 'a corrupt and conceited bureaucracy'. In a letter to a friend, written the day before the battle, he speaks with admiration of the 'world-soul', the Emperor, and dwells with satisfaction on the probable overthrow of the Prussians.

The Prussian spirit is, however, not confined to Prussia, and it is something more and something worse than 'corrupt and conceited bureaucracy'. What Hegel saw as the menace to Prussia, we see as a world-wide threat to individual freedom on the part of tyrannical, collectivist ideologies. The spirit which wants to impose on a nation a stereotyped economic theory and enslave the people by means of plausible collectivist schemes — this is the Prussian spirit which Hegel abominated and which is to-day the greatest threat to human life and happiness.

Throughout the world there exists a deep and rooted piety, guarding steadfast peasant communities, where fundamental social virtues are joined to simple religious faith. Prussianism, in the form of collectivist interference, uprooted men from these settled communities and forced them into collectivist farms, where the individual is deprived of his original myth and his instinctive relation to the soil. Real communism was destroyed in the effort to create an arbitrary intellectual communism. Is this not the very essence of Prussianism, this persistent and destructive interference in the lives of others?

Revolutionary ideas are charged with something more potent than gelignite; collectivist reformers might therefore be serving

[1] loc. cit.

humanity to better purpose if, instead of dressing up this Prussian spirit in idealistic ribbons because it has adopted their favoured political colour, they taught men how to work for their ideals without fanaticism. It is never entirely credible that brilliant humanists such as Mr. Wells and Mr. Shaw should still believe that a certain type of collectivist programme carries with it a kind of civilized sanction or guarantee, irrespective of the spirit which directs it. They would certainly not dispute the psychological axiom that if one seeks freedom by tyrannical means the result is tyranny, not freedom. Yet this fundamental canon of common sense is ignored when the so-called communistic experiment of Russia is being assessed. So long as socialistic experiments are actually controlled by a despot or an oligarchy, it is self-evident that no genuine result can be anticipated. Unless we are blind to psychological realities, we must realize that no communism worth the name can breathe in an atmosphere of despotic power.

Great collectivist schemes are to be distrusted. They lure men to heady dreams of power. The only defence against them is to make the individual human being the criterion of all our political planning, so that other factors have to relate to that one basic fact. So long as a statesman keeps the single human being in the centre of his field he remains comparatively sane, but once he loses this touchstone of common sense he proceeds to legislate as though psychology were mere sentimental nonsense, only fit for small nations and eccentric philosophers.

In calling attention to the interfering power-character of a large part of collectivist scheming, I do not underestimate the necessity for collectivist plans in the modern world. But just as there is a crucial difference between the spirit which founds an empire upon the principles of democratic freedom, and the spirit of militarism which sees the human subject exclusively as a unit of power, so I make an absolute distinction between a collectivist policy which *in its very conception* respects human individuality, and a collectivist ideology which regards the human factor as a mere detail of an organized political machine. Every reformer will assure you that he does not really agree with violence and tyranny, and that, as soon as his particular policy shall have won its way to power, he will grant freedom to the individual,

But these reformers delude themselves. There is no way to freedom over the pass of tyranny. The essential interests of the individual cannot merely be taken for granted; they are the goal of the whole political process, and must remain the living centre of all political effort.

The difficulty is that people are blind to their own aggressiveness. A man can usually recognize his moods — erotic, angry, depressed — but his aggressiveness is liable to remain hidden from his inner eye. This is largely due to a conscientious attempt to make human nature agree with the Christian ideal, which allows the aggressive instinct no honourable place among the virtues. Except in time of war, when this relic of unregenerate humanity finds honourable expression, aggressiveness must first put on a becoming garment before venturing into action.

But my fundamental ground for suspecting ideological attempts to transform human nature is to be seen in the degraded conception of individuality existing in every country where the collectivist schemer has enjoyed unrestricted scope. It is, to my mind, self-evident that if we spend all our labour and ingenuity in making a fool-proof world, safe for grown-up children to play in, we shall, therewith, obstruct Nature's aristocratic objective, the fully matured and differentiated human individual. Since the salvation of our culture rests upon the appearance of this mature human being, we can only hope that the exigencies of war will evoke those qualities of courage and faithfulness to an enduring purpose out of which a mature character is built.

The alarming spread of political aggression is due to a variety of causes. On the one hand, the increasingly complicated machinery of collective life has tended to estrange men too much from their original nature. People, thus estranged, are liable to reinforce a basic feeling of insecurity by fanatical adherence to parties and ideologies which seem to offer an outer substitute for the lost value within. Lacking insight into his own nature, such a man tends to identify his ego with the ideology he is trying to impose upon his fellows. This identification produces an inflation of the ego, which is, therewith, relieved of its former feeling of inferiority and insignificance. This, of course, is the inner story of the goose-stepping, the martial gestures, the braggart threats, and all the rest of the paraphernalia of power-madness with which the more sober portion of Europe has recently been nauseated.

A true relativist can discuss any part of his philosophy with detachment, thus allowing his fellow-man liberty to choose whether to accept or reject his ideas. But if I identify my ideas with my ego then at the back of every affirmation there lies a bludgeon. 'I am right,' also implies, 'You are wrong'. Thus Prussianism in the world of ideas arises from the same spirit which invaded Manchukuo, China, Abyssinia, Austria, Czecho-Slovakia, Poland, Finland, Denmark, Norway, Holland, Belgium, France, Albania, Greece and Jugoslavia.

Psychology can be proved to be the most essential as well as the most practical of all branches of knowledge. For if I attain sufficient enlightenment to see that an idea is not necessarily true because I happen to hold it, I have already minimized the possibility of war. There is, naturally, not the same punch in the relativist statement, but in the long run it will be found to have all the more persuasion for its lack of insistence.

A crucial psychological operation must, however, intervene between the absolutist and the relativist attitudes, an operation which might be called self-realization. When, for instance, the philosophical truism comes home to a man that the truth of a proposition is not self-evident merely because he has uttered it, he therewith rescues both himself and his proposition from that worst and subtlest intoxication of the mind — the lure of absolute truth. A proposition that retains enough modesty to be satisfied with the status of a relative truth maintains both itself and its human sponsor decently upon the human level. But as soon as the virus of absolutism has infected our gentle truth, it begins to thunder forth revelation, while its hitherto reasonable devotee assumes the air of a prophet.

This is no mere abstract issue; for with the former attitude the propounder is always willing to discuss, and even to negotiate; whereas with the latter he is liable, if we do not immediately agree to his proposition, to knock our heads off.

What appears, therefore, to be an imponderable psychological subtlety may actually decide the issue between peace and war. If, for example, in the recent phase of German expansion the rulers of Germany had been granted sufficient insight to see that a claim does not necessarily possess absolute merit because it happens to be German, it is clear, on the evidence of the British White Paper, that war would have been averted. Stated in this way, the issue is made to appear almost as an even chance. Whereas in point of fact, given the context of Hitler's possessed psychology within the framework of Nazi Germany, we know that the possibility of Hitler agreeing to a relative assessment of any issue was practically nil. Thus, although a psychological operation decides the issue between peace and war, it cannot become an indispensable attribute of leadership until civilized man makes psychological maturity his principal objective.

By a somewhat devious route we have now reached a conclusion which throws light upon the whole question of collective responsibility. Even if it were true, as Oscar Levy contends,[1] that Nazism can be traced back to the Judaic idea of the Chosen People, and that Bolshevism and Nazism have both a common root in Christ's promise of a Kingdom of Heaven, it does not follow, as he also contends, that because Christ's revolutionary ideas have led to disastrous consequences we ought, therefore, to seek our way by the light of other values and a new faith. We need not attempt to put out the sun because some people have distorted vision. Is it not more likely that we have reached the point when a new and vital understanding of the Christian problem is our only way to spiritual maturity? Perhaps the Kingdom of Heaven is a truth that was spoken directly to the loyal individual heart, and was never intended to serve as a char-à-banc image for those who cannot face the solitariness of the individual experiment. That His ideas became deflected from their original meaning is no argument that Christ's central spiritual principle was false. But a truth that is germane to the problem of individuation may lead to disaster if shouted through loud-speakers to the multitude. To lay the responsibility for the existence of mass folly upon the shoulders of those to whom the profoundest truths have been revealed, but whose message has been distorted or misunderstood, is to seek refuge from the problem of insufficient light in total darkness.

---

[1] OSCAR LEVY, *Idiocy of Idealism* (William Hodge & Co.).

6

The foregoing discussion has shown that two types of cause have to be considered when we attempt to answer the question why Germany, in particular, was liable to become the mad dog of Europe. The first type is racial in character and belongs specifically to the turbulent Nordic unconscious. We have discussed it under its mythological character of Wotan. The second is individual and, therefore, comes within the scope of personal analysis. I have described this cause as *alienation of one's original nature*. This I believe to be the fundamental evil of our time, and the reader will have doubtless observed that the one consistent critical aim of the present work is to invite his attention to just those factors and forces which effect the estrangement of individual man from his own being.

Prussianism is the spirit which inspires the modern collectivist policy of interference. Hence, Prussianism, according to my view, is essentially devilish. Jesus took as the foundations of his saying truth the primordial nature of man when He said: 'Suffer the little children to come unto me, and forbid them not: for of such is the kingdom of God.' What He sought to give His disciples was the translucent clarity of attitude which would allow the original nature of the soul to come out and thrive in the warmth of the sun. What He hated with a clear flame was the pharisaical spirit — the Prussianism of His time — which intervened like an opacity and, in place of the simple translucence of the child-mind, built up an attitude of self-righteous suspicion: that attitude which made every Pharisee a policeman spying enviously upon everyone else. Just as the Pharisees embodied and symbolized the dark power that would deny the freedom of the spirit in the very city of God, so Himmler, with his Gestapo, embodies and symbolizes the same evil power and the same single-minded aim to crush the spirit of man.

The reader may object that the Pharisees were the voice of tradition and custodians of the law, while the Gestapo is the repressive arm of a revolutionary party. But if we look beneath the surface we shall find that, although the Nazi party came to power by the revolutionary route, it soon ceased to be revolutionary in character. Ever since Hitler chose the way of militaristic power to solve his early embarrassments, he has marched true to the Prussian type, and he has made use of the very quintessence of Prussianism in his suppression of individual freedom. Both Stalin and Hitler have proved themselves to be entirely reactionary in their fundamental political attitude, however much they may dress their respective shop-windows with the latest ideological models.

The process of alienation by which a youth is seduced from his native individuality and converted into a Nazi bully, is both subtle and horrible. It is the direct negation of education, which consists in bringing out native quality and interest in such a way that individuality is fulfilled and a socially acceptable form realized. The Gestapo method of alienation, by which the ranks of Nazidom are recruited, consists primarily in the obliteration of every spontaneous reaction of human feeling. When the youth has finally learned to treat everything human with scorn and distrust, the slate is clean for Himmler to inscribe the required Nazi character. Thus the German youth, and indeed everyone who capitulates to Nazi power, is denaturalized, or spiritually gelded, for the sake of an already outworn power-fantasy.

In this work I am concerned with the crime of interference. The gelding is a far more serious matter than Hitler's power-fantasy. Hitler's fantasy will prove to be no exception to the rule: what is fundamentally unreal cannot survive. But the perversion of youth and the interference with individuality is a subtle, insidious disease which is liable to attack any highly organized collectivity.

It is clear that the state of dæmonic possession is, in a sense, secondary to that of alienation; inasmuch as a man who is convincingly rooted in his own being leaves no room in his house which a dæmon could inhabit. This is surely the meaning of the Mecklenberg legend, in which the peasant defeats the transporting fascination of Wotan. From the fact, therefore, that Wotan represents a latent indigenous character in the German unconscious, we may conclude that the disease of alienation has long tended to undermine the integrity of the German national character.

CHAPTER III

THE GOD CRIMINAL

I

Before we can come to the heart of our problem we need to understand the fluid, suggestible, unaccountable nature of mass-mentality. At first glance it would seem to be relatively simple to study the queer phenomena of the mass-mind. Mr. Tom Harrisson and his assistants, in their experiments in mass-observation, have already made interesting discoveries about the unlimited nature of collective foolishness. But the psychological roots of our major stupidities are still quite obscure.

During the course of his life every individual has, at certain moments, become more or less dissolved in the mass, and knows, therefore, from experience what this collective animal-state is like. Its essential content remains, none the less, beyond the reach of conscious introspection; almost as though it belonged to a different planet. For as soon as we have reverted to the collective state in which we become, as it were, mentally fused with the herd-mind, we are immediately subject to an altered state of consciousness, the chief character of which is a loss of objectivity. Our own light is temporarily extinguished. If in company with Mr. Harrisson we watch the condition of mass-folly from an objective vantage-point, we are, psychologically, as far removed from the level we are observing as is the field-anthropologist, for instance, from the level of an aboriginal orgy. A scene that is observed and recorded is not experienced. The moment one participates, submitting fully to the experience, one is already in an uncritical state of consciousness, not unlike that primitive condition described by Lévy-Bruhl as *participation mystique*; a state which, to a very large extent, precludes the objective functioning of the mind.

On many occasions I have watched the faces and gestures of a crowd listening to political harangues in Germany. I have observed human beings, with whom a few minutes before I was

99

in lively intercourse, assume the standardized mask and perform the abrupt motions of a mechanical doll, exactly as though, humanly speaking, they had ceased to exist. People living in Germany have learned how to discard their ordinary personalities and adopt this collective mask, very much as some people put on the required mask of respectability when attending church. If we exclude all those people who go to church for reasons of religion, we come to the residue, which submits to traditional opinion as a *force majeure* in much the same fashion as the Germans submit to political domination by the Nazis. From the viewpoint of the observer and the behaviourist these are identical phenomena.

It is clear, therefore, that the outside observer cannot make any very helpful contribution to our research unless he finds some means of inquiring into the nature of collective motive. Whenever we submit to collective requirements in a dutiful way, we do, in fact, assume a kind of mask of submission, and this mask appears much the same whether it is motivated by terror, or because we fundamentally agree with its necessity.

This descent, from the level where the individual is consciously navigating his own course, to that of collective submission, involves psychological change in which we temporarily hand over the direction of the situation into other hands. We cease to be responsible, just as we cease to take any further directional responsibility the moment we enter a train. We hand over control. But suppose everyone is concerned only with finding a seat in the train, the situation is open for some enterprising adolescent to realize his dream of becoming an engine-driver. What undoubtedly attracted Hitler was a vast train-load of politically passive Germans waiting for someone to conduct them to their unknown destiny.

Although collective submission is indispensable for any kind of government, it is none the less a state of primitive gregariousness. To go from a state of individual awareness and activity to that of collective submission is not unlike the descent from the freedom of one's work-room to the street. A relatively primitive state implies greater suggestibility. The frontiers of conscious personality, which are clear and established on the individual level, seem to dissolve away when one enters the suggestible collective state. Beforehand one could say: 'I am the master of my fate, the captain of my soul.' Now one is merely a blood-corpuscle circulating in the body of a vast animal. It is hard to realize this change and its implications, because at the moment we become part of the animal, we leave behind our objective, critical awareness.

The unchallenged power of the witch doctor or medicine man in primitive communities rests upon his instinctive capacity to hold this suggestible mass-animal under the influence of terror; and the terror he inspires comes from his traffic with the spirits. He can see what others cannot see. His spirit, taking the shape of lion, hyena, owl, etc., can pounce and kill, or it will inform him of hidden things, even of a man's secret thoughts. By his magic he can command spirits to do his bidding. The power of the medicine man extends over the whole range of primitive life because of his direct relation to the spirit-world.[1] He is not only a medium in the sense of being a kind of psychical conduit: he also personifies the contents of the unconscious by means of grotesque masks and fantastic disguises. With these aids he performs fearsome or grotesque dances in order to evoke the dæmonic contents from the general unconscious and fasten them, so to speak, upon himself. By thus becoming the dæmonic element, he can also charm it. His mastery over the dæmonic powers of the unconscious is the secret of his amazing ascendancy over the tribe. Were he to fail in this his whole power would collapse.

With this primitive figure in mind, we can begin to realize why Hitler, with sure instinct, used every means to repress and exclude the level of individual consciousness, why he wages war against individuality with its independent, creative spirit, and why he uses every kind of trick to reduce the general level of consciousness to a primitive level. He cannot converse with his fellow-man, but he can charm the great collective German soul. Essentially, as we shall presently see, his methods are those of the primitive medicine man. His prestige depends solely upon his power of calling to, and indeed personifying, the German unconscious. He performs this function in the same way as a weather-vane plays its appointed rôle as a function of the weather. While the

[1] The spirit-world is, for us, the unconscious.

wind blows, it is the visible manifestation of the force and changing conditions of the weather; but when the wind drops, the vane loses its soul. Hitler cannot, therefore, be said to possess a personal psychology in the ordinary human fashion. His human personality is practically obliterated by his specially cultivated magician's rôle. Were he a human being with a personal life of his own, he might be held accountable for what he has said and promised. But one cannot quarrel with a weather-vane because it says 'North' to-day and an equally convincing 'South' to-morrow. The vane is set where it is in order to make visible the ever-changing force and direction of the wind.

Whether performing before the microphone, or sitting in his eagle's nest on the Obersalzburg, Hitler is sensing and responding to the German unconscious. No stable direction is expected of a weather-vane, and before we can adjust our minds to Hitler correctly, we must abandon all ideas of ordinary good faith, and learn to view him primarily as a medium. The impression of sincerity which various people — especially women — have recorded of Hitler is not, however, due to skilful acting. There can be little doubt that Hitler has either lost or suppressed the function whereby a man is able to appreciate the inconsistency of his present behaviour with previous undertakings. He retains no continuity of personality, or at least not sufficient to make a clear junction between his inspirational or possessed state and his normal condition of semi-torpor.

That a man claiming to be the sole arbiter and spokesman for a nation of eighty million souls should cultivate this mediumistic unaccountability, must be infuriating for all who have to deal with him. The only way to treat him would be to cultivate an almost inhuman detachment. One must forgo all ideas of dealing with a personality, accepting instead the hypothesis of a stormy wind or a hysterical woman. When, after Prague, Mr. Chamberlain rounded on Hitler for betraying the Munich agreement, he was angry because Hitler had failed to act as a gentleman. Yet from the beginning of his career Hitler openly disclaimed any such pretension. Is not the man who casts the pearl more accountable than the swine? Mr. Chamberlain had had excellent opportunities for observing the unstable, hysterical being he had to deal with. Why, then, did he repress this knowledge and persist in regarding Hitler as the trustworthy leader of a great nation? Perhaps, like so many of his sanguine fellow-countrymen, he looked at his adversary down his own nose.

Hitler's unaccountability is more than usually discreditable, inasmuch as he deliberately exploits it for political ends. It is normal, for instance, for a man, temporarily possessed by a sudden passionate mood, to have no objectivity at the time, and only poor recollection afterwards, of what he said or did during the mood. But Hitler undoubtedly cultivates this state of dissociation, attuning his whole rhetorical art to the aim of intoxicating the mass-mind, whose voice he is, and for which, in Germany at least, such imponderabilia as truth and fair-dealing have no special significance. Intoxication is the German's greatest weakness, and it is this which has given Hitler his power. He trains for it, withholding himself from everything else. In order to cultivate his mediumistic *réagibilité* to the mass-psyche he tends to hold himself aloof from ordinary human situations, only coming into the limelight for the purpose of producing a dramatic impression. He is an emotional virtuoso, using his emotionality with conscious art. Accordingly, his relation to his hysteria is not unlike that of a *Heldentenor* to his voice. His expressionless, frowning face, his weak, mechanical handshake, his piercing but unfocused gaze, his inability to converse as man to man, or to submit to experienced advice — all are symptoms of his aloofness from ordinary life. His psychology lies either above or below the human level. In every direction in which a normal human being is organically related to his fellows by living emotional ties, Hitler appears deficient. But he is clearly in his element on the other side, where the human herd wallows at his feet, feeding him with power. It is for the sake of this that all normal relationships have been sacrificed.

2

Observers who are struck by Hitler's neurotic behaviour and uncontrolled humours find it hard to understand how so unstable a mind, that has never yet succeeded in mastering a task, can maintain the rôle of supreme power. It is not hard to understand how Hitler gained his position. His phenomenal ability to sway his audience, as well as his apparent harmlessness as an individual, commended him as a suitable political instrument in the designs of various powerful reactionary sections, industrialists, landed aristocracy, and conservative Generals of the Reichswehr. These sections combined to hoist Hitler into the saddle. But it is surely remarkable that a neurotic individual, having gained the position of supreme power, without education or traditional dynastic support, has been able to maintain absolute authority and steer a shrewd and consistently aggressive course for eight years under the most menacing economic and political conditions.

Three factors can be cited which make this feat intelligible. The first, and the most interesting psychologically, is Hitler's astonishing political intuition, by virtue of which he is able to sense the changing currents and eddies in the world situation. No one could deny Hitler's genius in this direction, though his emotional deficiency which deprives him of the smallest trace of understanding of any non-German standpoint is equally patent.

The second is his ability in finding associates of the type of Goering. For Goering combines a driving efficiency and organizing ability with a brutal, amoral unscrupulousness. The power which accrues to these accomplices in a gangster régime, where the only principle that matters is that which governs the distribution of meat in a pack of wolves, would of course be inconceivable in any other state. Nevertheless, Goering's effectiveness is undeniable.

The third is the most sinister factor in the whole situation, though its historical implications cannot yet be fully grasped, nor adequately assessed. I refer to Hitler's invariable choice of the criminal, instead of the honourable, way to his political objective.

But even more sinister than Hitler's obvious criminality is the fact that he has been supported in his crimes by the German people. We must conclude, therefore, that an unrecognized or latent criminality in the German unconscious finds in Hitler a kind of moral scapegoat. This pathological streak in the German character must be held responsible for the attempt to exalt the Führer into a divine being, superior to human laws. Feelings of guilt are avoided through a mystical transformation of the arch-criminal into the god. The blasphemous protestations

which follow become intelligible only when we regard them as
the frantic efforts of German spokesmen to stop the accusing
mouth of conscience:

He who serves Adolf Hitler serves Germany, and he who
serves Germany serves God —
BALDUR VON SCHIRACH, head of the Hitler Youth.

Hitler is a new, a greater and a more powerful Jesus Christ —
ALOIS SPANIEL, leader of the Nazis in the Saar.

The creator of mankind appeared 2000 years ago in the
form of Christ. To-day God reveals himself to the German
people again, in the form of Hitler — *Welt des Kaufmanns.*

Adolf is the real Holy Ghost — CHURCH MINISTER KERRL.

The following is quoted from Professor Hauer, a leader of the
German Faith movement, formerly a Christian missionary in
India, and subsequently Professor of Religious Philosophy at
Tübingen University:

The Germans have no feeling of guilt, or that they are born
sinners. Even if the German sins, he does not lose direct connection with God.

Again, from Baldur von Schirach:

The Nazi party has been proved to have better relations with
the Lord in Heaven than had the Christian parties which
disappeared.

Such protestations are more naively revealing than any direct
evidence of criminal intention. The need to exorcize this evil
conscience is also shared by women. The following comes from
one of the leaders of German women:

God has been merciful to us and given us two things; the one
we deserve, the other we did not deserve. The one we did not
deserve was the war, and this, so help us, we did not want.
But it was the will of God. In the midst of our great travail
and debasement, God forgave us and sent us the other,
Hitler! God breathed upon him; Germany and the German
soul received new strength![1]

Such fulsome affirmations of Hitler's divinity must express
some essential collective need, or they would surely have
appeared ludicrous, even to the persons who uttered them.

[1] FRAU SPANN, in *Deutsche Frauenvolk.*

A scene in the physiological laboratory at Cambridge returns vividly to my mind. I mention it as a graphic illustration of the compensatory excesses of a troubled conscience. In the course of their training, medical students have to use frogs that have been pithed (i.e. the brain is destroyed without killing the frog) for the purpose of studying the response of living muscle and nerve to electrical stimuli, and other experiments of a similar kind. One day the student who shared a bench with me complained to the demonstrator that his frog was not properly pithed. For a few seconds the demonstrator could not speak. He paced about white and agitated. Finally, he came over to my companion, and the red lava of Vesuvius could not have been more devastating than his anger. My friend had made his objection without being objectionable, and was naturally bewildered by the force of the storm which burst upon him. The demonstrator asked how he dared to question the pithing of the frogs. Did he imagine that he (the demonstrator) had not also been burdened by scruples? Either what they were doing was absolutely right, or it was manifestly and hideously wrong.

I do not want to complicate the issue by discussing the rights and wrongs of vivisection; but when I ask myself why the passionate, white face of the physiologist returned to my mind at this juncture, I see beside it the faces of thousands of good people in Germany who have tried desperately, like the tormented physiologist, to sanction the ultimate value of the cause they are working for. It is for this reason they have to insist upon their divinely-led mission: for if they did not, the accumulating horror of what Germany has done would devastate their peace of mind. The following statements from German leaders must surely be intended to put Hitler and his actions beyond the reach of criticism:

God placed Luther in a monastery and Adolf Hitler in a fortress. To these babblers in our ranks I say: 'Go and be silent in solitude also' — BISHOP HOSSENFELDER.

The question of the divinity of Christ is ridiculous and inessential ... A new authority has arisen as to what Christ and Christianity really are — Adolf Hitler —
CHURCH MINISTER KERRL, February 23rd, 1937.

THE GOD CRIMINAL

Hitler is lonely. So is God. Hitler is like God —
                    DR. FRANK, Reich Minister for Justice.

It is the duty of pastors, instead of quarrelling over dogmas,
to recognize in the leader of the German people one of those
great men whom the Lord has entrusted with mighty tasks on
behalf of his people and the whole world. The Church
should support, and not oppose, the will of God as represented
by Hitler.

It is important to note that the above quotations are from
official representatives of the Church and the Law, the natural
guardians of the state conscience. The last is from the address
of a judge passing sentence of six months' imprisonment on a
pastor for having forbidden children to give the Hitler salute or
to join in the clamour against the Jews.

Just as vivisection must not be challenged from any standpoint
other than that of the absolute necessities of medical science, so
the absolute superiority of the National Socialist revelation and
morality must not be questioned from any other ethical
standpoint.

National Socialism must not be judged from a Bibilical or
Ecclesiastical standpoint; it is the Bible and the Church
which must be judged from a Nazi standpoint. The Nazi
state embodies the totality of God — DR. KRAUSE, at a meeting
in Berlin-Pankow, January 17th, 1934.

Yet the need to go out and collect divine sanction for National
Socialism in the highways and byways is pathetically illustrated
in the following:

In the name of our chief, Hitler, we find . . . the first articulate
syllable stuttered by primitive man, the sound '*H—d*', an
expression signifying 'protection' or 'elevation'. The same
sound occurs in ancient German words like '*hut*', '*Huette*' and
'*hild*'. Adolf, the Leader's first name, is composed of '*ath*'
(divine or spiritual act) and '*uolfa*' (creator) — E. SCHMIDT-
FALK in *Voelkischer Beobachter*. Quoted in *The New Republic*.

It is unfortunate that the Führer's real name should be
Schicklgruber, though doubtless divine sanction could be
manufactured even out of this unpromising material.

The compulsive need to claim Germany as the sole source
of enlightenment is another symptom of a restless conscience.

The following is the considered view of Adolf Wagner, Bavarian Minister of the Interior, in a speech at Munich, July 16th, 1937:

> But transcending all else in greatness and security is the certainty that to-day and in all other ages there does not, and did not, exist a civilization without *Deutsche Kultur*. What a glorious privilege it is to belong to a people of which this can be said without presumption.

It would be superfluous to repeat such fables, if we could view them as the airy products of unguarded enthusiasm. But they are not. They are the official views of leaders of German opinion. The following, for example, is to be found in the programme of thirty points drawn up by the National Church of the German Reich:

> The National Church of the German Reich declares that the greatest written document of our people is the book of our Führer, *Mein Kampf*. It is completely aware that this book incorporates not only the greatest, but also the purest and truest ethics for the present life of our people.[1]

And this from a well-known professor:

> A people which desires honour can be no longer Christian.[2]

The following citations reveal the avowed criminal intention as well as the direct practical use of possessing a magical leader whose divine sanction can be called upon in any ethical 'emergency'. The first is cited from the instructions given by General Goering on October 23rd, 1932. The second is quoted from Adolf Hitler's funeral address at the bier of the Nazi Swiss agent, Gustloff:

> Anyone who makes the least difficulty is to be shot. It is necessary that the leaders should find out here and now the personalities who must be removed. One at least (meaning, one in every place) must be shot as a warning immediately after the revolution.

> Upon the path of our movement there lies not a single one of our opponents murdered by us, not one attempt on the life of our enemies has been made. From the first day to the

[1] Quoted in the *Manchester Guardian*, May 6th, 1938.
[2] PROFESSOR ERNST BERGMANN in his Foreword to *The Twenty-five Theses of the German Religion*.

present we have refused to use such outrageous methods. Never have we fought with such weapons.

What is so difficult for the onlooker to understand is why the Nazis should make these transparent attempts to whitewash criminal deeds which are in complete accord with the barbarous power-philosophy they openly teach. Why applaud barbarity in theory and then disown the deed? Following the analogy with individual psychology — which is permissible so long as we recognize that analogy does not necessarily mean identity — we know that a man who intends to do something forbidden by his conscience will land himself in a bog of ambiguity. Unless he is an old hand at crime, for example, he will almost certainly inculpate himself by excessive self-justification. If, on the other hand, he has contrived to conceal from himself his privy intention, he will tend to project his criminal motive upon some convenient scapegoat, wife, servant, partner, or rival, as malice and opportunity may provide. Supposing the intended, though half-repressed, criminal goal is so foul that his civilized personality will have none of it, he must either put his higher civilized centres out of action, or abandon the criminal plan. If he chooses, or is over-persuaded by his Iago shadow-dæmon, to carry through the crime, he will employ one of two methods, both of which are calculated to silence the higher, epicritic centres of moral judgment. Either he will descend to a brutal, archaic level of behaviour, undergoing a complete alteration of personality, as in the case of Dr. Jekyll and Mr. Hyde[1]; or he will yield to a sand-throwing attempt to sanctify the criminal motive by attributing it to the will of God. Unless inhibited by a sense of humour — a gift of heaven not vouchsafed to the fanatic — the criminal may even represent himself as the humble agent of God's mysterious will. This second method is not very plausible in the case of personal wrong-doing. But when the crime is done for the sake of an aggressive national policy, this method is, as we know, frequently practised.

The moral ambiguity in Hitler's Germany is also shown in the fact that it was the leaders of culture in every sphere against whom the Nazis aimed their fiercest persecution. In individual

[1] It is no mere accident that the concealed shadow-personality should be called Mr. Hyde.

psychology these would correspond to the conscience and the higher reasoning centres. The seat of the moral reason must naturally be overturned before an ordinarily decent man can be seduced to a criminal deed. When this occurs — and it is by no means impossible — the mask of the citizen, submitting decently to the law, is thrown off. The subject indulges in moods and outbursts of savage violence. He acquires a shifty expression and lashes out with resentment at the faintest breath of criticism. It cannot be ascribed to blind savagery, therefore, when a régime with an unsavoury background directs a cold-blooded persecution against its most cultured and outspoken citizens. For it is precisely these people who can recognize hypocrisy and will oppose a criminal policy with civilized resistance.

Although an accusing conscience is undoubtedly irritating, this cannot wholly account for the widespread outbreak of sadism in Hitler's Germany. Sadism is not a psychological entity, existing in and for itself. It is the negative of a very human positive. It arises out of frustration and resentment, and marks a character that has become twisted through the arbitrary deprivation of normal instinctual satisfaction. A brutal or cruel man is always unfulfilled. Cruelty is an inverted state in which the warmth of feeling and the light of the spirit have been extinguished. Accordingly, when the whirlpool of inversion can be made to flow forward again towards a realizable goal, cruelty and fanaticism disappear. From every point of view, therefore, it is wiser to cultivate love than to repress sexuality.

For the nationalistic dream of German power to be realized, it was essential that every generous, cultural tendency should be subordinated to motives of hatred and revenge. An official blight had, accordingly, to descend upon every organization aiming at international relationship. The whole moral attitude of the nation had to be anaesthetized, so that the rape of other nations' freedom and the wholesale enslavement of individuals might be effected without protest. It is not surprising, therefore, that the man destined to carry out this obscene policy was not only an alien, but a moral defective. We understand why the Christian Churches (the Catholic Church in particular) inter-nationally-minded scientists, artists and writers, the Jews with their international banking, commerce and racial organizations, the Freemasons, and every conservative institution with international affiliations, had to be attacked and persecuted. Hitler is proud of the title anti-Christ, and I doubt whether this is mere vanity on his part. He stands for criminality as a necessary implement of power, while the source of his inspiration is, admittedly, a dæmonic pagan god.

3

This regression to a more primitive level cannot be regarded as a mere process of degeneration. Men, or societies, who are slipping down hill, do not display enthusiasm or an increased vitality. The lowering of the level of consciousness in Germany is undeniable, but at the same time there is a powerful and purposive activation of the racial unconscious: a situation precisely similar to that found in schizophrenia, the disease of the split mind. Moreover, as with Nazi Germany, the schizoid man tends to emphasize a crude or tyrannical masculinity, because he feels split off from, and therefore suspicious of, his unconscious feminine soul. He cannot submit to, or go with, his own natural impulses. Therefore he is invariably cruel to his own feelings. Germany suffers from a similar split, and Germans are similarly undermined by a secret doubt as to the validity of their own nature. The only possible hope, therefore, of regaining her lost youth and former prestige was, for Germany, to recapture the pagan spirit of unreflecting, heroic action, whatever it might cost her in blood and treasure.

It was surely the fermentation of some such process as this which D. H. Lawrence describes[1] as the German mind turning away from the Christian West towards the Asiatic East, towards the floodgates which let in the hordes of Attila and the fabulous Jenghiz Khan.

But when the German nation instinctively turned to the alternative pagan hypothesis, rejecting the Christian spirit of co-operation and comradeship, it became involved in the problem of ambiguity. Its leaders had somehow to maintain a civilized front which would mask the underground recession from the Christian community. The problem was solved, for the Germans

[1] In a *Letter from Germany* quoted in chap. VI.

III

at all events, by reverting to the psychological state of the primitive tribe, which trusts itself implicitly to the god-man with his direct power over the spirits. It cannot be denied that Hitler performed a miracle for the German people, in so far as he conjured away the secret doubt and gave them instead a magical assurance in their national destiny. He performed this miracle by addressing himself to the expectant unconscious attitude which was identical with that of a primitive tribe. The following passage from Frazer's *Golden Bough* depict the primitive mental level which actually determines Hitler's functional relation to the German people:

> The persons in whom a deity is thought to reveal himself are by no means always kings or descendants of kings; the supposed incarnation may take place even in men of the humblest rank. In India, for example, one human god started in life as a cotton-bleacher and another as the son of a carpenter. I shall therefore not draw my examples exclusively from royal personages, as I wish to illustrate the general principle of the deification of living men, in other words, the incarnation of a deity in human form. Such incarnate gods are common in rude society. The incarnation may be temporary or permanent. In the former case, the incarnation — commonly known as inspiration or possession — reveals itself in supernatural knowledge rather than in supernatural power. In other words, its usual manifestations are divination and prophecy rather than miracles. On the other hand, when the incarnation is not merely temporary, when the divine spirit has permanently taken up its abode in a human body the god-man is usually expected to vindicate his character by working miracles. Only we have to remember that by men at this stage of thought miracles are not considered as breaches of natural law. Not conceiving the existence of natural law, primitive man cannot conceive a breach of it. A miracle is to him merely an unusually striking manifestation of a common power.
>
> The belief in temporary incarnation or inspiration is worldwide. Certain persons are supposed to be possessed from time to time by a spirit or deity; while the possession lasts, their own personality lies in abeyance, the presence of the spirit is revealed by convulsive shiverings and shakings of the man's whole body, by wild gestures and excited looks, all of

which are referred, not to the man himself, but to the spirit which has entered into him; and in this abnormal state all his utterances are accepted as the voice of the god or spirit dwelling in him and speaking through him. Thus, for example, in the Sandwich Islands, the king, personating the god, uttered the responses of the oracle from his concealment in a frame of wicker-work. But in the southern islands of the Pacific the god frequently entered the priest, who, inflated as it were with the divinity, ceased to act or speak as a voluntary agent, but moved and spoke as entirely under supernatural influence. In this respect there was a striking resemblance between the rude oracles of the Polynesians, and those of the celebrated nations of ancient Greece. As soon as the god was supposed to have entered the priest, the latter became violently agitated, and worked himself up to the highest pitch of apparent frenzy, the muscles of the limbs seemed convulsed, the body swelled, the countenance became terrific, the features distorted, and the eyes wild and strained. In this state he often rolled on the earth, foaming at the mouth, as if labouring under the influence of the divinity by whom he was possessed, and, in shrill cries, and violent and often indistinct sounds, revealed the will of the god.[1]

Naturally, this description of primitive possession by the god is not intended to correspond with the German's conscious attitude to the Führer. But no one for whom psychological evidence means anything at all will deny that it describes the general unconscious attitude to the Führer; nor will it be disputed, I think, that Hitler's seizures are of the same order as those depicted above by Sir James Frazer. When, therefore, we speak of Hitler as a medium, we need not envisage the professional type which is the despair of the Society for Psychical Research. Primitive mediumship always signifies not merely a conducting path, whereby human beings can gain contact with the spirits, but an actual state of possession, implying identity with the god. Thus the man who is possessed by a god comes to be considered as a god-man. His power is unlimited because it is magical.

Though the duality of the god-criminal does not play a large part in primitive mythology, we find the god linked to the criminal in significant juxtaposition in the sacred myth of Christianity.

[1] FRAZER, *The Golden Bough*, vol. I, pp. 376-77 (Macmillan & Co. Ltd., London).

It appears in the scene where Pilate invites the mob to choose the god or the criminal, and in the crucifixion itself where the god suffers a criminal's death between two thieves. The symbolism of this juxtaposition reveals depth beyond depth. Indeed the in-dwelling power of the Christian religion seems to abide most clearly in this symbolic descent of the god to the level of the criminal in man, in order that these most contradictory of all opposites might be reconciled ('to-day shalt thou be with me in paradise'). The choice of Barabbas by the mob is also significant. For when the individual leader or ruler renounces the responsibility of choice, leaving it to the mob to decide, the criminal is invariably chosen. The herd-mind, as we said before, is not the summation of a large number of individuals with all their powers of reason and reflexion. All that part of man which distinguishes him from the animal becomes latent when he is merged in a crowd. Therefore a crowd is an animal and responds like an animal. It demands leadership, which, if faithfully given, can transform the rabble into a marching, disciplined force.

The astrological sign of the fishes, which in a peculiar way marked the birth of the Christian Era, consists of two fishes pointing in opposite directions. The symbolism of these two fishes offers a wide field for debate, but the most obvious and probable interpretation points to the contiguity of two contradictory elements within the Christian field. Thus the idea of the God and the criminal is alluded to in the very constellation which presided over the birth of our era. And now at its close we find the same significant juxtaposition of god and criminal in the terrifying ambiguity of Hitlerism. But with what a difference! Jesus showed the way, the only way, in which the opposites can be reconciled within the soul of man: through the willing sacrifice of the deified superior function for the sake of the redemption of the whole. On the other hand, by identifying himself, and Germany, with both god and criminal, Hitler has confused all moral values, and reduced the god-value to his own primitive level.

CHAPTER IV

HITLER AS SYMBOL

I

NOTWITHSTANDING, or even, perhaps, because of, Hitler's criminality he became the function by which a listless, apathetic, beaten people were galvanized into the most formidable military power in Europe. We have merely to state this astonishing fact to realize that no unaided individual could deliberately have conceived, or carried out, so heroic a plan. The historian of the future who has to account for this achievement may well grope for hidden grains of gold in Hitler's character.

Its only intelligible explanation lies in the universal power of the symbol. Not as personality, but as symbol did Hitler become the great German transformer. And since it is altogether improbable that an adventurer will consciously set out to play the rôle of a symbol, we are bound to assume that Hitler was, in a sense, selected[1] for this purpose by the racial unconscious.

The word symbol is frequently used in the wrong sense to mean a sign or token. Jung has rescued it from its impoverished standing as intellectual counter, and has charged it with dynamic psychological content. For him, it is a vital function, through which antithetical elements are reconciled, and by which energy, contained in a latent or dissociated state, becomes transformed into available power. The universal, transforming symbols must always combine two principles of opposite or diverse qualities, as for instance high and low, great and small, universal and individual, heaven and earth, macrocosm and microcosm. Thus, birds with white wings and snake-like necks, such as the swan, goose, stork, etc., have always carried a symbolic value, inasmuch as they combine the idea of the earth-dæmon with that of the celestial messenger. Early theriomorphic deities, such

---

[1] Naturally when we speak of selection by the unconscious, we mean it in the Darwinian sense of a purposive, or teleological occurrence of a significant appropriateness.

as the sphinx, and the animal-headed Egyptian deities, such as Ra, Horus, Thoth, Anubis, Bast, etc., gained their divine character, as indeed do the totem animals of more primitive levels, from the fact that they combine animal and man, therewith transforming both into a new unity of power. The redeeming power of the crucifixion, the central symbol of Christianity, is due to its reconciling embrace, enfolding God and man, the heights and the depths of the soul, in a single transforming image.

In his definition of the symbol, Jung explains its value as follows:

> The living symbol shapes and formulates an essential un-
> conscious factor, and the more generally this factor prevails,
> the more general the operation of the symbol, for in every soul
> it touches an associated chord.[1]

Besides expressing this as yet unknown factor, the symbol must proceed from the most differentiated mental atmosphere, as well as from the most general, primitive levels of human nature. It is never a purely intellectual creation, since it must speak to every function and every type of individual. Thus, the living symbolical content necessarily expresses itself in a living plastic form, which can attract feeling and sensation, as well as convey meaning to thinking and intuition.

Another very important aspect of the symbol is brought out in the following passage:

> The attitude that conceives the given phenomenon as symbolic
> may be briefly described as the *symbolical attitude*. It is only
> partially justified by the behaviour of things; for the rest, it
> is the outcome of a definite view of life, endowing the occur-
> rence, whether great or small, with a meaning to which a
> certain deeper value is given than to pure actuality. This
> view of things stands opposed to another view, which lays
> the accent upon pure actuality, and subordinates meaning
> to facts.[2]

From this description, we can recognize the former attitude as corresponding with that which animates those within the experience. For all the multitudes of Germans, whether within

---

[1] C. G. JUNG, *Psychological Types*, Definition, p. 605. Trans. by H. G. Baynes (Kegan Paul & Co.).
[2] ibid., p. 604.

Germany or without, in whom a certain activation of the unconscious has taken place through the Nazi revolution, Hitler undoubtedly became the living symbol, combining god and barbarian, the venerated and the outcast, invincible conqueror and primitive medicine-man, in a single image. But besides this, he also contained that unknown future potential which he has promulgated as the New Order. Thus a collective symbolical attitude was produced which surrounded Adolf Hitler with an aura which had the effect of transforming him into a semi-divine being. Those outside the experience naturally tended to see the coin reversed.

With this general understanding of the working of the symbol, it becomes possible for us to appreciate why the Germans had to select an outcast to be the great leader. The decline of energy-value from the conscious level at the time of the German collapse meant that the energy-potential in the unconscious came to be the decisive factor in German political life. The reins, falling from weak and listless hands, were seized by men who knew neither what they were doing nor where they were going. All they were concerned with was to seize power by means of revolution. Under their hands the historical momentum of German aggression, combined with the pagan potential in the unconscious, gradually overwhelmed the opposing forces of conservative Christian culture. A cultural revolution is not unlike the capsizing of a boat. What was below now comes to the top. It was both symbolical and reasonable, therefore, that the representative of the repressed pagan antithesis should be an alien and an outcast. The symbol-bearer is always appropriate to his task.

Although it is rationally indefensible to speak of Hitler as being chosen by the unconscious, it is none the less true that his character corresponded, in a remarkable way, with the divided state of Germany at that time. In the same way the barbarian régimes of Stalin and Mussolini can be said to agree with some specific element in their respective peoples. But the equivocal nature of the German character makes the functions of leadership especially precarious. Cultured Germans despise and distrust militarism of the Prussian type; and the hard-headed Prussian realist reciprocates this distrust. No leader could hope to straddle such a basic antagonism with persuasive argument. The existence of an unbridgeable gap tends to breed an attitude of fatalistic acquiescence, an attitude which found appropriate expression in President Hindenburg, the senile figurehead of conservative inertia. The state of Germany during the Hindenburg régime was painfully reminiscent of Lear's incomparable limerick:

> There was an old man who supposed
> That the street door was partially closed.
> But some very large rats
> Stole his coats and his hats
> While that futile old gentleman dozed.

This immortal description of the provisional attitude of psychological infancy assists our understanding of the German political débâcle better than any long-winded analysis. German apathy precluded the possibility of achieving national unity, so that the machinery of government was left exposed for any marauder to seize. The eagerness with which Germany abandoned herself to Hitler's leadership is the logical result of her proved unwillingness to become politically responsible. When a people is ready to lay down its civic responsibilities in a mood of helpless despair, a dictator will always be found ready to take advantage of the occasion. But although Hitler suited the unconscious pattern, as the desired symbol of the pagan antithesis, he could not continue in this rôle without running the risk of meeting increasing opposition from the cultural side.

German colleagues who were by no means sympathetic with the Nazi spirit, have told me that, up to the seizure of Prague, Hitler was a generally positive symbol in their patients' dream-life. The invasion of Czecho-Slovakia had a damaging effect upon the basic allegiance to Hitler, even though this reaction was largely repressed. In modern Germany, political reactions are either misleading or absent. But dreams show the unconscious instinctual reactions and tendencies. We may conclude, therefore, that the German unconscious was almost solidly behind Hitler, so long as he remained loyal to the German racial myth, and could be regarded as a leader striving for the traditional German aims. It was only when he overstepped the limits sanctioned by his own theory that the national spirit recoiled. When the Prussian marauder emerged from behind the mask of the prophet

Hitler's value as a symbol began to dissolve. But by that time the army was on the march. He had succeeded in harnessing the immense energies of the nation to a grandiose programme of reconstruction, and the integrity of the symbol was no longer a matter of paramount concern. With the army behind him, no effective opposition was feasible.

The fact that we have to portray Hitler from one point of view as an unscrupulous political marauder, and from another as a kind of Messianic symbol, is the measure of the fundamental ambiguity of the German national psychology. Any attempt, therefore, to portray Hitler as merely evil must be unconvincing, since it is inconceivable that a mere charlatan could have achieved what, in fact, he has achieved, or have held the confidence of the German people during these testing years. Our portrait must embrace the constructive as well as the destructive genius of this human phenomenon.

2

The massive aspect of Hitler's achievement can best be seen under the phenomenon of the conversion of energy. This function, which also belongs characteristically to the operation of the symbol, has had a fundamental influence on the growth of civilization through the centuries. Culture, indeed, would be inconceivable without the displacement and conversion of the primal energy form (*libido sexualis*) into its various functional derivatives. Had there existed in human nature only enough biological energy for the satisfaction of elementary needs, including that of procreation, there would have been no culture, no science, and no religion. All that we value as sacred and eternal in our lives has, therefore, been created out of the surplus energy not taken up by biological necessity. And everything, which has had commanding power over man's feelings, has helped to prepare his mind for the operation of symbolic conversion.

Since man is the object of our study, every account we give of a mental process must refer primarily to individual psychology. The following description of Jung's is, I believe, the first psychological account of the process of conversion. Taking this as our model, it is possible to adapt our thought to the reverse process on a larger scale.

But, when the opposites are given a complete equality of right, attested to by the ego's unconditioned participation in both thesis and antithesis, a suspension of the will results; for the will can no longer be operative while every motive has an equally strong counter-motive by its side. Since life cannot tolerate suspension, a damming up of vital energy results, which would lead to an insupportable condition from the tension of the opposites did not a new reconciling function arise which could lead above and beyond the opposites. It arises naturally, however, from the regression of the *libido* effected by its damming up. Since progress is made impossible by the total disunion of the will, the *libido* streams backwards. The stream flows back, as it were, to its source, i.e. the suspension and inactivity of the conscious brings about an activity of the unconscious where all the differentiated functions have their common archaic root, and where that promiscuity of contents exists of which the primitive mentality still exhibits numerous remainders.

Through the activity of the unconscious, a content is unearthed which is constellated by thesis and antithesis in equal measure, and is related to both in a compensatory relation. Since this content discloses a relation to both thesis and antithesis, it forms a middle territory, upon which the opposites can be reconciled. Suppose, for example, we conceive the opposition to be sensuality versus spirituality; then, by virtue of its wealth of spiritual associations the mediatory content born from the unconscious offers a welcome expression to the spiritual thesis, and by virtue of its plastic sensuousness it embraces the sensual antithesis. But the ego, rent between thesis and antithesis, finds in the uniting middle territory its counterpart, its reconciling and unique expression, and eagerly seizes upon it, in order to be delivered from its division. Hence, the energy created by the tension of the opposites flows into the mediatory expression, protecting it against the conflict of the opposites which, forthwith, begins both about it and within, since both are striving to resolve the new expression in their own specific sense. Spirituality tries to make something spiritual out of the unconscious expression, while sensuality aims at something sensual; the one wishing to create science and art from the new expression, the other sensual experience. . . .

Should one side succeed in resolving the unconscious product, it does not fall alone to that side, but the ego goes with it; whereupon an identification of the ego with the most-favoured function inevitably follows. This results in a subsequent repetition of the process of division upon a higher plane. But if, through the resoluteness of the ego, neither thesis nor antithesis can succeed in resolving the unconscious product, this is sufficient demonstration that the unconscious expression is superior to both sides. . . .

When the mediatory product is preserved in this way, it fashions a raw product which is for construction, not for dissolution, and which becomes a common object for both thesis and antithesis; thus it becomes a new content that governs the whole attitude, putting an end to the division, and forcing the energy of the opposites into a common channel. The suspension of life is, therewith, abolished, and the individual life can compass a greater range with new energy and goals.[1]

This whole process, namely, the discrimination and conflict of the opposites, the damming-up of energy, its recession to a primitive, or archaic content, the liberation of energy which has accumulated through the tension, and, finally, the creation of a new symbolical expression, Jung has termed *the transcendent function*. The term is based upon the fact that, during the conflict, elements from the thesis flow across into the antithesis, and vice versa. Thus the opposing ways are transcended and a new way or attitude is created. This, however, is an ideal operation which is not always attained, since relatively few individuals have sufficient integrity or detachment to maintain a position of balance between the opposites. Clearly, if one side is preferred to the other, the whole process will be short-circuited and what should have been a transformation gives place to a more or less ferocious repression of the unsuccessful antithesis.[2]

Following the process in Germany, we see the fierce and bloody conflict between bitter opposites. We see the harking

[1] loc. cit., pp. 608-10.
[2] The Freudian conception of sublimation involves a deliberate interference with the transformation process on behalf of the socially preferred standpoint.

back to an archaic content, the consequent activation of the unconscious, and the creation of a new social pattern (Hitler's New Order) from the recession of the national *libido* from the former conscious level.

The heat of political feeling is so persuasive, that it is difficult to regard political history in terms of a more or less indifferent mechanism. Men engaged in partisan warfare are naturally convinced that they are directing the course of events, and everyone taking part in the struggle feels that everything depends upon his particular support. Thus an illusion is produced, whereby the factor of human personality is thrown into relief, while the age-old processes of the collective unconscious, which to a great extent determine the course of events, remain as invisible as the Gulf Stream. It is the business of the psychologist to give these processes their place in the total picture.

The first thing to note, however, is that the conversion of energy under Hitler is in the reverse direction from that described above. In Jung's account the conversion is upwards from undifferentiated collective elements to integrated individuality. Whereas the conversion-process in Germany is downwards from the individual level of conscious judgment to the vast collective reservoirs of the state. This naturally involves a wholesale delegation of political responsibility upon the leader; and so long as it is assumed that what is done by the state is not subject to ethical laws, this downward conversion must entail a catastrophic decline in ethical standards.

The creation of an equitable political system needs the cultivation of individual responsibility towards the machinery of collective power, and demands a high standard of integrity from political leaders. The political arena invites the gambler and the gangster only when human folly has left the incalculable power of a modern state for anyone to seize. To guard against this eventuality, democratic states have long since devised constitutional safeguards.

To resume the problem of energy-conversion, we have yet to understand why there must always be a harking back to an archaic content, before a solution of the conflict becomes possible. The reasons for this regression are much the same as those for the mining of coal. In other words, consciousness can restore its energy-supply only from the inexhaustible energy-content of the unconscious. What Jung has termed the primordial image is really a rich deposit of latent energy contained in a general image of age-old emotional value. Thus any personality, whether living or historical, when identified with such an image, becomes transformed by powerful mythological projections which both magnify him and lend him certain mystical attributes.

In general the primordial image has an absolutist, all-or-none character. It tolerates no rivals and no equals. It is isolated and autonomous, like Plato's world-soul. Being self-contained it needs no organs of relatedness. In its pristine naivety it knows nothing of the relativist world with its complicated network of reciprocal claims. Whenever it gives voice it speaks in the terrific manner of Sinai:

> For I the Lord thy God am a jealous God, visiting the iniquity of the Fathers upon the children unto the third and fourth generation of them that hate me.[1]

This absolutist character is also the distinctive mark of the autonomous or dissociated complex. As soon as it becomes adapted to other factors in consciousness, its all-or-none character disappears. In psychological language this represents the transformation of the protopathic reaction into the epicritic. It represents the whole long ascent from the primordial level to the cultural. Hence the treatment of a case of possession, where an autonomous complex rules, is the same as that by which a sound democracy cures itself of an autocratic ruler; the complex is reduced from an absolute to a relative status. In other words, it is allowed to exist only in so far as it relates to other functions.

The autonomy of the primordial unconscious process can be observed in a child absorbed in fantasy-play. Fantasy tends to reveal the characteristic all-or-none character. It creates its own living world without relation to other factors. The child shows the same self-contained independence. He is, as it were, enclosed in a state of primordial timelessness.

When the primordial image, latent in the collective unconscious, is activated through a leader at a time of national crisis, it becomes, as it were, humanly realized on the contemporary

[1] Exodus, xx, 5.

political stage. This is achieved by the unwitting transference of the associative contents of the image from the collective psyche to the human object. Through this projection of mythological content on a wide scale, incalculable streams of energy are released from the unconscious, centring in a commanding concentration of purpose upon the acclaimed leader. This conversion of energy is accompanied by certain well-defined and predictable effects.

Inasmuch as the primordial image belongs primarily to the myth-making mind of the race, it is intelligible that its projection upon a living representative will endow him with certain mythological attributes. It is commonly assumed that mythical qualities are showered upon prominent figures in the past only where their historical outlines are blurred by the lapse of time. This is by no means the case. There were, until recently, certain parts of Ireland where people still believed that Parnell was alive, as there were many people in the last war who could not believe that Kitchener had died. He would surely appear again in the hour of need. A London engineer, a cultivated man of varied experience, once said to me with intense conviction, that it was not possible for Mrs. Eddy to die. Everyone knows the feeling of living continuity with the past, the sense of the timeless moment, of having known this person or lived this experience before in a past life, the feeling of awe and wonder that sometimes takes hold of one in a sacred place — all these effects belong to the quickening of the primordial image, when, for a moment, we are dissolved in the impersonal continuity of the racial psyche. The essence of these experiences lies, however, in the fact that consciousness is intensified; so that the event has the unmistakable character of individual experience. Whereas, when the image is projected upon a leader, the experience is shared with many millions of one's fellow-beings, so that one's individual connection with the total event is dissolved in the general pool.

3

There is another aspect of the conversion process which has a direct connection with the problem of morale. The building up of energy reserves, through the cultivation of individual responsibility and initiative, is analogous to national thrift. Whereas the conversion of energy downwards, from the individual to the collective level, is like the spending of the nation's accumulated treasure.

From this point of view, the cultivation of political individuality, as in the Swiss Republic, represents a relatively high energy-potential. Whereas the totalitarian régime, which survives only through a mythological magnification of the leader, results in a correspondingly low level of individual value and responsibility. It is impossible to exalt the leader by means of a continual transference of magical value without, at the same time, depleting the herd. In other words, overvaluation of the object involves a corresponding impoverishment of the subject. This law was exemplified in the low-level phase of Christianity towards the end of last century, when a magnification of God, which depended upon an unworthy abasement of man, went hand in hand with an irresponsible delegation of the most vital human problems to divine management. Behind the continual protestations of childish helplessness there lurked obstinate spiritual laziness.

When we ask ourselves what is the purpose of the deification of the Führer or the Duce, we discover that the totalitarian system offers a constant inducement to the individual to return to a childish state of dependence upon the all-knowing parent. The great leader is looking after everything. There is nothing to worry about. He will see to it. Thus the complete attitude of faith which formerly leaned on God becomes the property of the Führer. Hitler has deliberately tried to take the place of Christ, stealing the values created through centuries of Christian discipline.

This misappropriation of psychical reserves must in time be exposed. It is also predictable that the collapse of German morale will immediately follow this exposure. The man who pretends to magical or divine powers invites the expectations which mankind, in his weakness and inferiority, has always laid at the feet of God. When these expectations receive a rude shock, faith turns to execration.

This reversion is already in actual operation in Italy, where the omnipotent pretensions of Mussolini have been effectively exploded by the Army of the Nile. In relation to the conversion process, this exposure is not unlike that of a company promoter who has persuaded a multitude of investors to put their savings in a fraudulent concern. Thus the transference of psychical value from the individual citizen to a mythically inflated leader necessarily results in a precarious national morale.

Hitler has fostered superhuman expectation by dramatizing his public appearances to the limit of human tolerance. Sometimes he would keep his vast audiences waiting for hours in order to heighten the moment when, out of the rim of darkness, he would step magically into the spotlight. From this brilliant focus he would deliver his speech, and then withdraw into the darkness.

All the tricks used by Hitler to effect the maximum impression on his audience, including the powerful aid of the microphone, must be regarded as means of conversion, whereby the latent energy of the collective unconscious is brought over into available political force. It is hardly necessary to point out, however, that the goal of this mass-phenomenon is the obverse of the aims of individual therapy; this being to restore value to a deprived individual. Whereas the totalitarian conversion-process fattens the deified leader with the individual energy-value milked from the herd.

There are three grounds on which the process of downward conversion will always be preferred by a dictator régime. In the first place, energy at the individual level is not amenable to crude, totalitarian manipulation: independent judgment tending to stand in his path when a leader attempts fraudulent methods. In the second place, the quantity of available energy is naturally much greater on the collective level: so that, judged quantitatively, the downward conversion has everything to be said for it. The third reason, and it is the most cogent of the three, relies upon the fact that energy on the collective level is primitive and, therefore, available to every kind of suggestion. All the means by which Hitler intoxicates the German masses, whipping up the collective psyche into a state of frenzy, can be paralleled by examples from primitive life.

Tribes living in or near the primitive level are readily subject to mass excitements. The savage war dances, and the famous spring dances, preceding the work of the agricultural season, are by no means a mere outlet for superfluous energy. The intoxication of the dance is the means by which energy is pumped up from a latent, inert condition in the unconscious to the active state in which it can be harnessed to the necessary seasonal tasks. It is doubtful if any savage people could be induced to fight unless they had first lashed themselves into war-frenzy with the dance. In the same way the conversion of energy from the primordial level of the *libido sexualis* to the relatively higher potential needed for agricultural work in spring-time must be regarded as an indispensable cultural process. The magnificent and grotesque painting of the body, the technique of ornamentation, the feathers, the masks, and the whole impressive crescendo of the dance, are all effective in arousing the inert *libido* into action. Thus the dance is really the power-station of the primitive community. The more we study the Hitler phenomenon with its formidable means of mass-intoxication, the more clearly it emerges that the immense disturbance he has caused in the European family is due to the fact that, in every crisis, he resorts to primitive means. The mass-emotion, generated at the later Nuremberg rallies, became an annual threat to world-peace, because Hitler deliberately fomented the incalculable force of primitive affect in the German unconscious, in order to use the excitement thus generated as a threat in his 'war of nerves'. He is indeed a magician who stumbled upon a new way of using the primitive forces of nature for dark, satanic ends.

Primitive consciousness is spasmodic and occasional. It is not a continuous stream of recorded time in which events and purposes are related to an active and controlling I. Much more is it an undirected stream of natural happenings, its course running frequently underground. For considerable tracts of time consciousness absconds to a level where the flow of mental life is lost to view. But when consciousness is present, the primitive mind is deficient neither in memory nor accountability. In this respect Hitler is by no means primitive. Primitive man is instinctively conservative of custom, and values accountability as a primary virtue. Hitler's repudiation of responsibility in respect to previous pledges and undertakings is simply pathological. It is civilized snobbery to describe German trickery and faithlessness as a reversion to the jungle. Primitive life in the jungle is grounded upon nature's law of reciprocity. It is because Germany abides by no law that she is an outlaw in the world to-day.

From what has been said above, it will be seen that at certain crises of national existence the downward-conversion of energy to the primitive level may become essential on grounds of racial survival. From this point of view, it is possible to regard the temporary magnification of the leader-archetype as a teleological necessity. Its disadvantages are, however, so many and so perilous that only a nation threatened by imminent disruption could willingly acquiesce in it. For example, the fundamental incredibility of the leader's pretensions makes it necessary for him to insist upon an attitude of absolute faith. Relativity, even in the most modest degree, is not permitted to come near him. Revelation is his; hence one of the central tenets promulgated by dictatorship is that the leader has been sent by heaven, the result being an arrogant assumption by his followers that they are the Chosen People.[1]

Every recent case of aggression — Japan in Manchuria and China; Italy in Abyssinia, Albania, and Greece; Russia in Poland and Finland; Germany throughout more than half Europe — each has been justified by national spokesmen as the mission of a people chosen by heaven to carry peace and civilized order to backward and barbarous lands. It seems impossible that any people could remain so grotesquely self-deceived; yet the day of enlightenment never dawns. The state of nationalistic possession corresponds to the compulsive state met with in individual psychology; it is a blinkered condition, a state of restricted insight, in which neurotic sensitiveness is constantly defending inflamed prestige. Everyone knows that aggression is a crime against humanity, but by dint of collective repression and the use of some plausible slogan, an essential evil is converted into a national virtue and the arbitrament of heaven is invoked, not to excuse a necessary crime, but to honour a heroic manifestation of the racial spirit.

---

[1] There is an obvious implication here which might well have been a major incentive in the Nazi persecution of the Jews, since within the precincts of a single national faith there cannot be two absolutist deities, still less two Chosen Peoples.

HITLER AS SYMBOL

4

It has been contended that this aggressive spirit is the inevitable expression of national feeling; and that if national boundaries could be eliminated, wars would cease. This argument is vitiated by the assumption that the spirit of fanatical nationalism is identical with genuine national feeling. The Swiss, the Scotch, the Welsh, the Scandinavian peoples, the peasant folk of nearly every country, are capable of intense patriotic devotion. But they are not easily caught by ideological nationalism. When patriotism is rooted in feeling it remains human and relative; whereas ideological passion is all in the head.[1] Nationalistic fanaticism continually does things in the worst of taste because it is artificially motivated. If the German, for instance, could experience spontaneous pride at the thought of being a German, he would not need to inflict his unaccepted inferiority upon the rest of the world. Even his love for his own land is never quite enough; it must always be supported by derogatory contrasts. Thus his overweening arrogance has little to do with genuine pride. It is as though the German had to foster the idea of superiority in order to shout down a traitorous feeling of worthlessness.

It is undeniable that Hitler conjured away the doubt which undermined every national effort after the defeat of 1918. In this respect he proved hiself to be a true medicine-man. The most positive aspect of the conversion operation can be seen in this transformation of a disabling sense of inferiority into flaming national faith. Hitler's reputation was built upon this apparently miraculous achievement.

It is hard for us to see in Hitler anything but a gesticulating charlatan. The fact that he is not ridiculous to the Germans is sufficient proof that he is defended by his sacred office. When Hitler tells his people that they are the descendants of the gods, he is not repeating ethnological facts; he is speaking with the tongue of men and angels, that is, with the authority of the racial un-

[1] The chief of the Pueblo Indians at Taos, New Mexico, explained to Jung that the craziness of the white man was due to the fact that he identified himself with the head. The Indian feels himself centred in his heart. If he thinks too much there is something wrong with him.

I

129

conscious, and no breath of criticism can pierce the primordial mantle which enfolds him.

But notwithstanding the manifest efficacy of this conversion operation, it is not exempt from the peril which attaches to all magical procedures. Fundamentally it rests upon illusion. It is not true that the Germans were not beaten in battle. It is not true that the Versailles Treaty was a harsh and unjust sequel to their defeat. It is not true that the Germans have been chosen by heaven to be the rulers of the world. All these fantastic notions by virtue of which Hitler has thrown his magical allure over the mass-mind can be substantiated only by exterminating everyone who knows them to be false. Magic is a spell, and Hitler has so arranged it that no free mind shall enter a German home, lest the spell be broken. Naturally, Hitler's magic cannot eradicate the doubt which haunts the German soul. Moreover, the German is right to doubt the validity of his German nature. It is assuredly not for nothing that he belongs to the most hated nation in the world. That is a truth he will have to live with for years to come.

For the time being, however, the doubt is invested in Hitler, and so long as he succeeds, it is safe in his keeping. Were it possible with the aid of subtle propaganda to strike at this vulnerable spot the end of the war would surely be in sight. For the brittle nature of German morale — so clearly proved by the despicable German censorship — could never withstand a searching exposure of this psychical Quisling.

Jung has stated that wherever a feeling of inferiority exists, it is related to the existence in the unconscious of an undeveloped function which should be playing its part in consciousness. In other words, the so-called inferiority complex is the expression of a one-sided psychological development. This definition certainly tallies with the general German leaning towards the intellectual and the *Geistig*, and with the corresponding deficiency on the side of instinct and feeling. A people, for instance, that had not already been alienated from their own instinctual nature, could not have given themselves with suicidal abandon to such abandoned leadership. In a free country, individual mettle is flexible, sure-footed, and ancestrally guaranteed. Whereas faith in the Führer is the faith of despair. He has to be the invincible, infallible god-man, because the Germans have, literally, nothing else; they have no other instinctual resource to fall back upon. The experiment has to succeed.

Again we are reminded of the parallel with ancient Jewish history. The Jews were also fanatical and one-sided. They too were a conquered people, and temporarily estranged from their original nature. They too accepted the leadership of an alien, who demanded the same absolute submission to his rule. And, according to Freud, they too reverted to an earlier deity during their perilous passage from Egypt to Palestine. Time and again Moses had to wrestle with a vacillating morale, which showed itself in a childish spirit of revolt. But one essential difference stands out clearly: the Jews obeyed a God they could trust. With this power encompassing them, they kept their tradition sacred and inviolate in the Ark of the Covenant throughout their long and perilous migration. Often they were tempted by wayward impulses, but under Moses' leadership they preserved their national soul from evil.

The greatness of Germany is not to be disputed; but her fatal weakness is revealed in the fact that she had to put her faith and her fate into the hands of a cultural renegade. In this fact alone we can detect the desperate impulse towards self-destruction. Yet fanatical belief is notoriously impervious to propaganda. The Germans will hate the Führer before they allow themselves to distrust him.

The Achilles' heel of Germany is perhaps to be found in Mussolini, the original model of modern dictatorship. If, by a series of ignoble defeats, Mussolini could be made to look sufficiently ludicrous, the German nation would feel its world beginning to rock. For Hitler modelled his whole style upon the Italian prototype, and told the world in resounding phrases of the identity, both of heart and mind, of the two dictatorships. For ridicule to bite deep, it is important that Mussolini should not merely suffer defeat: he must be ignominiously worsted. When doubt has returned, the essential kinship of the two dictators argues the possibility of a similar fate. From the moment Mussolini rolls down the hill like an empty barrel, the forces of retribution will swing into their stride. As in 1918, we shall then find our best ally in the German impulse towards self-destruction.

5

We have seen how the squandering of psychical reserves in the process of downward conversion leads inevitably to catastrophe. Is it possible to link up this destructive tendency with the paranoidal psychology of her leader? In cases of paranoidal homicide, the morbid fantasy-system can be discerned increasing in explosive intensity, until the criminal outbreak becomes inevitable. We have observed the increase of German aggression following the same steep curve as Hitler's mounting paroxysms of hatred. Which, then, is the cause, and which the effect? It is questionable whether a leader could be seduced into a suicidal policy of aggression unless he were himself, in part, either criminal or insane. For no one now believes the specious reasoning that an action which is criminal for the individual is justifiable and proper for the state.

The paranoidal tendency became clearly visible in Germany with the aggressive incline which led to the world war in 1914. In precisely the same way as a paranoiac weaves around himself the fantastic plot, which isolates him from his fellows, German statesmanship led the nation into the position of an isolated and hated people. Like a man who does not see that isolation is the result of a certain behaviour, the Germans had to assume that they were a chosen people, surrounded by a ring of hostile and envious neighbours; an assumption for which, once again, an earlier parallel could be found in the Jewish attitude to the hostile world they themselves had created.

This whole development, the idea of the chosen people, the plotting ring of enemies, followed by the outbreak of violent aggression, impelling Germany to hit upon England as the arch-enemy, resembles the classical unfolding of the homicidal paranoiac system. It is undoubtedly the presence of this delusional system which has added a sinister twist to the whole of Germany's policy in recent years. Nazi mentality is completely modelled on the mechanism of paranoia. It is characteristic of paranoia, for example, for the delusional system to be built up with fanatical one-sidedness, so that facts or inventions from every source are given the tendentious colour needed to maintain the delusion. These are then built into the substance of the delusional system.

Everything feeds it, while nothing refutes it; since all evidence which might fail to corroborate the delusional premises is immediately repressed. A paranoiac does not tell the truth, or if he does, it is with the object of concealing the delusional system from critical observation. The more the major complex monopolizes the mental field, the more impossible does it become for the subject to entertain any other point of view than that asserted by the complex.

The paranoidal system, like every autonomous psychic factor, insists upon absolutism. From this feeling of absolute rightness proceeds the feeling of persecution which, with irrational and therefore unassailable logic, fastens upon some person of the milieu as the cause of the whole plot. The paranoiac is dangerous, because his conviction of utter rightness leads inevitably to the idea of exterminating the evil influence which is secretly working against him. The dissociation and independence of the complex is liable, through constantly being fed with subtly conditioned facts, to increase to the point when its contents become projected in the form of auditory hallucinations or voices. According to Dr. Rauschning's evidence, Hitler has long since been hearing voices. It might, indeed, be argued that the inspirational character of Hitler's authority rests upon a shrewd political exploitation of psychopathic states of mind.

6

While the pathological aspect of Hitler's psychology is under review another essential element in the process of energy-conversion should be mentioned. I refer to the effect of the massed projection upon the leader himself. The danger of inflation can be regularly expected whenever a person allows himself to become identified with a primordial image. These contents are truly primordial, inasmuch as they have always existed, and no man thought or invented them. Because of their immense antiquity, they are charged with energy in a very different measure from the more homely contents of the personal unconscious. It is as though the voltage of the primordial image came from a general power-station, while that of the personal contents from a 12-volt battery.

Everyone, therefore, who identifies himself with a content of the collective unconscious is liable to become galvanized with energy. Psychotic inflation is so regularly associated with mystical states of revelation, that in cases of high-powered mediums, like Mary Baker Eddy or Adolf Hitler, opinion is sharply divided between those who hold them to be divinely inspired and those who think them insane. As the term implies, inflation means to become blown up, unreal, lost in fantasy, sometimes to the point of becoming psychologically unrecognizable. The subject is led, as it were, by the hand of fate to play a rôle, without knowing that the rôle which lures him on is, as it were, a baited trap. If it does not destroy him completely, it will surely test him as he has never been tested before.

The energy-content of the image naturally varies according to its value or significance in the collective hierarchy. The images clustering around the idea of the Leader contain, as we might expect, the highest possible potential of energy. In this constellation are gathered the archetypes of Saviour, King, Emperor, War-chief, etc. In the professional hierarchy we find Magician, Medicine-man, Old Wise One, Elder, Orator, etc. On the shadow-side we note the inviting rôle of the Victim; also the Renegade, Scapegoat, Outcast, Criminal, Dwarf, or Hunchback. There are also many feminine archetypes, the most powerful of which are the Mother and the Queen. Around the image of the Mother cluster archetypal derivatives, such as Matriarch, God-mother, Nurse, Foster-mother, etc. Woman's intuitive relation to the unconscious is canalized in such figures as Medium, Soothsayer, Prophetess, Witch, Enchantress, and Sibyl.

Such images are very numerous, and some of them dispose of far more collective energy than others. Sometimes, the instinctual image is deeply rooted in the animal ancestry of man, as, for instance, the wolf-like conquistador enacted by the dictator of Russia. Whereas in the case of Mussolini, who identified himself with the Caesarean archetype of ancient Rome, the image was excavated from the specific racial tradition. Or the archetype may be inherited from the ancestors, as a living mythological heirloom, as in the case of the Mikado or of our British King.

These ancient images, rooted in every case in the age-long continuity of the tribe, naturally have enormous power and prestige. The image of the Führer, for example, touches an unconscious chord in the German psyche sounding back through national and tribal memory, to the general biological matrix of instinct, to that condition where the survival or extinction of the herd depends upon the instinctive flair of the leader. Besides this, Hitler is endowed with the *mana* of the medicine-man. In primitive communities the prestige of the medicine-man is often greater than that of the chief, because of his power to control the awful potentialities of the unseen. The authority of the chief rests upon the actual and visible forces he can command, but the power of the medicine-man is almost unlimited, since the whole of life on the primitive level is dominated by fear of the unseen. The third cultural image invoked by Hitler is that of the saviour of his people. It is on the strength of this identification that he claims to supersede Christ and His Church. Whether he believes this claim or not, the fact that he has made it will surely be read by history as the claim of a madman.

Since these images cover a wide field of human longing and ambition, it must follow that a relative degree of inflation is a familiar malady. It is doubtful, indeed, whether it should be called a malady, since people of the milieu suffer more than the person afflicted. The only remedy — and it may avert much suffering — is an education in self-criticism and detachment for all who aspire to play governing rôles. The practical value of a dynastic succession consists primarily in the fact that its members are trained to carry the burden of the archetype without suffering inflation. When we compare the limitless fantasies and inflated antics of Mussolini or Hitler with the disciplined composure and dignity of a trained monarch, we can appreciate the wisdom of our ancestors in instituting dynastic succession.

Sometimes with individual subjects undergoing analysis, the state of inflation, through a sudden activation of the unconscious, produces a certain oddity of behaviour; almost as though the possessing image would not tolerate any rival claim or viewpoint.[1] But when the man charged with the primordial image is supported in his divine claim by tumultuous throngs of his fellow-men

---

[1] A good example of psychotic inflation is to be found in H. G. Wells's *Christina Alberta's Father*. Mr. Preemby was more fortunate than Hitler in the fact that he was alone in believing himself to be Sargon the Magnificent, King of Kings.

it can be readily imagined how, in a time of crisis and revolution, a political impostor may be converted into the heaven-sent leader.

Hitler does not tally either with the image of the saviour or the leader in our racial unconscious. On the contrary, he corresponds with Judas, the betrayer of the god. Thus we return in our spiral to the problem of Hitler's ambiguity. To what extent is his double nature a question of viewpoint? If it could be shown that everyone in Germany held him to be divine, while everyone on our side of the water could see him only as a criminal, we should have to agree that the ambiguity was relative, not to the man, but to the viewpoint. This, however, is clearly not the case. Moreover, his ambiguity is not merely a matter of opportunist adaptability; that is to say, he is not simply a criminal who also happens to know what the Christian ethic demands of a man. He is, without doubt, a split personality. The window that opens to the heavens is contradicted by the trap-door which leads down to hell. His maniacal fanaticism, together with his lack of humour and self-criticism, all accord with the presence of an opacity or psychical split which allows no free interplay between the two sides. If, standing on the bright side, he could appreciate the point of view of his own shadow, he would also be fitted to recognize the existence of different standpoints in his fellow-man. His split denies him, therefore, not merely the elements of enlightenment, but also that balance between seriousness and humour with which alone the fruits of enlightenment can be enjoyed. Since the mere possibility of self-criticism rests upon the ability to see oneself differently, it must be possible to step outside one's habitual mental orbit into that of another function before one can reasonably aspire to a balanced maturity.

Viewing individual psychology with an architectural eye, one discovers the fact that the ground-plan of the psyche is naturally four-square. That is to say, the four main psychic functions are given as part of the basic psychic structure. They represent the differentiated reactions of consciousness, in the same way as the four limbs of the body represent the response of the living organism to the elementary needs of movement and adaptation to terrestrial conditions of life. Among the less differentiated forms of life, there would seem to be a greater liability for a dangerous overdevelopment of one bodily function and the consequent retrogression of

HIMMLER

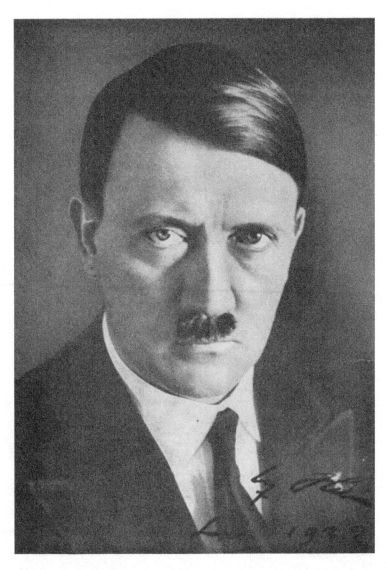

HITLER

others. The vast reptiles of the Mesozoic swamps were early experimenters in exaggeration. Conditions of life were such as to encourage the evolution of extreme hypotheses. Nature attempted a multitude of experiments in sheer mass, unenlightened by sufficient adaptability or intelligence. The results, compared with the more differentiated mammalian form of Tertiary conditions, seem monstrous and ill-considered.

There are certain ill-formed or undifferentiated types of psychology which give one somewhat the same disagreeable feeling of top-heaviness or lop-sidedness. An examination of the condition of the unconscious in cases of this kind often reveals an atavistic state of the emotions which makes ordinary feeling relationships impossible.

On the opposite page are reproduced photographs of the Führer, and of Himmler, infamous head of the Gestapo. If these faces are studied side by side one notices in both a fixity of gaze, as in the eye of a man aiming at one's heart with a rifle. In this fixed gaze there is an expression of ferocity, cold-blooded, like the eye of a reptile. It seems to look past one into a world which knows nothing of warm-blooded life, with its mating, its care for its young, and its decent loyalties. We know at once that both these men are fanatics; but there is something in the eyes more terrible than fanaticism. The first thing we instinctively look for in a face is the basic human quality of good faith. We need to know whether this person can stand by a pact. This is as much an animal as a human sense, since reliability is a fundamental need even for coexistence in the same environment. One's relation to a dog or a horse, for instance, is based upon a tacit instinctual pact between man and animal. All the qualities upon which the bare possibility of human relationship is grounded, such as reliability, steadfastness, loyalty, trust, good faith, honest dealings, and fair play, are derived from this basic warm-blooded pact. It follows that the inhibitions which bridle savagery, whether in animal or man, are also rooted in this same deep fraternity. In opposition to this feeling for community which, as we have shown, is an inherent and necessary condition of warm-blooded animal life, the renegade, separatist, secretive element has always been present as a latent tendency, threatening the foundations of human society.

This renegade tendency is by no means necessarily criminal; it can also serve as the individual point of departure, the irrational deviation from the existing pattern which may eventually lead to a new evolutionary phase. Whether its issue be beneficent or criminal depends upon the aegis, or determining motive, which governs its operation.

I have selected this photograph of Hitler, because what it reveals does not rely upon some fleeting· expression. The uncanny fixity of the eyes involves a deliberate threat to the human subject. Just as the fixed eye of a snake is a menace to the bird it lights upon, so Hitler's threat to seize and rule the German unconscious, or indeed any susceptible human creature, by the power of magic, can clearly be read in this pitiless, boring eye. More directly than words can voice thought one sees the determination to penetrate the mind of his victim, and to impose upon it his fanatical will. It is the gaze of a hypnotist, but not of one who uses hypnotism in the service of man. Rather does it express the passionless insistence of a man who has learned how to exert a magical effect upon his fellow-beings; intending, moreover, to use these tricks, without pity or scruple, in the gaining of his ends.

There are many expert psycho-therapists who, at one time or another, have practised hypnotism in the relief of mental suffering. The fact that scarcely anyone of repute employs the hypnotic method to-day, is not because it was ineffective. On the contrary, it often appeared to work miracles. It was given up, because its effects, both upon patient and doctor, were found to be morally dangerous. The patient would invariably project the image of the magician upon the doctor; usually coming to depend upon him, as Germany now depends upon Hitler, with a kind of slavish sub-servience. The doctor, on the other hand, even though he may have explained to the patient that he was only using a natural function, would unconsciously absorb the patient's magical pro-jections; until, after a time, he began to show symptoms of deplorable inflation. Secretly preening himself upon possessing special and magical powers, he would enjoy the aura of authority to which a magical reputation always gives rise. He would perhaps heighten this effect by monocle and mannerisms, until his colleagues would reluctantly avoid his company. In those days the psycho-therapist had not yet learned how to disinfect himself from the magical projections coming to him from his patient's unconscious; perhaps the most subtle danger to which the doctor is exposed.

The expression in Himmler's face has not the same armour-piercing character as Hitler's, though the glint of the barrel can be discerned behind the glasses. In order to place one's finger accurately upon the right key, one would have to ask what functional pair would correspond to these two Nazi leaders in a primitive society. Hitler, as we have seen, is the shaman, the magician, the wizard, the one who has relations with the spirits. Himmler, on the other hand, is clearly the witch-doctor, the one who smells out the enemies of the chief, and whose spies can always inform him who it is that is putting witchcraft upon the chief's favourite wife, or making the cattle sick. His is the power of terror. The whole machinery of terroristic espionage is in his hands and, since Nazi terrorism takes no heed of justice under the law, Himmler's power is as uncontrolled as Hitler's. What we see in these two faces is the awful aloofness of men who possess unchecked power over human lives. No soul, however faithful, could stand this constant and devastating temptation. And these are not faithful souls.

We need only select from history the worst instances of terroristic tyranny, from the power of the Inquisition, the Cheka, the Ogpu, and the Gestapo (an evil smell seems to cling to their very names) to the witch-doctors of Cheka, the Zulu tyrant, and other similar abominations in Africa, we shall find in every case unchecked terror going hand in hand with unchecked power. There exists, in other words, a logical and inevitable relation between the totalitarian claim to power and the witch-doctor. The former apparently cannot exist without the latter. A fact, which has such momentous consequences for mankind, must be worth more than a mere cursory statement. Something that happens regularly, predictably even, must be capable of explanation from basic principles.

When discussing the one-sidedness of fanatical psychology, we discovered that the psyche is naturally four-square, and maintains equilibrium through the tension of the opposites. But when, through overvaluation, one function assumes a totalitarian sway it pushes the other functions into the unconscious, where they undergo a remarkable change of character. The systematized suspicions, for example, which become attached to everyone in the neighbourhood of a paranoiac, are produced by the exiled functions in the patient's unconscious. Just because they are excluded from normal functioning, they can operate only by means of projection from beyond the pale.

A paranoiac, as we have already seen, is a man whose mind is possessed by a dissociated, autonomous complex which allows no place for any other standpoint. But paranoidal symptoms are also liable to appear wherever a man accumulates money, power, or notoriety in an uncontrolled crescendo. The multi-millionaire with his electrical fence, armed guard, and secret password, is an example of the same psychology. Anything which grows to excess transgresses the laws of balance and reciprocity. Through losing connection with its original meaning and setting it necessarily creates a condition of insecurity. Since this condition is also associated with deficiency in insight, the subject is unable to see that his sense of insecurity is bred from his excess. He is therefore bound to assume that secret enemies are aiming at his power. These must naturally be eradicated. Thus the justifiable stings of conscience are converted into accusations of plots and conspiracies against his associates.

The witch-doctor is therefore the outward and manifest sign of the dictator's paranoia. Yet the disease cannot be regarded as purely subjective, since the whole entourage of the tyrant becomes infected with paranoidal ideas, and the court honeycombed with intrigue. Paranoia in high places, as witnessed both in the Kremlin and at Berchtesgaden, often produces an acute psychical infection which may involve a hideous toll of victims.

7

Looking once again into the face of Himmler, is it not possible to read the fate of Germany in that arrogant, defensive mask? An attempt to analyse the features might perhaps afford a clue. The eyes are mean and set close together. The falling lines from the corners of the mouth form a querulous oval in which mouth and chin are isolated, as though to emphasize their adolescent truculence. The slit-eyes and high cheek-bones give a mongoloid character to the face, suggesting the impenetrable mask of the Asiatic.

Having made an inventory of the features, the badly-formed, asymmetrical ears, the weak, obstinate chin, the contemptuous mouth, the cruel, evasive eyes, the thin inquisitive nose and thick unprofitable neck — one is left with an impression of the whole which is more than, and to some extent independent of, the sum of its ignoble parts. Beneath all is an expression of self-distrust and inferiority which the studied air of ferocity cannot conceal. The soul that looks out of this visored face has never known the confidence and faith of manhood. It is an adolescent soul, with all the suspicion and distrust of emotional immaturity congealed into cruelty and contempt. This man must surely have been tyrannical with his own feelings. It may be that as a result of some early treachery to his original nature, a pitiless hatred and scorn of his fellow-beings has been engendered. Though, naturally, a man does not attain to the position of the most hated man in his own country merely on the strength of an overcompensated inferiority complex. Himmler must also be credited with a certain native genius for cruelty. What part perversion has played in his make-up we cannot, of course, say; but the diagnosis of emotional infantilism gives us a significant sidelight into the hidden springs of Nazi cruelty.

Ferocity, deliberately developed and employed, as the chief instrument of a vast political system, is a very different thing from the spontaneous outbursts of savagery among primitive peoples. It has no true affinity with the basic instincts of man. Such deformities of the soul have, of course, to do with the general psychological environment. Psychological hygiene depends to a very great extent upon the spontaneous reaction of the psyche to surrounding events and conditions. The child-psyche responds to injustice, cruelty, consideration, unreliable moods, impatience, suspicion, trust, etc., immediately and appropriately. But supposing these spontaneous individual reactions are repressed at an early age by a terrorist atmosphere, and assuming that the subject acquiesces in the repression, as he surely must, the soul is inevitably warped. Estranged from his own truth, he begins to react according to an altered, or conditioned, pattern which is established in the place of his own individual nature. If this becomes permanent a kind of spiritual gelding results.

Maturity is not something that can be superimposed on the

adolescent psyche by education. It is the product of an inner development. It must follow, therefore, that where the character of emotional response is conditioned by an arbitrary political recipe which suppresses individuality in favour of mass-reaction, psychological maturity will be frustrated. We have only to imagine the cumulative effects of this wholesale collective inter-ference upon the delicate sensibilities of the individual soul to recognize the means by which systematic cruelty has become installed in Germany as a normal process of government.

The adolescent immaturity of the Nazi leaders is self-evident even to a distant observer. The bombastic swaggering, the silly boasting and goose-stepping, the undignified public style which always relies upon creating a butt at which volleys of schoolboy insults can be levelled, the widespread homosexuality, and, above all, the tragically irresponsible character of recent German policy — from the top to the bottom we find the same flamboyant juvenility.

Inasmuch as the collectivist mentality in Russia conceived individuality on the nursery level, a political and military associa-tion between Nazi Germany and Russia was always a feasible proposition, notwithstanding Hitler's affectation of scorn and superiority. The very conception of regimenting and coercing millions of human pawns in accordance with the ideas of some magically-endowed leader is so essentially childish that only a nation of grown-up children, like the Russians, or a nation of spiritually gelded adults, like the Germans, could be attracted by it. The fact that they have been so seduced, and that the two largest nations in Europe have sunk to a purely quantitative estimation of the meaning of culture, reveals a spiritual landslide which is all the more terrifying because of its inherent stupidity.

We cannot help ascribing intelligence to members of our species. It is a fundamental premise underlying all our dealings with our fellow-men. Doubtless the thousands of Russian soldiers, lying frozen in the forests of Finland, and the Italians among the mountains of Albania, also accepted this fatal hypothesis. Yet no intelligible ground exists for the wrecking of these in-numerable homes and the daily sacrifice of life. A monstrous obtuseness in regard to vital human feelings impels this cruelty and senseless slaughter.

For this reason it is useful to study the face of Himmler. He symptomatizes a disease which is, I believe, the most dangerous of all human afflictions. For what can be worse than the crippling of the individual human soul, with all its miraculous potentialities, by ignorance, cruelty, and stupidity?

That the crippling of individuality is a deliberate part of German policy can no longer be doubted. It is explicit in the whole Nazi *Weltanschauung*. Leisure, privacy, personal savings — everything which nourishes the individual principle in its life-and-death struggle with a tyrannical régime, is foreclosed. The German citizen is told: 'Since Adolf Hitler came to power you have a private life only when you are asleep. There can be no private life beyond this.' Before you satisfy any individual need you are told to 'think ten times before you decide you want a thing'.

Is it not possible that the arrested development visible in the face of Himmler, and the repression of individuality throughout the whole German people — revealed especially in their tragic lack of civic courage — are both due to the same fundamental cause? The mature part of the human soul in Europe is that part which has submitted to the Christian discipline. If it is true for the Eastern man that spiritual maturity can be reached only in the way revealed by the Buddha, it is surely as true for the man of the West that the Christian way, in its most profound meaning, represents this unavoidable path of development. This path is not to be found through a regressive, downward conversion to the irresponsible, collective state of mass-feeling. Two world wars within a quarter of a century are evidence enough that the Western soul is still immature. Yet only the collective, sheepfold way of saving mankind has been seriously attempted in the West. We have forgotten that the individual path to-spiritual maturity through self-realization is also contained in the Christian way.

Because people have either been born, or shepherded into one or other of the religious folds, relatively few individuals in the West have tried to discover the way that leads to their solitary individual truth. This conception of maturity involves the acceptance of responsibility for one's unconscious as well as for one's conscious motives. It aims at the completeness of individuality with its unique potentialities, and at a greater intensity of life than can be provided by the comfortable compromises and expedients of collectively guaranteed existence. But the man who longs unreservedly for completeness must also know what it means to be crucified upon the opposites. Not till then does he realize the full meaning of the Christian path.

Although maturation through a denial of our Christian truth is for us inconceivable, this does not mean that the Christian way is the final statement of our truth. It does mean, however, that the Western man, who denies the validity of the Christian way must remain warped and juvenile. It also implies that the man who refuses to go beyond the accepted Christian teaching, if life should demand it, has forgotten to be fully human.

CHAPTER V

THE MESSIANIC POSSIBILITY

I

In view of what has happened in Europe since Germany invaded Poland, it must appear utterly ironical to many of my countrymen to speak of a Messianic possibility in Germany. But everyone who is familiar with Germany, and has watched the expressions of despair and resurgent life pass across the face of Europe during the decade after the last war, will agree that the Messianic need and hope were surely there. Indeed the present mood of dogged apathy which, if reports are true, did not even relax its grip at the news of German victories, is almost certainly due to the dashing of the Messianic hope in the hearts of the German people.

For a time after 1918 Germany was crushed and hopeless. Then, with the Youth Movement, a flicker of hope and interest began to revive. Underneath all the rather confused political experimentation and revolutionary agitation, there grew a widespread longing for deliverance. This longing had the indefinite character of something emerging out of the darkness, towards a light that was still in the distance. It was not concerned with any of the existing forms, whether religious or political, neither could it be canalized into desirable channels.

When Hitler appeared on the scene he was, at first, no more successful in relation to this inarticulate longing than the rest. Through his art of political mediumship, however, he soon learned to respond to the emergent need in a directly primitive fashion. At the early Nuremberg rallies Hitler evoked the Messianic enthusiasm with consummate art and skill, and reliable observers, who were 'outside the experience', have testified to the genuine religious fervour that was generated among those enthusiastic bands of youths. We may conclude, therefore, that the sincerity of Hitler at that time need not be questioned.

Psychologically, the Messianic possibility consists in a state of spiritual readiness due to the activation of the saviour-archetype in the collective unconscious. This primordial image expresses a fundamental emotional content of the unconscious. In it is contained the deepest, as well as the most primitive, longings of the human soul. Hitler appeared upon the scene as a magical leader when the restless, collective urgency was greatest. As a stranger and an outcast, he could respond emotionally to this need for deliverance. These conditions also agreed mythologically with the activation of the saviour-image, or heaven-sent leader, in the national unconscious.

The appearance of 'the chosen one', naturally, tends to synchronize with a specific anticipation in the collective psyche, the essential precondition of which is a period of oppression, giving rise to a state of inner division. The Jews had suffered severely, as a subject or enslaved people, for hundreds of years before the coming of Christ. Prophecies of His coming had also had the effect of creating a subjective state of preparedness for the recognition and acceptance of the Messiah. The Messianic archetype belongs essentially to the natural order; during times of adversity, hope and expectation accumulate like the anticipation of rain during a drought.

Primarily, the Messianic symbol is a function of deliverance; through its operation a state of spiritual hunger is satisfied. An unstable people is liable to become one-sided, as though imprisoned in certain fatalistic assumptions which make it impossible for the opposite qualities to thrive. The man who can embody the Messianic symbol for a given people must, therefore, comprise the essential human quality that is needed to complement and heal the one-sidedness. The Jews, for example, were oppressed by an arbitrary, inhuman conception of divine law which had little sympathy with man's native ethical feeling. It was personified by the rigid, upright Pharisees. The Mosaic law, the stern, unbending attitude of the prophets, the harsh conception of deity as the lawgiver, and the whole pharisaic attitude to sin and retribution, weighed upon the spirit of the Jewish people just as much as their alien oppressors. The Messianic redemption in this case consisted of a passionate embodiment of the opposite truth: God was the Spirit of love and all men were brothers. The image of the Father was needed to replace that of the Law-giver in man's relation to God.

But what, one may ask, has this talk of the Messianic image to

146

do with Hitler's Germany? We are still too near the evil to see the redeeming possibility which lay waiting and expectant in the German unconscious. But Hitler sensed that the fated hour had come when the primitive longing could be satisfied. Of this there can be no reasonable doubt. We must also give Hitler the credit for a passionate concern for the greatness of Germany, and for an intuitive understanding of the post-war neurotic attitude.

When we speak of the one-sidedness of the pharisaic mentality, the rigid quality which Jesus hated above all, we refer, by implication, to a balanced image of man as a mature whole, existing somewhere, like a Platonic form, in the background of the mind. For every judgment we make, whether about the architectural planning of a house, the growth of a tree, the shape of an arch, or the character of a human being, must be related to a certain abstract optimum. We have in our mind's eye, as it were, an archetype of balanced wholeness which determines our feeling about the individual case.

Sometimes this archetype of wholeness appears as a phantasm in dream or vision. I remember the case of a terribly one-sided, extraverted American doctor who came to me in a distraught condition of mind. In the course of his life-history he told me of an occasion when, having come home after an overfilled day, limp and dazed with exhaustion, he sat half-dozing in his surgery. In a kind of trance he saw, standing upon the table beside him, a little image, which he tried to describe to me. It was merely the figure of a mature man in a simple robe, carrying a staff in his right hand. As he described this figure my patient broke down and wept. He knew that this apparition, which he had seen standing in front of him as a simple image, was the real desire of his whole being.

The concept of individuality comprises the totality of a man, as well as his unique quality. Hence in judging individuality, the archetype of balanced maturity presents itself naturally to the mind. Similarly, in our attempt to discover what is the matter with a possessed people, such as the Germans, we have to apply this archetype of balanced wholeness to the normal, or characteristic, German mentality.

To begin with, the prevailing attitude of German philosophy and scientific thinking is decidedly introverted. With a few notable exceptions as, for instance, Richard Wagner or Mendelssohn,

German music and art follow the same introverted direction. Until the Prussian element ran off with the German State, the independent States of Germany were apparently content to live a conservative, self-contained life within their borders, and without any tantalizing thoughts of colonial expansion. The cultured German mind was pre-eminent in the realm of painstaking scholarship, specialized erudition, scientific technology, in the detailed organization of ideas and classification of facts; indeed in every department of civilized achievement requiring thoroughness and inventive industry. As a whole the German nation has been hard-working and docile, with an immense respect for intellectual achievement, and for the art of music, the one creative field in which the German genius is supreme. It showed small inclination, on the other hand, for spontaneous, extraverted initiative. Except for the calamitous bouts of military aggression, when the split-off Prussian antithesis took control under Bismarck, Wilhelm II, and Hitler, there have been few extraverted adventures, no political initiative and, until quite recently, no special inclination to look longingly across the seas towards possible rich conquests in other lands.

Once, walking in the company of a German professor down the Unter den Linden in the golden days before the Great War, I stopped to watch the goose-step of the soldiers changing guard. My companion, seeing me smile, observed: 'It is all very well for you English to smile. You are natural fighters. Your people enjoy fighting. But we are studious and love the arts of peace. If we did not show off like this we should never fight at all.' This blindness of a cultured, intelligent German to the whole meaning of Prussianism — that split-off other half of the German character — illustrates not only the typical one-sidedness, but also a tendency to reason away the unacceptable. This split might, therefore, be represented as a dissociation between the cultural introverted and the aggressive extraverted aspects of German psychology.

Extraverted energy naturally runs out to gain the world. It creates an instinctual attitude of out-going interest, finding a field of operation in the development of every kind of objective possibility. Introverted energy, on the other hand, flows in the contrary direction from the object, or thing, towards the subjective world of the idea. The introverted subject tends to feel that the frontiers of his inner world must be defended from the encroachment of the menacing and lawless world of objects. As he sees it, therefore, fighting is something that is forced upon him by the necessity of guarding the orderly world he has created from chaotic intrusions. Both the antipathy and the moods of mutual attraction of these opposing types derive from the fact that they naturally complement one another; each being strong where the other is weak. The premises of extraverted psychology are as different from those of the introverted as man is from woman. Misunderstandings are bound to multiply, because if an introvert were to behave as an extravert, he would feel lost and disintegrated; whereas if the extravert tried to live as an introvert, he would soon become sick and neurotic, devoured by his own thoughts.

The term introverted merely signifies a prevailing tendency, or an habitual direction of the psychic energy inwards to the subject. Similarly, the extravert is a man whose energy runs habitually and spontaneously outwards to the object. Neither direction is neurotic. The terms come into play in psycho-pathology only when the habitual direction tends to become exclusive.

Like every other habitual psychic mechanism, introversion and extraversion are liable to assume an exclusive bias and develop a dæmonic character. The exaggeration of one or other mechanism, therefore, affords a valuable criterion in the clinical diagnosis of psycho-pathological states. The dæmonic extraversion of a man like Hitler, for example, is the sign of a fundamentally pathological mentality. In a well-balanced psychology these opposite directions of the psychic energy have a natural tidal swing like the ebb and flow of the sea. Whereas the presence of an underlying instability is liable to produce a functional exclusiveness that is broken by spasmodic interludes in which the repressed antithesis comes to the surface in an abrupt or explosive fashion. Thus an habitual introvert may, at times, be seized by a mood of compulsive extraversion almost manic in character. To a true extravert this forced extraversion appears spurious and even somewhat ludicrous. Similarly, a pronounced extravert may be liable to depressive, introverted, almost paranoidal moods, which, in their turn, lack the serenity and productive poise of true introversion.

This phenomenon of what should be called the *dissociated antithesis*, though not unfamiliar in our daily experience of our fellowmen, has not yet been observed and described as an aspect of national psychology. In the case of Germany, however, we have clearly to do with a radical dissociation between the introverted, cultural, peace-loving aspect of the German nature, and an explosive, militaristic extraversion which, when it breaks loose, completely denies and falsifies the true national spirit. The mutual attitude of scorn and distrust, which has become an historical factor of disunity between the cultural and aggressive aspects of the German nation, is clearly symptomatic of this divided national will.

Normally, the introverted idea is the ruler of Germany. In no other land has the idea such a supreme value. The spiritual exaltation and intoxication, to which the Germans are collectively prone, might be regarded as a kind of forced ideological extraversion; the manic phase of an idea which only a creative introverted attitude could handle reasonably. Again, no extraverted Anglo-Saxon, and certainly no logical, objective Frenchman, could have seen the world as will and idea, as Schopenhauer did. Just as the Jews have lived under the Law, the Germans have been shaped and moulded by the Idea; but chiefly as a subjective introverted power, not as part of an extraverted scheme of life.

2

We can now resume our discussion of the Messianic symbol in relation to the Führer. The picture of Germany as inhabited solely by swaggering, bullying fanatics is no truer than that of Hitler as nothing but an insane, possessed criminal. Both Germany and Hitler are split, and in neither case can the mind succeed in welding together a composite image of the two antithetical aspects.

In his mountain eyrie, Hitler restores his inner man in the true introverted fashion. At these times he seeks and enjoys solitude. When he descends from the mountain, he will have nothing but extraverted action. It was this call to action and the effective deed which rang through a dispirited post-war Germany like a martial challenge. Every attempt to recreate a healthy political structure after the collapse of 1918 came to grief on the morbid introverted fatalism of defeated Germany. Faced by what seemed a super-human task, and lacking the inspiration of far-seeing leadership, the collective *libido* withdrew from existing forms and tasks and went underground, where it waited in a state of suspense for some new direction.

German temperament is more prone to moods of fatalism and despair than to hours of faith. The extraordinary thoroughness of organization, which anticipates every possible eventuality, is due very largely to this basically introverted disposition. Having no spontaneous faith in what the future may bring, the German leaves nothing to chance and, having no friendly relation with his instinct, he cannot trust to improvisation. Accordingly, prodigious value is given to the planning, foreseeing intellect which makes up for temperamental deficiencies and onesidedness, and creates safeguards against a hostile fate.

Since a one-sided attitude necessarily produces a yearning for its opposite, it will be appreciated that the condition of Germany described above was likely to create Messianic anticipations. It is the unbalanced man with infirm will who seeks supernatural support. A man, poised soundly on his own base, will follow good leadership, but he will not expect magical or miraculous aid from the leader; nor will he allow himself to be herded, regimented, or dragooned.

It would be interesting to know to what extent Hitler acted consciously when he took upon himself the rôle of magical leader. Did he choose to be the Messianic symbol, the Chosen One, or was he drawn into it willy-nilly by the strength of the unconscious longing? Those who habitually play the rôle of the medium are often compelled, by their own function, to embody a symbol which has been activated in the group unconscious, and is seeking expression in the real world.

Hitler came upon the expectant German scene with a trumpet-call to action. The time for thinking and reflection was past. He did not want any subtle analysis of the situation, no carefully planned or nicely adjusted moves. He was steeped in Wagnerian ideas — an unspeakably vulgarized Wagnerism, it is true, but none the less effective for general consumption. Here was something truly indigenous. Inflamed by the spirit of the early German gods, he felt himself possessed by the unconquerable spirit of Siegfried, the hero who killed the lazy, covetous, plutocratic dragon Fafnir, and whose coming was the sign of the downfall of the old order. Behind everything Hitler said and did, in every suggestive throb of his voice, there lurked the assurance: 'You are the descendants of our gods. You are the unconquerable people, appointed from the beginning of time to rule and dominate the peoples of the earth. You were not beaten in the war, you were betrayed by Jews, Bolsheviks, and Freemasons. Throw out these hidden traitors. Rise up in your greatness and seize your inheritance. The German gods are with you.'

With this battle-cry the fortress of the German intellect, with its timorous conservatism, was stormed; since when there has been no real intellectual life in Germany. The intellect has been active and industrious, but with the industry of the ant-heap. Its true function has been enslaved by the power of the primitive idea which took possession of the German soul.

In so far as he originally embodied this idea, Hitler comes into the Messianic succession. In exactly the same way Enkidu, by reviving an earlier primordial truth, played, as we shall presently see, a Messianic rôle in the Gilgamish epos. The fact that Germany is now accelerating towards destruction, depends not upon the symbol, but upon two conditions which made a favourable outcome practically impossible. One is the instability and one-sidedness of the German mentality, with its tendency to swing over to the previously excluded antithesis with a suicidal abandon. The other is the Führer's fatal lack of integrity and his insensate greed for power.

But when he first sprang into the ring, whirling the sword of Siegfried around his head, the transformation that came over Germany was much as though Hamlet were suddenly imbued with the freely-acting spirit of Horatio. The primitive energies suspended in the unconscious came rallying to the horn of Siegfried, while, under the spell of his rhetoric, the people began to hear from the other side of the Rhine, and across the Channel, the sleepy muttering of the conservative custodians of the world's treasure-house: '*Ich lieg und besitze, lass mich schlafen.*'[1] Can we not

[1] 'I lie still and possess, let me sleep' – sung by the dragon Fafnir, the possessor of the Rhinegold, as Siegfried approaches.

hear Horatio upbraiding Hamlet with characteristic Hitlerian vehemence: 'Contemplative natures, retrospective like all intellectuals, are dead persons who miss the meaning of life'?[1]

And Hitler was undoubtedly right. The overvalued German intellect was, politically, beating the air. While it was preoccupied with unrealities, the real factors, that were destined to shape the future, were forming below in the embryonic activity of the unconscious. Embryonic processes demand immense supplies of vital energy. Hence when something new is forming in the racial unconscious, there is a necessary shifting of energy downwards to the revolutionary counter-position. This swing-over of value to the opposite principle is the sign for the excluded, outcast elements, which had had no place or function in the previous order, to force their way to the top.

Hitler himself was an outcast, excluded largely by his own neurosis, it is true, but consumed with the outcast's resentment and hatred of the established order. Hence, the danger of the swing-over was intensified. The sudden regression from order to anarchy is all the more perilous where there exists no effective opposition. What the fanatic cannot realize is that a swing-over from a one-sided state into its opposite only changes the position of the pieces on the board; it cures nothing. The process of healing takes place when thesis and antithesis stand freely opposed, and are able, through an open conflict of reciprocal viewpoints, to bring about a new attitude.

This new factor possesses the character of the reconciling symbol, inasmuch as it is born of both sides, and supersedes the one-sided dominion of either. Jung has called this the transcendent function, because it is produced by the transcending of virtue from A to B as well as from B to A. For the operation of this function in the political arena, we have only to look at the development of national unity through conflict during the last three decades in this country. Realistic enthusiasm and practical common sense have succeeded in bridging the antagonism between conservative capitalist elements and revolutionary socialism without fanaticism and bloodshed. But reconciliation of opposite principles is only feasible where the opposites stand in relatively balanced conflict. And before conflict can generate this creative reciprocity, the opposites need to

[1] *Hitler Speaks*, p. 221.

forgo their respective claims to absoluteness, submitting to relativity within a circumscribed field.

3

The evil and corrupt spirit, against which the whole moral force of civilization is now enrolled, has been engendered, not by the revolution, as Dr. Rauschning assumes, but rather by the disastrous lack of that effective opposition which could have held it upon a firm and settled course. When we have to deal with acute inflammatory conditions within the body, the first efforts of the protective elements in the blood-stream are aimed at localizing the inflammatory area. If the poison becomes general, there is a total febrile reaction. The situation only becomes deadly when bodily resistance is weak, and there is no longer any effective reaction to the poison.

The lack of firm opposition to National Socialism was tragic, because without it, the revolutionary dynamism was bound to fail in its constructive aim. The forces of the revolution were let loose in every direction, producing an intoxicating sense of *élan* and acceleration, but having no realizable goal. Dr. Rauschning expresses this tragic unsettlement with great force:

> Ruthless dynamism has won against all other political conceptions of aims and methods. This is the natural outcome of the doctrinelessness of the whole German revolution. The foreign policy of National Socialism consists simply of universal unsettlement: it is revolution for its own sake. And this characteristic prevails over all else, over all that might confine the revolution within assigned paths and to definite purposes. Accordingly, all day-to-day arrangements, axes, friendships, pacts, even enmities, are only of tactical importance. And the party pushes into the background those of its members who are insufficiently 'revolutionary', insufficiently elastic to see power as the one aim of the movement, and universal unsettlement as its one method. [1]

It is important to note how this description of the revolution's

[1] HERMANN RAUSCHNING, *Germany's Revolution of Destruction*, p. 262 (Heineman, London).

fundamental lack of form accords with our earlier description of Hitler's personal inability to concentrate upon a task, or to hold his attention upon any given problem. Similarly, the transitory, fluid character of all his alliances, pacts, and enmities can be seen as the inevitable consequence of the same dæmonic urge. In a subsequent chapter we shall see that we are dealing here with the most vital problem of conscious life, the struggle between the archaic dynamism of the unconscious and the directing control of consciousness.

When the controlling intellect becomes apprehensively tyrannical and repressive, the spontaneous, instinctual play of the mind is cruelly checked, breeding the spirit of revolt. On the other hand, the controlling and integrating power of consciousness may be overborne by the unconscious dynamism. In this case the result is insanity.

The senseless brutality and slaughter of the Nazi régime is not the expression of political necessity, it is a pathological dæmonism. To seek power for its own sake is no aim for a reasoning consciousness. It is not even as reasonable as the snarl of a tiger. But when an enterprise, motivated by will-to-power, is opposed by effective criticism from an opponent of almost equal standing, the situation begins to assume a new form. For now the dæmonic will is forced to limit itself by declaring a definite aim and direction. Thus a coherent policy moulded on existing realities is generated when a power-psychology is controlled by determined and directed opposition. The converse is also true, that without opposition either without or within, no durable resultant can be achieved.

In this connection it is interesting to note how Hitler seems almost to crave opposition, how he complains that his antagonists are nonentities, and how he is able to bring off an effective performance only when he has set up something or someone to attack. Hitler's cleverness and so-called initiative are apparent not in open combat, but rather in the cheating or outwitting of his enemies. Concerning this side of Hitler's character, Dr. Rauschning writes:

> He has the two contrasting qualities of a supreme capacity for cool calculation and the irrational gift of intuition . . . It is always opposition, an enemy, that awakens these qualities. This arouses his sense of superiority, on which he is

dependent, his confidence in his giant's power over the 'dwarfs', democracies, the 'respectable' people ... It is these elements which made him. Anyone who had seen how Hitler will almost deliberately grow heated over some small issue in conversation, will raise his voice and begin to gesticulate excessively, thus raising himself out of a lethargic dullness in order to say something; how he will grow indignant or rapturous in the effort to fight his way out of mental shackles, will realize that similarly in great questions it is not cool calculation and superior tactical ability alone that bring him success, but that he needs these emotional outbreaks, in order to maintain his combative intensity and to gain his power of influencing by suggestion, to which almost everyone who meets him succumbs, the foreign statesman no less than the German citizen.[1]

There is surely an ironic justice in the fact that the very thing which Hitler needed most, in order to mould his movement into a humanly adapted shape, was effectively wiped out by his own ruthless methods. Opposition was a *sine qua non* for the success of Hitler's revolution, but without self-discipline, opposition cannot be tolerated: and this is just what Hitler lacked. Hence the whole gathering impetus of National Socialism went over into destruction, avidly seeking some new enemy or goal. A movement which seemed at one time to have incalculable regenerative possibilities, both for Germany and for the whole of Europe, thus drove relentlessly towards chaos. Dr. Rauschning describes this progress as follows:

Hitler has manifestly moved away from the ideas of the first economic 'experts' of the movement. The radicalization of National Socialism into dynamism is like Salome's dance: one veil of ideology is cast off after another. Rosenberg's foreign policy is too dogmatic, too static, to be in tune with the present day. Hitler's policy to-day is entirely a policy of stirring up universal unrest, with the actual aims of the régime kept undefined. This absence of principle suits his gift of recognizing and promptly seizing every political opportunity for increasing his power.[2]

The inevitable result of this uncontrolled dynamism, which none of the National Socialist leaders has either the wisdom or the

[1] loc. cit., p. 288.   [2] loc. cit., p. 265.

THE MESSIANIC POSSIBILITY

integrity to direct into constructive channels, is a rapid increase of ill-considered enterprises and unwieldy pretentious organizations. Like vast parasitic organisms, they drain the vitality of the whole of German industry, without contributing anything in return. Dr. Rauschning can see only one end to it:

> For us Germans, the issue is plain and simple. Everyone who is still capable of thinking for himself must know that National Socialism is leading us to self-destruction.[1]

In spite of his temperamental conservatism, Dr. Rauschning is fully alive to the positive achievements of National Socialism. But he distinguishes sharply between the constructive achievements of the revolution and its main course. Something analogous could be observed in the actual work of reconstruction. Magnificent schemes were being put through, but at headlong, crazy speed. There was hardly time, one felt, for the windows to be glazed or the doors painted, before the next gigantic scheme came crowding along. It was this indefinite acceleration of National Socialist ambition which ruined the whole experiment. Dr. Rauschning's comment is as follows:

> German Conservatives and Nationalists defended their capitulation to National Socialism by saying that there was much that was open to objection in National Socialism, its methods were reprehensible, non-moral, as one Minister expressed it, but on the whole the National Socialist course was the right one for Germany. The truth is almost the opposite: National Socialism has some splendid achievements to its credit, and even much of its work in foreign policy cannot be seriously objected to from the national standpoint, having in view the difficulties with which Germany has had to contend; but its general course is mistaken, unfruitful, and in the long run, infinitely disastrous.[2]

On the next page the author sums up his criticism with the sentence: 'German aims are indefinite to-day only because they are infinite.' This conclusion agrees fundamentally with our psychological diagnosis, that Germany is possessed by the unconscious. The aims of the unconscious (if one can be allowed to speak of the unconscious having an aim) tend always to be boundless

[1] loc. cit., p. 282.   [2] loc. cit., p. 289.

157

and infinite. Representatives of the collective unconscious such as Ayesha, for instance, in Rider Haggard's myth; or, on another plane, Nietzsche's Zarathustra, with his aim of transcending man; or again, Gilgamish, with his mighty ambitions and his pursuit of the secret of immortality — such figures seem to embody an unappeasable longing or an indefinable goal. A man possessed by the unconscious is as though swallowed by a myth. The limits of his ego are dissolved among the fluid, timeless imagery of the unconscious. In this state he may easily become identified with a divine figure or with a quasi-mythical ruler, as, for instance, Mr. Preemby's sudden expansion into Sargon the Magnificent, King of Kings. [1]

We can even discern the boundless character of the unconscious in the familiar figures of legend and folklore, and in the almost infinite powers ascribed by primitive man to wizards, magicians, and medicine-men; just those persons, in fact, who claim to have special knowledge of, and traffic with, spiritual powers. The legendary hero is capable of infinite endurance, his courage and strength have no limits; the king is infinitely wise or powerful; the princess is infinitely beautiful, and the treasure which accompanies her is beyond price.

People who are temporarily invaded by unconscious contents are apt to lose their orientation in reality. One form of mental symptom is fear of space, which means fear of the unconscious, the boundless element. The opposite symptom is the fear of being confined or caught in a situation where immediate escape is impossible. People under the influence of the unconscious are liable to be vague and indefinite in expressing themselves, oblivious of time, and never quite clear or explicit about their objectives. Those, on the other hand, who have created an integrated personality have a clearly defined limit to their territory. There are no blurred edges, and no indeterminate frontiers confuse the issue between the I and the not-I. The vigour of consciousness can indeed be estimated by the way in which individuality is established, as a defined and ordered territory, over against the boundless fluidity of the unconscious. Individuality is a contained and ordered kingdom; the unconscious, the boundless sea.

Hitler evoked a limitless mythological response from the German

[1] H. G. WELLS, *Christina Alberta's Father.*

people. Everything was possible. But the leader lacked an integrated consciousness. He was swept along by the power he had aroused and no one dared withstand him. Not until it was a matter of life and death, and the whole of Europe was in danger of being swamped, did the conservative powers take up the challenge. At last the man appeared who could draw the sword Nothung from the tree. Until Churchill assumed leadership there was no real unity. The attitude of acquiescence and unconcern which paralysed the shaping of British policy under Baldwin had lured the nation into mortal danger. So long as Britain lay like the dragon Fafnir, coiled around the treasure, pretending that Hitler was no concern of hers, her spirit was weak and infirm. But with the change of leadership the unity of the nation was restored. From the moment that she seized the problem with a resolute grip, the true quality of the people answered to the need.

Some abiding truth for Germany may also come out of chaos, now that her destructive dynamism has at last been firmly opposed. But the Messianic possibility, that was ready and waiting in post-war Germany, is dead. It has been betrayed and murdered by a leader who was bankrupt in virtue, and who could not tolerate the discipline of opposition, without which nature can create nothing durable.

CHAPTER VI

ACCELERATION AND DESTRUCTION

I

In his remarkable book *Germany's Revolution of Destruction*, Dr. Rauschning gives an impression of National Socialism that reminds one of a landslide or an avalanche. His evidence is all the more valuable psychologically since the catastrophe, which he saw approaching, is now actually upon us. From the standpoint of the present work, his most significant testimony has to do with the destructive effect of the avalanche upon human individuality. The following passages contain the gist of his indictment:

> It is the essential task of every revolution to produce a *tabula rasa*, to make a clean sweep of the past political forces; but the nihilist revolution of National Socialism sets out to destroy everything that it cannot itself take over and convert to its own pattern. This explains its *Gleichschaltung*, or forcing into conformity of all elements of society and of every independent activity, or else their total suppression. It explains why the revolution ignores the very conceptions of a private sphere in life and of legality . . . The new social order will consist of universal and equal servitude, a general mobilization, not only for the purpose of military preparedness, but as a permanent revolutionary system — a servitude which will remove human labour from the sphere of economic and social considerations and subject it to the principle of blind obedience to an absolute despotism. . . .

> Thus National Socialism is at issue with every independent activity or ordering of life. It is bound to make an end of freedom of initiative, of all that in the past has made for creative ability and progress: these things make its dominion incomplete. Nothing is more intolerable to it in its revolutionary course than originality, individuality, character, or true public spirit. Whatever it cannot dominate it must destroy; whatever it cannot absorb and master must go. . . .

160

This destruction is not brought to a halt before the things of the mind. The fight against the intellectuals and against the freedom of science is not in the slightest degree the outcome of any inferiority complex; it arises from the clear recognition that in the field of the intellect the indissoluble unity of Western civilization remains active. In this field, independence of thought and resistance to the revolution are bound to show themselves sooner or later.[1]

Dr. Rauschning's idea that National Socialism has to destroy everything it cannot absorb into its own low-grade collective pattern, agrees perfectly with the known facts. National Socialism is not a political party that is responsible to a tradition with honourable antecedents. It is a revolutionary party arising out of despair and defeat. It had no ground of its own, no possessions, and no past. All that it now is and has, has been taken from other parties and interests, mostly by violence. As an organism, it developed the habit of robbery and violence and, as a revolutionary party seeking power, it had to do away with everything and everybody which stood in its path.

Dr. Rauschning is a conservative Prussian who has spent a large part of his life as an officer of the state. He sees not only the obvious brutalizing of German life under the Nazis, but he has watched the disintegration of established standards of morality and integrity among permanent officers of the state. He has seen the state departments, with their disciplined, vigilant officers, reduced to impotence. He writes:

> To-day the State is nothing but an administrative machine. There is no true sphere of the State in the Third Reich.[2]

Intelligence, sense of responsibility, individual quality, even adequate training, are all waved aside as no longer desirable among the governing personnel:

> Any man will do who will exercise power with ruthless brutality. Only in a revolutionary period can the difficult problem of selection of personnel be treated with the negligence, indeed the criminal negligence, shown by National Socialism.[3]

---

[1] HERMANN RAUSCHNING, *Germany's Revolution of Destruction*, pp. 93-5, (Heinemann, London).
[2] ibid., p. 28.   [3] ibid., p. 34.

A state officer nurtured in the principles of responsible government is naturally filled with bitter feelings, when he sees men in
high positions of the state openly encouraging corrupt, unprincipled
practices and pouring contempt upon those who still stand for
civilized principles.

> It is impossible [Dr. Rauschning says] to demand scrupu-
> lous correctness in a member's private life, when any crime
> may be required of him in the interests of the party.[1]

Hitler's habitual attitude of scorn for the docile German citizen
is related to the fact that he himself has jettisoned all the
ethical standards by which the decent citizen lives. He is bound
to assume therefore that people who still direct their lives by
moral standards are lacking in intelligence. Although the passage
was subsequently deleted from later editions, Hitler wrote in
Mein Kampf:

> The German has not the faintest notion of the way the nation
> has to be swindled if one wants mass support.

To the British mind, nurtured from Arthurian days in the tradition
of fair-play, a leader who openly confessed that the policy he
stands for can succeed only through swindling the whole nation,
is an incredible phenomenon. Yet Germany's leader, having first
warned the people that he was about to swindle them, proceeded
to do so, and succeeded.

2

We should have to go to the East, or back to the dawn of
civilization, to find a parallel to Hitler's attitude of god-like
arrogance towards the people he rules. Gilgamish, the mythical
tyrant of early Sumerian civilization, had many points in common
with Hitler. He too was a magician. He is described as being 'two-
thirds divine and one-third human'. He too had a special relation
with the spiritual powers, claiming Shamash, the sun-god, as his
father. He was also instructed by dreams and was, above all, a
dæmonic personality. In building the thick-walled city of Erech

[1] ibid., p. 36.

he is described as 'masterful, dominant, subtle'. In his tyrannical, civilizing will:

> Gilgamish leaveth no maid to her mother, nor daughter to hero,
> Nay, nor a spouse to her husband. [1]

At last, finding his tyranny unbearable, the people of Erech, prayed to Anu for release. He passed the matter to Aruru, the earth-goddess, telling her to make a champion like unto the primeval seed of mankind'.

> So when the goddess Aruru heard this, in her mind she imagined
> Straightway the conception of Anu, and, washing her hands, Aruru
> Fingered some clay: on the desert she moulded it. Thus on the desert
> Enkidu she made, a warrior, as he were born and begotten. [2]

Since all myths originate in human experience, we can treat this material as we do dreams, viz. as an emotional record. From this point of view, we may infer that when a leader becomes possessed by a fanatical, tyrannizing will a compensatory, underground, seceding movement is liable to take place among his people. The regression naturally flows back towards the source. All life flows from the mother. Accordingly, Aruru combines the idea of the fruitful Earth, or Nature, with the human image of maternal source. The primordial state is the original condition of man; the state when he abides unquestioningly within the laws of nature, i.e. the natural state. The prayer to the gods represents the recession of the collective *libido* into the collective unconscious. The early gods are the primordial images which are activated, or come to life, through the introversion of the vital energy. Purposive introversion into the unconscious results in a creative activity, in which the primordial relation with nature, and with the instincts, assumes a fresh and alluring aspect. Enkidu is described as being covered by a luxuriant growth of hair and

> In the way of a woman he snooded his locks in a fillet.

[1] R. CAMPBELL THOMPSON, *The Epic of Gilgamish* (Luzac & Co., London), p. 10.
[2] ibid., p. 10, line 34.

He knew neither people nor land: he pastured with the gazelles
and drank his fill with the cattle.

With the beasts did his heart delight at the water.

This description of Enkidu as the image of primordial longing,
quickened in the soul of the people by a recession of *libido* from
the terrible civilizing fury of Gilgamish, brings this mythic parallel
right into the present scene. Here, for instance, is a picture of the
methods of interference and domination practised by National
Socialism as seen by Dr. Rauschning.

> . . . Crimes are arranged and attributed to opponents. The
> people are kept in a state of fear, utterly intimidated. At the
> same time they are stirred up into a blaze of indignation,
> given the sense that they have been saved from destruction,
> and made to feel thankful to a strong régime that gives them
> security. . . .
>
> One word, finally, on the most elementary, but perhaps most
> . . . characteristic . . . method of domination employed by
> National Socialism — the marching. At first this marching
> seemed to be a curious whim of the National Socialists.
> These eternal night marches, this keeping of the whole
> population on the march, seemed to be a senseless waste of
> time and energy. Only much later was there revealed in it a
> cunning purpose, based on a well-judged adjustment of ends
> and means. Marching diverts men's thoughts. Marching
> kills thought. *Marching makes an end of individuality.* Marching
> is the indispensable magic stroke performed in order to
> accustom the people to a mechanical, quasi-ritualistic
> activity until it becomes second nature.[1]

Rosenberg offers the following explanation of the Nazi's
marching policy:

> The German nation is simply out to discover at last its own
> style of living, a style of living that is fundamentally dis-
> tinguished from what is called British Liberalism . . . It is
> the style of a marching column, no matter where or to what
> end this marching column may be directed.[2]

It may be, as Dr. Rauschning says, that this frenzied activity is
'just to distract men's minds'. But if this is really the case, this

---

[1] HERMANN RAUSCHNING, *Germany's Revolution of Destruction*, p. 51.
[2] Quoted by RAUSCHNING (loc. cit., p. 51) from Rosenberg's *Gestaltung der Idee*.

bankrupt political party ought surely to have collapsed long since. Is it not more probable that we have to deal, in both instances, with the same conversion-process, whereby energy can be shifted from the sphere of the individual and his personal interests downwards into an organized collective mechanism?

The chief mistake made by those who see in their fellows nothing but the means whereby some pinnacle of power can be reached, is that they overlook the essential realities of the human soul and recognize only transitory impulses. They imagine that it is possible to obliterate the dangerous individual reaction by merely accelerating the collective machine. The only problem which concerns the power-addict in his conception of leadership is how to make the people pliable to every command. It is a tragic fact that Hitler can still think like this notwithstanding his own early experience of human misery. Mankind is more prone to reproduce his early experience than to learn from it. Recruits, who have been savaged into submission by a rough-tongued sergeant, are only too liable to reproduce the tough tradition when they eventually find themselves in the sergeant's place.

Hitler, we know, suffered terrible humiliation and repression in his early years. Now, having stepped into the oppressor's shoes, he takes his neurotic revenge in the repression of others. But what the oppressor does not see is the underground recession of the life-stream, moving away from his inhuman ideal. The creation of Enkidu is predictable wherever a fanatical ideology weighs too heavily upon a nation's spirit.

As long ago as 1938 I saw evidences of this recession in Germany. Nowhere, of course, were there overt signs of resistance, but with everyone with whom confidence was established, the longing for release from tyranny constantly obtruded itself, often in the form of eager questions about the conditions of life in England.

But without speculating as to the time or occasion of Enkidu's emergence, we can say with psychological certainty that an underground migration has already taken place in Germany, and that what is now taking form in the unconscious is diametrically opposed to the spirit of Hitlerism. There cannot be a Gilgamish without an Enkidu.

From Gilgamish to Hitler, a despotic power has always bred the same illusion. History is full of examples of how the fanatic and the revolutionary bring things about; yet only rarely are they able to effect what they so passionately intend. If this be true, we might well ask why myth, legend, and history are full of the deeds of these possessed beings. The reason is, of course, that the dæmonic personality is a most impressive phenomenon. It is as though men realized that a Gilgamish, or a Hitler, was the agent of fate. The power that possesses such a man, using him as its agent, is clearly something beyond the personal. He captures the minds of his contemporaries like a magnet. Everyone is curious to see what his dæmon will make him do next; almost as though the force of a cyclone were personified in a human being.

3

From this angle of approach it is interesting to see how our picture of Hitler compares with that of his dæmonic elder brother. Both Gilgamish and Hitler have a peculiar and psychologically significant relation with the mother. The myth is unusually explicit about this relationship. We are given a picture of the mother as a seer to whom Gilgamish takes his dreams. She foretells coming events from them. When Gilgamish and Enkidu have striven together for mastery, and for possession of the sacred prostitute whom Gilgamish sends to entice Enkidu to Erech, Gilgamish brings Enkidu to the mother, who thereupon accepts him. Thus the mother seems to personify in a special way the hero's relation to the unconscious. This symbolism is intelligible when we recall the fact that the unconscious is the womb of emergent reality. It is the source of everything that man creates. Hence the mother-image is the natural deity of the unconscious.

The medium's psychology is constellated in an especial way by the mother. This fact will be more readily understood when it is recalled that the mediumistic type is related more to events and contents of the unconscious than to the world around. Analysis of men who are mediums invariably reveals, according to my experience, a typical mother-complex; while the maternal type of woman usually plays an important rôle in his love-life. The connection between the mediumistic function and the infantile dependence upon the mother is, indeed, so apparent, that we might even regard the function of mediumship as a primitive expression of the *libido* that has never been detached from the mother.

From his description in the myth, it is clear that Gilgamish, like Hitler, was possessed by the unconscious. His uncanny power, intimated in his semi-divine constitution, was derived from his mother, the prophetess, and from the sun-god Shamash, whom he claimed as his father. In his fanatical building activity, in his quest of, and victory over, the monster Chumbaba, in his relation to Enkidu, and above all, in his unassuageable pursuit of the secret of immortality, Gilgamish reveals the features of one possessed. But, just because he is possessed and pursued by his dæmon, his goal always recedes and his soul remains unsatisfied. At the outset (as with Hitler) his dæmon urged him to apparently realizable concrete objectives. But as the possession grows on him, his ambition becomes transformed, reaching out towards infinite or metaphysical goals; until at the end of the myth, his quest for Enkidu's spirit, and for the secret of immortality, completely displace all earthly ambitions.

This strange combination of concrete realism with the high metaphysical quest is, to some extent, also characteristic of Hitler. The analogy may possibly throw some light upon his bewildering ambiguity. Dr. Rauschning's evidence on this point is as follows:

> Hitler's realism deceives the onlooker. This man, who can calculate with such icy clarity, who can await the right moment, who feels his way forward, one might say, with mastery, who is constantly testing and trying the weak spots — a man who so realistically examines everything surely cannot at the same time be a fantast, simply out to overturn everything, trusting himself to a limitless movement that is to bear him to some dimly sensed new order. And yet this duality is, in fact, the essential characteristic of those great 'destroyers' of whom Jakob Burckhardt writes. Men of this type are 'inventive in destruction', they have a flair for the weak points, the points at which they can apply pressure in order to bring down the old order. And it is their destiny to do this until a really creative will opposes them, or until their environment is exhausted. These are the men of great tactical gifts. They are also the men possessed of dæmons,

of second sight, dreamers urged on by visions, who regard themselves as men like unto gods, and who live in an unreal world in spite of all the realism they can assume on occasion. [1]

Dr. Rauschning also claims that the secret of Hitler's swift and successful strokes is that he has no fixed aims, but waits until his dæmon tells him to move, keeping his immense force in reserve like a coiled snake, always ready to strike. A leader without policy or principles, ready to take advantage of any situation with overwhelming strength, has, of course, immense tactical advantage over any possible opponent. Dr. Rauschning repeatedly insists upon this opportunism in the direction of National Socialism. He writes:

> National Socialist policy has only impulses, no fixed political aims — impulses and a system of tactics. There is no degree of saturation in the political aims of National Socialism: there can be none. Thus, nothing can be more irrational than to ask what are the final demands of its 'dynamic' foreign policy.
>
> In particular, therefore, it is not correct to regard the new German foreign policy as simply the final form of the policy of the pan-German. The foreign policy of the Third Reich goes beyond the most extreme limits any nation has consciously set itself in the past. It is supposed to be a 'peace policy of justice' — but: 'A new peace shall make Germany mistrèss of the globe, a peace not hanging on the palm-fronds of lachrymose pacifist womenfolk, but established by the victorious sword of a master race that takes over the world in the service of a higher civilization.' Such is the main political principle of National Socialism as expressed by Rosenberg. Hitler's language is more general, but it conveys no less ambitious perspectives. [2]

Without omitting to enjoy the lachrymose palm-fronds of Herr Rosenberg, we can also see that this infinite policy allows infinite latitude of objective. The programme is always fluid, so that any aggressive intention can always be denied when expediency demands. It is significant also to note that no representative of the Nazi régime would dream of allowing himself ever to say a word in favour of peace. This is the true dæmonic style, explosive, virile, masculine, and unassuageably

[1] loc. cit., pp. 193-94.   [2] loc. cit., p. 194.

bloodthirsty. Obviously, the women must carry all those gentler human characters which do not suit this heroic Nordic style.

The trick of using scapegoats to bear one's inconvenient motivations is one of the first psychological signs of an ignoble state of mind. But fanatical psychology cannot function without scapegoats. In daily life we commonly judge the integrity and maturity of a man's character by his attitude to this vital moral problem. Not to make use of a scapegoat to ease one's soul of shame, is the law of psychological maturity. Though this principle is implied in the whole Christian attitude, it has been left for our time to state it explicitly as the foundation of ethical conduct.

This principle stands as the touchstone of maturity, because, in a peculiar way, it concerns the problem of the primitive sublayers of our mental structure. When we speak of a person, or of a nation, going through a regressive phase, we actually mean that his mode of behaviour has reverted to the primitive type. This contamination from the unconscious primitive levels produces reactions of a very dubious character. Everyone is familiar with the trickily evasive answer, the slippery movement away from accountability and a definite standpoint, the readiness to leave everything hard or unpleasant for somebody else to tackle — that whole devil's fry of procrastination, tardiness, and unreliability which makes our best effort of self-criticism seem inadequate. Maturity demands not only a genuine submission to the analytical moral law, which no longer allows the primitive to slip away out of focus by merely blaming somebody else. It also requires of us an honest coming to terms with the primitive needs of our nature.

Since Hitler's Germany is passing through a regressive phase in which the contamination from below has all but obliterated the reliable German character, we might explain the contemporary maelstrom by assuming that Hitler symbolizes — in an exceedingly menacing form — the shadow-aspect of civilization.

Civilization was founded, as we saw in the Gilgamish myth, on a psychologically exclusive basis which tended to repress the primordial inheritance of mankind. But the psyche itself is living history; it is the unedited chronicle of the ascent of man from the first beginnings of life on this earth. Only the last, thinnest layer of adaptation is civilized — seven thousand years at the outside. The whole of the remainder is primitive, and it is this tremendously ancient psychic potential which civilization has attempted, quite vainly, to exclude.

For many years after the war the Germans tried, with increasing signs of exhaustion and revolt, to fulfil their obligations under the pressure of the victors. The victorious allied powers naturally seemed to the Germans very much as Gilgamish must have appeared to the oppressed people of Erech. At all events, it was during this period that the heart of Germany seceded away from the Western style and the Western civilized goals, back to the alternative primitive hypothesis lying dormant in the unconscious. This recession of national *libido* away from the half-hearted Weimar attempt, and the painstaking, civilized pathway, corresponds with the prayer to the gods and the creation of Enkidu in the myth. Actually, what was brought to light through the pressure and operation of the Versailles Treaty was the latent split within the collective German psyche. Versailles did not create this division: it merely produced the occasion which forced it again to the surface. What was lacking in Germany was the desire for unity which always creates an atmosphere of human tolerance. The Gilgamish way is the repression of human weakness by a cruel and arbitrary intensification of superiority. The psychological way is the acceptance of inferiority, and the reconciliation of the opposites through this acceptance. This is also the way developed in the myth. After Gilgamish has accepted Enkidu as his brother, the latter acts as the indispensable corrective to the hero's headstrong ambition.

4

In the absence of this spirit of tolerance and acceptance of inferiority, the life-stream of German culture began to abscond, seeking an earlier solution and a more congenial climate in the unconscious. This spiritual migration away from the civilizing tasks of the West was sensed as far back as 1923 by D. H. Lawrence who, at times, discerned conditions under the threshold with astonishing accuracy. In a 'Letter from Germany' Lawrence tells

of his impressions as he crossed the Rhine into the Black Forest
after an absence of over two years. It is an amazing prediction of
coming events:

> It is as if the life had retreated eastwards. As if the Germanic
> life were slowly ebbing away from contact with western
> Europe, ebbing to the deserts of the east. . . .
> Germany, this bit of Germany, is very different from what
> it was two and a half years ago, when I was here. Then it
> was still open to Europe. Then it still looked to western
> Europe for a reunion, for a sort of reconciliation. Now that is
> over. The inevitable, mysterious barrier has fallen again,
> and the great leaning of the Germanic spirit is once more
> eastwards, towards Russia, towards Tartary. The strange
> vortex of Tartary has become the positive centre again, the
> positivity of western Europe is broken. The positivity of
> our civilization has broken. The influences that come, come
> invisibly out of Tartary. So that all Germany reads *Beasts,
> Men and Gods* with a kind of fascination. Returning again
> to the fascination of the destructive east, that produced
> Attila. . . .
> But at night you feel strange things stirring in the darkness,
> strange feelings stirring out of this still unconquered Black
> Forest. You stiffen your backbone and you listen to the
> night. There is a sense of danger. It is not the people.
> They don't seem dangerous. Out of the very air comes a
> sense of danger, a queer, *bristling* feeling of uncanny danger.
> Something has happened. Something has happened which
> has not yet eventuated. The old spell of the old world has
> broken, and the old, bristling, savage spirit has set in. The
> war did not break the old peace-and-production hope of the
> world, though it gave it a severe wrench. Yet the peace-
> and-production hope still governs, at least the consciousness.
> Even in Germany it has not quite gone.
> But it feels as if, virtually, it were gone. The last two years
> have done it. The hope in peace-and-production is broken.
> The old flow, the old adherence is ruptured. And a still older
> flow has set in. Back, back to the savage polarity of Tartary,
> and away from the polarity of civilized Christian Europe.
> This, it seems to me, has already happened. And it is a
> happening of far more profound import than any actual
> *event*. It is the father of the next phase of events.
> And the feeling never relaxes. As you travel up the Rhine

valley, still the same latent sense of danger, of silence, of suspension. Not that the people are actually planning or plotting or preparing. I don't believe it for a minute. But something has happened to the human soul, beyond all help. The human soul recoiling now from unison, and making itself strong elsewhere. The ancient spirit of prehistoric Germany coming back, at the end of history.

The same in Heidelberg, Heidelberg full, full, full of people. Students the same, youths with rucksacks the same, boys and maidens in gangs come down from the hills. The same and not the same. These queer gangs of Young Socialists, youths and girls, with their non-materialistic professions, their half-mystic assertions, they strike one as strange. Something primitive, like loose, roving gangs of broken, scattered tribes, so they affect one. And the swarms of people somehow produce an impression of silence, of secrecy, of stealth. It is as if everything and everybody recoiled away from the old unison, as barbarians lurking in a wood recoil out of sight. The old habits remain. But the bulk of the people have no money. And the whole stream of feeling is reversed. . . .

And it all looks as if the years were wheeling swiftly backwards, no more onwards. Like a spring that is broken, and whirls swiftly back, so time seems to be whirling with mysterious swiftness to a sort of death. Whirling to the ghost of the old Middle Ages of Germany, then to the Roman days, then to the days of the silent forest and the dangerous, lurking barbarians. . . .

It is a fate; nobody now can alter it. It is a fate. The very blood changes. Within the last three years, the very constituency of the blood has changed in European veins. But particularly in Germanic veins.

At the same time, we have brought it about ourselves — by a Ruhr occupation, by an English nullity, and by a German false will. We have done it ourselves. But apparently it was not to be helped.

Quos vult perdere deus, dementat prius.[1]

Lawrence was averse from expressing his intuition in psychological terms; accordingly some of his metaphors demand

---

[1] D. H. LAWRENCE, 'Letter from Germany', in *Phoenix*, pp. 107-10 (William Heinemann Ltd.). I am indebted to my colleague, Gerhard Adler, for the above reference.

interpretation. The essence of the matter lies in his feeling that 'something has happened to the human soul, beyond all help. The human soul recoiling from unison, and making itself strong elsewhere'. In view of recent political transformations this early gravitation of Germany towards Russia (which Lawrence insists upon calling Tartary) is of especial interest. Tartary is a rather indefinite semi-barbaric area of eastern Russia, while Russia itself is vast and almost boundless. It is accordingly fitted to represent the indefinite realm of the unconscious. Tartary might represent the Moslem or non-Christian aspect of Russia. When Lawrence wrote he was not concerned with the possible political manipulations of a future Ribbentrop, but rather with the receding of the German soul away from the Christian community of the West, with its hard-won Christian values, to that other latent possibility, the ruthless, primitive dynamism of the pagan unconscious. Is it not possible that, in his insistence upon Tartary,[1] Lawrence's intuitive antennae may have been sensing the same extra-Christian dynamism which Jung has designated Wotan?

In Lawrence we have a witness of the German scene who is politically above suspicion. It is as though he had just wandered into the German unconscious (as one might wander into the Black Forest) and had met Enkidu face to face. Lawrence's detachment from his own civilized roots gave him an uncanny insight into what was happening in Germany. It helps us to a true understanding of what happened in Germany between the two wars. Without this understanding we can easily go astray.

The vital energy of an individual, or of a people, is a living stream. Either it is flowing onwards towards a potential goal in the future, or backwards towards its source. With the individual life-stream, the source is, naturally, the mother. But with the great stream of the racial unconscious, the backward flow leads towards the original, or primordial, state. When a crisis emerges in the life of the individual, or the nation, there is a tendency for the stream of energy to divide against itself in the manner of a watershed: one portion streaming onwards, the other back. This

---

[1] The eastern heart of Russia, largely inhabited by Mongols, who were carried there by the Mongol invasion of the thirteenth century.

backward-flowing stream may be merely a recoil from the increasing psychical strains of the next evolutionary phase. If this is the case a negative regressive phase must follow. But the harking-back can just as well be a *reculer pour mieux sauter*; in which case, we must regard the regression as a movement in search of a simpler, more unified, and, therefore, more primitive solution.

The analogy with the Gilgamish story is instructive in regard to the latter possibility. The harshness of the rule of Gilgamish, as already said, would correspond, from the German point of view, with the dictated peace treaty and the rather uncompromising attitude of the victor powers. The revolt of the people and their prayers to Anu represent the phase of division, in which the stream of energy divides against itself. In recent German history this would correspond with the increasing division, both politically and psychologically, between the conservative elements, resolved to follow the path of traditional culture, and the Communists and Revolutionaries who turned their faces away from the West towards a more hopeful dawn in the East.

Seen from the angle of the myth, the movement away from Gilgamish is also the movement towards Enkidu and the renewed covenant with nature. We can, therefore, regard it as a teleological regression. From the teleological standpoint one always looks to the end, viewing the whole process that went before in relation to what emerges from it. It may be objected that Enkidu is a rather doubtful gain. This, however, was not the view of Gilgamish, for whom the relation with Enkidu had supreme value. But first he had to catch the wild man and bring him to Erech, for which purpose he borrowed one of the sacred prostitutes from the temple of Ishtar. He had then to overcome Enkidu, and finally come to a basis of understanding which accepted the other's very different nature.

In analytical practice a similar sequence of events is frequently enacted under one's eyes. The harsh uncompromising rule of a one-sided conscious function is more than likely to bring about a recession of *libido* into the unconscious. A primitive shadow-figure is thereupon created, personifying the excluded human attributes which compensate the one-sided conscious attitude.

The anima[1] regularly plays the rôle of go-between, whereby the two antithetical parts of the subject are made to relate. The most important part of the analytical experiment is this coming to terms with the representative of the unconscious. If the shadow wins in the trial of strength, the previously existing conscious values are overturned and chaos rules for a time. It is essential, on the other hand, that the old régime of blind repression should not be re-established. The ideal solution, therefore, is mastery through acceptance, which, after all, is the solution of every relation between master and servant. The neurotic character, which seeks to avoid the responsibility of mastery, also fails to find any genuine service.

In the relation between the civilized conscious and the primitive unconscious, the conscious function should naturally be master; while the unconscious, as naturally, serves. But there must first be a fundamental acceptance of the primitive standpoint. This is a *sine qua non* of a real coming to terms with the unconscious. It is beautifully illustrated in the myth, in the scene where the mother, from the temple steps, says to Gilgamish: 'This day I have born thee a brother.' Indeed, in the birth of friendship between the two, the fact that the relation rests upon mutual respect is clearly indicated. The text informs us that immediately after the combat:

> . . . his fury abated,
> Aye, and his ardour was quelled: so soon as was quelled his
> ardour,
> Enkidu thus unto Gilgamish spake: 'Of a truth, did thy
> mother
> Bear thee as one, and one only: that choicest cow of the steer-
> folds,
> Nin-sun[2] exalted thy head above heroes, and Enlil hath
> dower'd
> Thee with the kingship o'er men.'[3]

The fight for mastery is ostensibly for possession of the sacred prostitute of Ishtar. But, immediately they have made their pact of brotherhood after the fight, the dæmonic energy of Gilgamish

---

[1] The soul-image or feminine personification of a man's unconscious.
[2] The mother of Gilgamish.
[3] R. CAMPBELL THOMPSON, *The Epic of Gilgamish*, p. 19.

turns towards the forest of Cedars, guarded by the fire-breathing monster Chumbaba. Enkidu is against this enterprise, but he is overpersuaded by the passion of Gilgamish, who has set his civilizing eye on the great cedar trees. In this way competitive animosity is transformed into an excellent working combination, from which both gain what they previously lacked. But, before this understanding is reached, Gilgamish makes the mistake of trying to adapt Enkidu to the sophisticated, luxurious life of his court, where he tries to show him off and make much of him. Very soon this becomes impossibly tedious for Enkidu, whose taste for real things and real pleasures cannot be debauched. He runs away and finds his way back to the wild uplands, cursing the girl who had seduced him from his original estate. But Gilgamish, who cannot endure life without his other half, seeks him out, offering him his own conditions so long as he will not forsake the pact.

The logic of these events is psychologically transparent. Gilgamish is a one-sided genius who oppresses his people because he is repressing the other half of his own nature. In Enkidu he finds this excluded other half and, through the pact of brotherhood, he becomes whole, which also means healed. Once having experienced totality, he cannot again tolerate a partial, or divided, state. Thus when Enkidu dies — as a punishment for hybris, an attitude which he has clearly caught from Gilgamish — Gilgamish is distraught, and the rest of his life is spent in an unappeasable quest for the soul of Enkidu. He is committed to this metaphysical quest as whole-heartedly as he was formerly given to the pact. Thus, led on by his fate and his own longing for unity, he pursues the quest of immortality which, at bottom, is the problem of the supra-personal element in the structure of individuality.

I have given this brief account of the myth, because it depicts a condition which, in certain essential respects, resembles that sensed by Lawrence. What Lawrence discerned was a seceding, a migration, and an acceleration. He sensed the dæmonic element, because something in his own nature answered to it. This took place, it must be noted, before Hitler had appeared on the scene. Was it not this same backward streaming tide which attracted the outcast and dreamer of dreams? Was he not lured to play the Messianic Enkidu rôle without even knowing what he did[1]? Impressions of Hitler, from various sources, give one the picture of a man being whirled along on an immense flood in a flimsy boat, without any means of navigation, or knowledge of his destination. Indeed Hitler himself refers to the acceleration of the Nazi movement, and his own inability to control it even if he would.

Acceleration belongs to all movement that is assisted by natural force, whether this be gravity, dissolution, conflagration, panic, or the attraction of chaos. At its outset, nearly every movement can be controlled, opposed, or directed. But massive acceleration makes reasoned control impossible. On the other hand, things that are stable, firmly rooted, or established, are not liable to destructive acceleration.

What I have termed the dæmonic factor in human psychology, although immediately recognizable, is not easy to define. We have to deal with a phenomenon of vital energy, proceeding from a state of instability, which tends at times to be accompanied by violence and uncontrolled acceleration. The instability arises from a psychical split, or state of inner division, as, for example, the split between the cultural and the militaristic aspects of German life. Because these contradictory aspects cannot be reconciled, they are liable to bring about violent explosions and disturbances, or, alternatively, moods of impotent despair.

We shall have more to say about this schizoid condition of the German psyche in a later chapter. For the moment it is enough to record the phenomenon of the split soul in the Gilgamish myth, and the characteristic dæmonic nature of the hero, with his compulsively accelerating tempo: a condition which wise counsel and every kind of obstacle proved powerless to check. With regard to the German acceleration, Lawrence's impression is vividly expressed:

> Like a spring that is broken, and whirls swiftly back, so time seems to be whirling with mysterious swiftness to a sort of death.[2]

Also the later impression of Dr. Rauschning:

> The radical dynamism into which National Socialism has developed is a dangerous destructive fever which spreads at an uncanny rate.[3]

---

[1] It is noteworthy that Hitler has also caught the hybristic infection, the sin which heaven never forgives.
[2] loc. cit.　　　[3] *Germany's Revolution of Destruction*, p. 267.

And again:

> Hitler was abandoning himself to forces which were carrying
> him away — forces of dark and destructive violence. He
> imagined that he still had freedom of choice, but he had long
> been in bondage to a magic which might well have been
> described not only in metaphor, but in literal fact, as that of
> evil spirits ... We witnessed the development of a man
> possessed, the helpless prey of the powers of darkness.[1]

Finally Hitler himself is recorded as saying:

> We have been drawn into a movement which will carry us
> along with it, whether we like it or not. If we resist it we shall
> be annihilated.[2]

These impressions of something as irresistible as an avalanche
are very convincing. This irresistible something for which
we have no name, but which is akin to the *furor teutonicus* of pagan
Germany, has its subtle as well as its gross effects. One had only
to visit Germany, and make some kind of human relation to the
people one met, to discover an irrational obstinacy that would
suddenly intervene, almost like a little lump of fanaticism,
which had broken away from the main mass. On two occasions
I have watched this piece of the German avalanche melt away
under a foreign sun.

The first case was that of a young German scientist, who had
been sent to England as a kind of cultural envoy to put the Nazi
Weltanschauung in a true light before the English people. A
marked lack of sympathy with his Nazi philosophy left him
puzzled and discouraged. After a time, he became swamped by
feelings of inferiority and neurotic despair, which he attributed
to difficulties between himself and his fiancée in Berlin. When he
came to me his morale was not far from zero. He brought me his
dreams and discovered, to his surprise, that, in spite of his conscious belief in the Nazi ideas, the régime was represented in the
unconscious by the notorious Von Killinger, a man whom
he had special reason to detest because of his brutality
to members of his own circle at the University. Then, in a whole
series of dreams, the Nazi standpoint was vigorously pilloried
and caricatured.

[1] *Hitler Speaks*, p. 213. [2] ibid., p. 112.

ACCELERATION AND DESTRUCTION

What had happened was clear. My patient had suffered, more even than most Germans, from a sense of inferiority tinged by introverted fatalism. In company with a great many of his contemporaries, sheer spiritual hunger had prompted him to project upon Hitler fervent Messianic expectations. A kind of semi-religious conversion took place, in which he allowed himself to be swept along on an extraverted collective wave. When his inferiority became magically converted into Führer-worship, he became an ardent member of the party. As a scholar and intellectual, he soon won distinction in the party, and was eventually chosen as an envoy for England. Installed in London, he felt like a wandering ice-floe that had been carried into the path of the Gulf Stream. No longer contained by the Nordic myth, the Nazi complex began to melt away. But his whole conscious orientation made it impossible for him to accept what was happening to him. Accordingly, in order to repress the anti-Nazi influence which was undermining him he would lash himself to greater missionary efforts. The conflict was too pressing to remain unconscious indefinitely. When he came to me his depressed state was due to the fact that he had not only found his Führer-worship to be dead, but his old feelings of inferiority had returned.

The other case was that of a well-known German professor, an authority on Oriental religions, and a man of wide experience outside Germany. He had been invited to Zürich to give a course of seminar-lectures on his own subject of Oriental religious philosophy. During his first lecture certain assumptions crept in concerning the so-called Nordic culture which, although accepted in Germany as part of the basic 'Aryan' creed, have been entirely discredited elsewhere. The professor was manifestly taken aback when, at the close of his lecture, these presuppositions were subjected to a competent scientific scrutiny by certain members of the class. A devastating critical fire was levelled at the whole Nordic race-theory, a fire that was all the more destructive because of the detached scientific standpoint from which it was directed. The professor was unable to continue his theme and had, in consequence, to reorganize the rest of his lectures. Later he explained that he had imagined these ideas could be taken for granted everywhere, as they were throughout

Germany. The specious reasoning supplied by Nazi apologists
had always seemed to him sufficient. He was evidently disturbed
to find his ideas subjected to a criterion of truth radically different
from the one used in Germany. What was true and sufficient
for him was the emotional content of the Germanic myth, and it
had obviously never occurred to him that people who were not
contained by the German Faith would see truth differently.

As in the former case, signs of deflation and inferiority were
immediately evident, but such traitorous feelings were naturally
over-compensated at once by vigorous counter-measures. That
the melting process had begun was evident from the heat
generated by the criticism.

In both instances, the intellectual content of the Nazi ideology —
which in point of fact is negligible — had been taken for granted
for the sake of its emotional and mythological significance. This
is the blissful state Jung describes as being 'within the experience'.
In neither case was it possible to focus down upon the emotional
content, as is usually possible when we are dealing with an
individual experience. For example, the emotional content which
we spoke of as Führer-worship, bears no resemblance to the usual
experience of hero-worship. Everyone remarks that the Führer
is not impressive as a personality. His attraction resides in his
function, in his provocative shaman's voice, and his sensitive
relation to that common myth which contains all who participate
in the experience. Thus the Führer becomes the associative
nucleus, or symbol, of that whole collective experiment. It would
be impossible to localize this feeling in any individual psyche,
because the essence of the experience lies in its participation. But,
though difficult to localize and control, these collective emotional
states are all the more binding upon the unconscious. We
acquiesce in them without owning responsibility for them. In
this way such factors can easily become our fate. The example
of the Gadarene swine goes to show that acceleration and
destruction through dæmonic provocation, is, in point of fact,
one of the most plausible forms of suicide. And yet, so difficult
is it to seize these collective motivations in a comprehensive term,
that we have to fall back upon mythological figures like Wotan
in our attempts to describe them. The reason for this elusiveness
is not far to seek. We look for the source of all motivations within

the lit arena that is open to personal introspection, i.e. our individual psyche. We are naturally sceptical of everything which eludes this scrutiny, and when the chill breath of scepticism falls upon a thing, we are inclined, like Peter, to disclaim all connection with it. Hence our strange ignorance of the unconscious.

5

The phenomenon of dæmonic possession has always gripped the imagination of mankind, particularly when it concerned a king, or one of the mighty ones of the earth. History provides a large gallery of portraits of possessed war-lords and tyrants, from Nebuchadnezzar to Hitler. There is a significant similarity in these portraits. The prophet Daniel, noting this similarity, based his prophecy upon an indefinite repetition of the type. Not only does he give us a faithful picture of the present crop of lunatics, but one that is equally true in essentials for their ill-starred antecedents. Naturally a touch of variety is needed here and there to give individuality to the features, but the basic traits are identical.

> And the king shall do according to his will; and he shall exalt himself, and magnify himself above every god, and shall speak marvellous things against the God of gods, and shall prosper till the indignation be accomplished: for that that is determined shall be done.
> Neither shall he regard the God of his fathers, nor the desire of women, nor regard any god: for he shall magnify himself above all. But in his estate shall he honour the God of forces: and a god whom his fathers knew not shall he honour with gold, and silver, and with precious stones, and pleasant things.[1]

One can enjoy true satisfaction in the discovery that the peril which darkens our world and threatens to extinguish our culture has already been met and vanquished by our forefathers. It would be more comfortable if we could regard madness as a purely medical problem. But when it spreads like a plague over

[1] Daniel, XI, 36-37.

a large part of the earth, it assumes an almost apocalyptic character.

It is this world-shaking disease which is revealed in the famous dream of Nebuchadnezzar. This king performed a double service to posterity. Not only did he leave his most valuable dream-material eternally enshrined in Holy Writ, but he even kept at his court the most enlightened analyst of that time.

Nebuchadnezzar's account of his dream is as follows:

> Thus were the visions of mine head in my bed; I saw, and behold a tree in the midst of the earth, and the height thereof was great.
> The tree grew, and was strong, and the height thereof reached unto heaven, and the sight thereof to the end of all the earth:
> The leaves thereof were fair, and the fruit thereof much, and in it was meat for all: the beasts of the field had shadow under it, and the fowls of the heaven dwelt in the boughs thereof, and all flesh was fed of it.
> I saw in the visions of my head upon my bed, and, behold, a watcher and an holy one came down from heaven:
> He cried aloud, and said thus, hew down the tree, and cut off his branches, shake off his leaves, and scatter his fruit: let the beasts get away from under it, and the fowls from his branches:
> Nevertheless, leave the stump of his roots in the earth, even with a band of iron and brass, in the tender grass of the field; and let it be wet with the dew of heaven, and let his portion be with the beasts in the grass of the earth:
> Let his heart be changed from man's, and let a beast's heart be given unto him; and let seven times pass over him.
> This matter is by the decree of the watchers, and the demand by the word of the holy ones; to the intent that the living may know that the Most High ruleth in the kingdom of men, and giveth it to whomsoever he will, and setteth up over it the basest of men. [1]

The following is Daniel's interpretation of it:

> ... My lord, the dream be to them that hate thee, and the interpretation thereof to thine enemies.
> The tree that thou sawest, which grew, and was strong, whose

[1] Daniel, IV, 10-17.

height reached unto the heaven, and the sight thereof to all
the earth:
Whose leaves were fair, and the fruit thereof much, and in it
was meat for all; under which the beasts of the field dwelt,
and upon whose branches the fowls of the heaven had their
habitation:
It is thou, O king, that art grown and become strong: for
thy greatness is grown, and reacheth unto heaven, and thy
dominion to the end of the earth.
And whereas the king saw a watcher and an holy one coming
down from heaven, and saying, hew the tree down, and destroy
it; yet leave the stump of the roots thereof in the earth, even
with a band of iron and brass, in the tender grass of the
field; and let it be wet with the dew of heaven, and let his
portion be with the beasts of the field, till seven times pass
over him;
This is the interpretation, O king, and this is the decree
of the Most High, which is come upon my lord the king:
That they shall drive thee from men, and thy dwelling shall
be with the beasts of the field, and they shall make thee to
eat grass as oxen, and they shall wet thee with the dew of
heaven, and seven times shall pass over thee, till thou know
that the Most High ruleth in the kingdom of men, and giveth
it to whomsoever he will.
And whereas they commanded to leave the stump of the tree
roots; thy kingdom shall be sure unto thee, after that thou
shalt have known that the heavens do rule. [1]

Daniel's handling of the dream is clear and direct. But there
are certain psychological sidelights which it is possible to glean
without presuming to improve upon Daniel's inspired interpretation. In spite of every natural human prejudice, we have
to believe that the fruit of the tree which tried to reach heaven,
both in the case of Nebuchadnezzar, and of Hitler, was good and
plentiful, so that 'there was meat for all'. In nearly every case of
dangerous dictatorship, the growth of excessive power has been
accompanied by many collective boons. Indeed, if the aspiring
dictator failed to improve the lot of his subjects by systematizing
the means of livelihood, his tree would not gain the necessary
collective sanction. Tyrannical methods alone never made a
tree grow to heaven. Napoleon gave the Napoleonic code and

[1] Daniel, IV, 19-26.

other great boons to France. Hitler cured unemployment and improved the lot of millions of his countrymen on his path to world-dominion. These things are not just the bread and circuses of decadent Rome. The tree of the world-conquerors assuredly gives meat to all, before it becomes an offence to heaven and the natural order.

So far as the dream goes, nothing is said about the king being wicked or criminal. His tree is merely excessive. It became an offence in the eyes of the watcher simply because 'it reached unto heaven, and the sight thereof to the end of all the earth'. The relativity of nature had been overstepped; therefore down it must come. The fig tree that had no fruit, the rule of a despot that knows no bounds — these are in themselves accursed. The watcher makes articulate the silent judgment of nature.

The only enigmatic part of his doom is the injunction to 'leave the stump of his roots in the earth, even with a band of iron and brass'. The metal band is clearly associated with the idea of constriction and punishment. Following this suggestion we might conclude that the stump of the tree is to be left in the earth that all who run may read and remember. But the brass and iron bands might also signify the necessary measures which should evermore be kept in readiness to check the megalomaniac ruler. From this point of view Nebuchadnezzar's dream is a celestial warning intimating to future peoples the need for safeguards against the repetition of Nebuchadnezzar's crazy attempt. Even if madness cannot be prevented, it is not inscrutably ordained that mankind must continue to submit to endless torment, because every now and again a tree forgets its proper place in the order of nature. It is also the sin of excessive growth which determines the nature of the punishment. The stump is to be bound 'with a band of iron in the tender grass of the field', and the king is to be turned into an animal that eats the grass. The grass of the field is the lowliest herb, the standardized biblical unit of growth; as the candle, not the star, is the humble unit of light.

According to this rendering, the tender grass would represent the humble stature of the children of Man. By identifying himself with Zarathustra, Nietzsche lost touch with his common humanity. Through the fatal allure of Moby Dick, Herman Melville lost his ordinary human stature. Mussolini tried to expand himself to the Caesarean level: Hitler to that of Napoleon and Charlemagne. Throughout the ages, these power-maniacs have exiled themselves from the state of the dew-laden tender grass. In their fever to become gods and supermen, they forsook their own law-abiding human nature ('neither shall he regard the God of his fathers, nor the desire of women'). The further implication of this rendering is to be found in the nature of his punishment: 'and let his portion be with the beasts in the grass of the earth'. This means that the king is to be compelled, by his own madness, to participate with the humblest and lowest creatures on the earth. The thing that became too high must be cast down among the lowest, in order that balance may be restored, and the claim of a man to be superior to man, refuted. The justice of heaven is more perfect than that of man; the punishment is entirely appropriate. The ignominy of Mussolini and the ineffectual pathos of the Exile of Doorn have something of this same natural excellence. Celestial justice is also more merciful. Daniel's interpretation of the stump symbolism is as follows:

> And whereas they commanded to leave the stump of the tree roots; thy kingdom shall be sure unto thee, after that thou shalt have known that the heavens do rule. [1]

Inasmuch as Daniel was speaking to the king, this must be regarded as interpretation *ad hominem*. But since the prophet is unflinchingly interpreting the justice of heaven, even Nebuchadnezzar is given his chance of learning what it actually means to endure the opposites, by which all related things are conditioned; and, through learning, to be healed.

The crime which always brings down retribution from heaven is that insane arrogance (the hybris of the Greeks) which will not submit to any superior power. The essence of the crime, implied in the tree that reaches to heaven, is that Nebuchadnezzar claimed divine status, and admitted no power above himself. A man possessed by the dæmon of power is always tempted to deny the existence of God, i.e. any power to which he must unreservedly submit. The power-mirage which tempted Christ on the mountain came from this same subtle dæmon; only He was

[1] Daniel, IV, 26.

wise enough to recognize whence the idea originated. It was the most crucial moment of His life.

Nebuchadnezzar's dream, as is usually the case with great dreams, also contains the healing principle. His cure is certain, if he can summon the grace to submit to the rule of heaven. Statesmen of to-day prefer to term this act of grace a 'change of heart'. Admittedly, such an event is rare amongst dictators, mainly because they tend to lose that spiritual sensitiveness which could warn them of their mortal state.

A final most valuable implication is contained in the peculiar form of Nebuchadnezzar's insanity. He is degraded, or ennobled, into the animal state. The suggestion here is that, since it is a dæmonic animal mechanism that possessed him, he shall appear as such before the world. What we have termed dæmonic acceleration is dynamically indistinguishable from that of a stampeding herd of cattle or a charging rhinoceros. Dynamism that is under the control of intelligence is dirigible power, but when we are in the grip of a process, the momentum of which is independent of conscious control, we are actually being driven, carried, urged, compelled by blind animal force. The fact that the possessed subject can always provide some rationalization for his compulsive activity does not alter the case. Either consciousness is riding and directing the animal, or the animal is making off with the man. In the latter event, the dæmonic energy is liable to appear as compulsive sexuality or will-to-power. Or again, it may take the form of dæmonic extraversion, or compulsive work, or unbridled acquisitiveness or talkativeness. Not the form of the activity, but the compulsive energy which informs it, is the essence of the matter. Instinctual energy can assume a thousand different forms, but the compulsive character of dæmonism is recognizable whatever form the force may assume. It drives with increasing momentum towards explosion or crisis. Its derivation from the original energic source, the *libido sexualis*, is therein manifest.

6

In our analysis of the sequence of events in power-mania we started with temperamental instability as the initial term.

But when the idea of instability is conceived in relation to the energic factor, we should have to state it as follows: In the unstable or split psychology instinctual dynamism tends to break loose in unbridled forms. We can speak of the phenomenon of dæmonic acceleration when the compulsive factor, impelling action or movement, regularly precludes the possibility of intelligent control.

This analysis of the dæmonic element is concerned with the field of individual psychology. In respect to human collectivities the phenomenon is, naturally, very much more impressive, and is further complicated by the general susceptibility to psychic infection, whereby the dæmonic momentum can be imparted to a vast multitude, with devastating consequences. This infection takes place when the *libido* streams away from individual goals, with their stabilizing clarity, to the dark unconscious levels, where the differentiated energy suffers conversion downwards into a pooled emotional state, or mass movement.

This conversion downwards, from responsible individuality to irresponsible collective momentum, is analogous to Janet's conception, *l'abaissement du niveau mentale*. But again, we need to discriminate between the spontaneous downward movement, described by Lawrence and Janet, and the arbitrary conversion of individual energy to regressive forms, through the collective regimentation, the lying radio-propaganda, the universal espionage, the stirring-up of venom through the creation of scapegoats, and all the infamous paraphernalia of Nazi rule. The one is a process of nature, while the other is a callous interference with the natural order of life. But when we describe the conversion as arbitrary, we should remember that no régime could convert *libido* to political purposes on this wholesale scale, if the latter had not already been seduced away from its former differentiated channels. Hitler will be known to history as the great seducer of German energy.

CHAPTER VII

THE SOURCE OF HITLER'S IDEAS

I

BEFORE we finish with Hitler it is necessary to probe a little into the source of his ideas. For whatever view we may take about his qualities as a man and a medium, it can be said with complete confidence that he is not the author of the ideas he brings forth. Mediums who broadcast their personalities in the grand fashion, like Mary Baker Eddy or Adolf Hitler, are seldom, if ever, original thinkers. But, like their humbler colleagues, they do not say, even if they have not repressed the knowledge, where their ideas come from.

In the case of Mrs. Eddy, there is no question but that she got her central idea of mental healing from Quimby, one of the earliest mind-healers in America. Originally a clock maker, Quimby's interest in psycho-therapy was awakened by a series of lectures on hypnotism, as far back as 1838. He studied the subject and gave many lectures about it. He advanced from hypnotic suggestion to mental healing, which he sometimes accompanied by physical manipulation. Mrs. Patterson, later Mrs. Eddy, came to him as a patient and was apparently cured. In any case, she was profoundly impressed by Quimby's teaching which she absorbed while undergoing his treatment. Her experience of the actual healing effect of a new idea became the pith and centre of the new teaching. From this humble source sprang the Christian Science Church.

Mrs. Eddy's discovery consisted in her recognition of an active spiritual principle in Quimby's new method and teaching. She was also shrewd enough to see that this dynamic content was the vital thing which the Church lacked. We need not assume that Mrs. Eddy realized the fact that, at the primitive level, the functions of healing and religion are one. It is, however, a matter of interest that the priest is, in fact, identical with the medicine-man in the primitive hierarchy. It is also significant that the cult

THE SOURCE OF HIS IDEAS

of Aesculapius embraced an introverting religious discipline, and that, etymologically, the root of healing, health, whole, etc., is identical with that of holy. From the fact that Mrs. Eddy valued her experience in the way she did, we must conclude that her instinct for spiritual matters was keen and realistic.

What almost certainly happened was that her therapeutic experience with Quimby aroused a primordial echo in her unconscious. An age-old religious conception, lying latent in the unconscious, was thereby activated, and with mediumistic sensitivity her mind responded to this archaic thought. It was as though Quimby had inadvertently dropped a spiritual ferment into the depths of a waiting mind, converting a rather crazy American woman into the founder of a new religion.

As in the case of National Socialism, the instability of its founder is also represented in the one-sidedness of Christian Science ideology. For Christian Science exists upon the proceeds of an idealistic conspiracy to delete one half of human reality. It is not insignificant, therefore, that in the orthodox account of Mrs. Eddy's life in the *Encyclopaedia Britannica*, her whole experience of mental healing with Quimby is also deleted. Christian Science systematically represses the real and exalts the ideal. Yet in view of the undoubted efficacy of its spiritual principle, and of the world-wide influence it has achieved, we must, in justice, give its founder a place in the succession of Messianic symbol-bearers.

I have mentioned this case because it forms an illuminating parallel to National Socialism, both Hitler and Mrs. Eddy representing a Messianic or healing idea seen with a tragically one-sided vision. Although Mrs. Eddy's psychotic unscrupulousness was, of course, in no way comparable to Hitler's criminality, there are none the less many significant points of resemblance. Both are fundamentally unstable subjects, each having developed a characteristic paranoiac psychology.[1] With only a meagre education to prepare them, both became possessed of a highly charged mythological content from the collective unconscious. As regards their psychological type, both belong to the hysterical, grandiose type of medium; a type that is only too liable to mistake

[1] In the latter years of her life, in the full tide of her carefully preserved power, Mrs. Eddy had a psychical bodyguard of specially selected virgins, who were trained to ward off the vibrations of 'malicious animal magnetism' which she asserted were being aimed at her by old friends and pupils.

his intuition for the voice of heaven, and himself for a divinely
inspired prophet. It might also be added that both tend to be
somewhat secretive as regards the source of their world-shaking
ideas.

In this respect Hitler is more communicative than Mrs. Eddy.
The following account of a conversation given by Dr. Rauschning
tells of Hitler's eager discovery of Richard Wagner and of the
profound influence Wagner's ideas had upon his development.
Dr. Rauschning records:

> Hitler recognized no predecessors — with one exception:
> Richard Wagner. He said: 'None of these lesser lights know
> the real Wagner. I don't mean simply the music, but the
> whole revolutionary doctrine of civilization, down to the
> details that may seem trifling and immaterial.'
> . . . Wagner had attributed much of the decay of our civiliza-
> tion to meat-eating. 'I don't touch meat,' said Hitler,
> 'largely because of what Wagner says on the subject, and
> says, I think, absolutely rightly'. . . He did not touch meat
> or alcohol, or indulge in the dirty habit of smoking; but his
> reason had nothing to do with considerations of health;
> it was a matter of absolute conviction. . . .
> Wagner, said Hitler, had really proclaimed the eternal
> tragedy of human destiny. He was not merely a musician
> and a poet; he was the supreme prophetic figure among the
> Germans. He, Hitler, had come early to Wagner, by chance
> or by the disposition of Providence. He had discovered, with
> almost hysterical excitement, that everything written by that
> great man that he read was in agreement with his own inner-
> most, subconscious, dormant conviction.
> 'The problem,' he cried, 'is this: How can we arrest racial
> decay? Must what Count Gobineau says come true? We
> have acted politically on it — no equality, no democracy!
> But are we to allow the masses to go their way, or should we
> stop them? Shall we form simply a select company of the
> really initiated? An Order, the brotherhood of Templars
> round the holy grail of pure blood? . . .
> 'We must interpret Parsifal in a totally different way to the
> general conception, the interpretation, for instance, of the
> shallow Wolzogen. Behind the absurd externals of the story,
> with its Christian embroidery and its Good Friday mystifica-
> tion, something altogether different is revealed as the true

content of this most profound drama. It is not the Christian-Schopenhauerist religion of compassion that is acclaimed, but pure, noble blood, in the protection and glorification of whose purity the brotherhood of the initiated have come together. The king is suffering from the incurable ailment of corrupted blood. The uninitiated but pure man is tempted to abandon himself in Klingsor's magic garden to the lusts and excesses of corrupt civilization, instead of joining the *élite* of knights who guard the secret of life, pure blood.

'*All of us are suffering from the ailment of mixed, corrupted blood.*[1] How can we purify ourselves and make atonement? Note that compassion, through which man gains comprehension, is only for the corrupted man at issue with himself. And that this compassion knows only one treatment — the leaving of the sick person to die. The eternal life granted by the grail is only for the truly pure and noble!'

Hitler continued with vivacity:

'For myself, I have the most intimate familiarity with Wagner's mental processes. At every stage in my life I come back to him. Only a new nobility can introduce the new civilization for us. If we strip *Parsifal* of every poetic element, we learn from it that selection and renewal are possible only amid the continuous tension of a lasting struggle. A world-wide process of segregation is going on before our eyes. Those who see in struggle the meaning of life, gradually mount the steps of a new nobility. Those who are in search of peace and order through dependence, sink, whatever their origin, to the inert masses. The masses, however, are doomed to decay and self-destruction. In our world-revolutionary turning-point the masses are the sum total of the sinking civilization and of its dying representatives. We must allow them to die with their kings, like Amfortas. . . .

'Imagination is needed in order to divine the vast scale of the coming order. But when a situation is created that favours noble blood, the man of the great race always comes to the top, as, for instance, our own movement shows. The creation and maintenance of this situation is the great preparatory political action of the Leader-legislator.'

'Once,' I mentioned, 'I heard you say that the days of conventional nationalism are over. Did I rightly understand you?'

'The conception of the nation has become meaningless. The

---

[1] Italicized by the present author.

conditions of the time compelled me to begin on the basis of that conception. But I realized from the first that it could only have transient validity. The "nation" is a political expedient of democracy and Liberalism. We have to get rid of this false conception and set in its place the conception of race, which has not yet been politically used up. The new order cannot be conceived in terms of the national boundaries of the peoples with an historic past, but in terms of race that transcend those boundaries. All the adjustments and corrections of frontiers, and of regions of colonization, are a ploughing of the sands.'

I tried to object that there were very great difficulties in the way of this for Germany, but Hitler cut me short with a wave of his hand.

'I know perfectly well,' he said, 'just as well as all these tremendously clever intellectuals, that in the scientific sense there is no such thing as race. But you, as a farmer and cattle-breeder, cannot get your breeding successfully achieved without the conception of race. And I as a politician need a conception which enables the order which has hitherto existed on historic bases to be abolished and an entirely new and anti-historic order enforced and given an intellectual basis. Understand what I mean,' he said, breaking off. 'I have to liberate the world from dependence on its historic past. So I have to fuse these nations into a higher order if I want to get rid of the chaos of an historic past that has become an absurdity. And for this purpose the conception of race serves me well. It disposes of the old order and makes possible new associations. France carried her great Revolution beyond her borders with the conception of the nation. With the conception of race, National Socialism will carry its revolution abroad and recast the world.'

Hitler concluded, with growing fervour:

'Just as the conception of the nation was a revolutionary change from the purely dynastic feudal states, and just as it introduced a biological conception, that of the people, so our own revolution is a further step, or, rather, the final step, in the rejection of the historic order and the recognition of purely biological values. And I shall bring into operation throughout all Europe and the whole world this process of selection which we have carried out through National Socialism in Germany. The process of dissolution and reordering will run its course in every nation, no matter how old and firmly knit its social system may be. The active section in the nations, the militant, Nordic section, will rise again and become the ruling element over these shopkeepers and pacifists, these puritans and speculators and busybodies.

'This revolution of ours is the exact counterpart of the great French Revolution. And no Jewish God will save the democracies from it. There is a stern time coming. I shall see to that. Only the tough and manly element will endure. And the world will assume a new aspect.

'But the day will come when we shall make a pact with these new men in England, France, America. We shall make it when they fall into line with the vast process of the reordering of the world, and voluntarily play their part in it. There will not be much left then of the clichés of nationalism, and precious little among us Germans. Instead there will be an understanding between the various language elements of the one good ruling race.'[1]

I have quoted this conversation in full because I want to show how directly Hitler's fundamental conception of the all-conquering Nordic race, as a supra-national political conception, is related to Wagner. It also gives us a vivid impression of one of Hitler's Pegasus flights into that mirage-world he calls the future. The *Leit-motif* of all this turgid fantasying has to do with the Amfortas disease of tainted blood, and no great psychological insight is needed to see that Hitler identifies himself with the king who suffered from the never-healing wound. With this unconscious identification, Hitler reveals the nature of the conflict in his own soul. We know that Amfortas was vulnerable to the enchantment of Kundry because he belonged exclusively to one side. As king of the Grail he was a partisan of the upper, ideal aspect of human nature and, because he was a partisan, he was seducible. An extreme, one-sided psychology is an offence against nature. In order to restore the balance of the opposites, nature intensifies the allure of the excluded other side. Thus seduction and betrayal become the inevitable bogies of limited minds.

So long as the knights of the Grail are exclusively identified with the spiritual hypothesis, Kundry is doomed to use her bewitching

[1] HERMANN RAUSCHNING, *Hitler Speaks*, pp. 226-30.

arts against them. Amfortas receives his wound when caught in her snare. Parsifal, on the other hand, is detached from either side, and follows the command of his heart. Therefore, he is able to resist Kundry and recover the Holy Spear from Klingsor.

Hitler, with his extreme fanaticism, is tormented by the Amfortas wound, which is nothing but a subjective reminder of the repressed other side of his own soul. Every man who refuses to accept the duality of his nature is liable to suffer from this never-healing wound. It is nature's retribution for the crime of non-acceptance. His ideal *Herrenmensch* of the 'pure and noble blood' is merely another attempt at a one-sided solution and, therefore, he is forced to identify himself and his *corps d'élite* with the knights of the Grail, completely ignoring the fact that Amfortas is the symbol of failure. His blindness to the real significance of the myth is the sign of his own malady, even indicating an unconscious prescience of his own doom.

But behind his fatuous interpretation of the Parsifal myth and his significant insistence on the idea of corrupted blood we can discern the sinister shadow which hangs over his own origin. Is there not an attempt to exorcize a haunting, derogatory ghost, for example, when he proclaims: 'But when a situation is created that favours noble blood, the man of the great race always comes to the top, as, for instance, our own movement shows'?

It will, I think, be conceded that if Hitler knew himself to be the son of the inconspicuous custom's official Alois Schicklgruber, he would not have dwelt so emphatically upon the idea of noble blood. On the other hand, the fantasy of nobility is a frequent accompaniment of illegitimate parentage. The mystical value Hitler gives to the idea of 'pure blood' must, therefore, derive, to some extent, from his own personal antecedents.

To come back to Wagner, we may be quite sure that Hitler's veneration for the composer was not based, primarily, upon musical appreciation. To the Germans, Wagner is, of course, much more than a composer of operas. Wagner himself, especially during his earlier years, was passionately absorbed in political dreams of a greater Germany.

Wagner's faith was threefold. He believed in himself, in the ordained supremacy of the German race, and in the immense, almost mystical power of the theatre. This curious attitude towards the theatre may have been partly due to the fact that, in Germany at that time, it was the best available avenue for the presentation of ideas. But it was also almost certainly derived from his close friendship with Nietzsche who, in his *Birth of Tragedy*, had traced the origin of Greek drama back to the collective religious ecstasy which seized the worshippers of Dionysos. Wagner's mythological drama is frequently inspired by religious feeling. Often one senses a deeper, mystical trend reaching beyond the quasi-historical scene of the myth into a world where the *dramatis personae* are living spiritual forces.

Neither Wagner nor Nietzsche were popular with their own countrymen, and both were brutally outspoken in their scorn and contempt for the ordinary German. Certainly, it was not the real Germany which inspired them with their mystical belief in the German race and its future. Nietzsche, in particular, railed against German philistinism, its narrow-minded, herdlike stupidity, its anti-Semitism, and its foolish, conventional prejudices. He was in love with the Superman, his own spiritual creation, and he hated the Germans in so far as they were a constant reminder that his creation was remote from human reality. But through Nietzsche's Zarathustra, as through Wagner's *Ring*, there runs a prophetic stream of inspiration, the source of which is that same urging potential in the racial unconscious which now bears Hitler's Germany along its path of destiny.

In view of the fact that the characteristic Nazi arrogance is strongly reminiscent of Nietzsche, we might wonder why Hitler's attitude to Nietzsche is so much cooler than it is to Wagner. Presumably Hitler could not stand Nietzsche's real superiority. Crowned with all his political obscenities, Hitler cannot tolerate the ruthless psychological scrutiny of the introverted philosopher. Wagner, with his extraverted exuberance and political out-pourings, is a genius more easily to be patronized. But a Hitler cannot take liberties with a Nietzsche. The fire of Nietzsche's spirit keeps political jackals and hyenas at a distance. Wagner, on the other hand, was habitually amoral in all his dealings. He allowed no ties to fetter his genius. Like Hitler, he sacrificed everything which other men hold sacred to the dæmonic spirit which possessed him. The actual human material upon which Wagner's genius was grafted was little better than Hitler's own, though in sheer creative power the creator of *Tristan*, the *Ring*, and *Meistersinger* towers majestically above his inflated disciple.

As we shall presently discover in his political utterances, Wagner's vision of Germany's future was no less exalted than Hitler's. But Wagner was wise enough to know that his vision could never come about in the stupid Prussian way. He despised nothing so much as the arrogant new Reich of 1870 with its vainglorious Prussian spirit, fomented by Bismarck. His attitude to militarism is expressed in a savage letter to a friend in which he dreads the day when his 'little Siegfried will become a soldier, and be put out of existence by a stupid bullet in one of the miserable wars brought on us by Prussian politics'.

Nietzsche and Wagner were visionaries in the true sense. They strove always for the essential truth of their vision in the realm of the spirit. Neither knew nor cared anything for *Realpolitik*. Nietzsche's vision led him to his conception of the Superman, an ideal embodiment of the incalculable spiritual potential awaiting discovery in the unconscious. Zarathustra presents in visionary outline the Aquarian man of the future, the man of the new epoch whose ruthless passion for life strips away every vestige of Christian weakness and sentimentality.

Wagner's vision, on the other hand, was never clearly expressed as a philosophy, though in his imaginative grasp of Teutonic myth-material he found a means of instilling his vision into the unconscious of every German. In his treatment of mythological themes the principal *motif* is usually concerned with the advent of the young untried hero, whose indwelling power and genius claims the victory over the forces of established interest and traditionalism. Isolde rightly belongs to King Mark but the youthful knight Tristan intervenes. Siegmund rescues Sieglinde from the house of Hunding, and from their love a new order springs to life, personified by Siegfried. Walther turns up out of nowhere at the meeting of the Mastersingers and, by the strength of untutored genius, breaks through the bars of tradition and prejudice, personified by Beckmesser, winning Eva with his new and wondrous song. Always it is the theme of the downfall of the old gods and the advent of the victorious hero.

2

Some of Wagner's early political writings reveal rather crude attempts to adapt his vision of the new man to the political stage of his day. Speaking of his Republican vision of a classless community, he outlines a political picture in which the existing aristocracy is wiped out, and a new and vital relation established between the Monarch and his folk. He says:

> Let us be quite clear and settle in the first place what is to be the gist of our Republican effort. Are we seriously to believe that if we press on from our standpoint we shall immediately arrive at a bare kingless republic? I will tell you the aim of our unmitigated Republican effort. And first, our efforts for the good of all must treat the so-called achievements of the immediate past, not as a goal in themselves, but as a beginning. This goal held firmly in view is quite frankly to abolish the last glimmer of the old aristocratism. [1]

Advocating the extinction of every favoured class he says:

> There shall be no more lords and pages of the Chamber. Be done with this court of idle sustenance for nobles. It shall become the court of the whole blithe, happy Folk, where every member of the people, through its joyous deputies, may smile upon their Prince, telling him he is first of his Free Folk.

In pursuit of his vision Wagner wants to dissolve the Army and Communal Guard, creating a *Volkswehr* without class-distinction. Proceeding to the next step he proclaims:

> When all classes, hitherto at enmity and parcelled off by envy, have been united in the one great class of the Free Folk, embracing all who shall have received human breath on the dear German soil from God — think ye that then we shall have achieved our goal? No, then shall we begin in earnest.

This next task is to liberate mankind from bondage to gold, the 'sallow metal', presumably reverting, as Hitler has done, to methods of barter and exchange.

[1] RICHARD WAGNER, *Prose Works*, vol. IV., translated for the Wagner Society by W. A. Ellis (Kegan Paul & Co.), 1892-99. Speech addressed to the *Vaterlandsverein* in Dresden, June, 1848.

His attitude to Communism is identical with Hitler's:

> Does this smack to you of Communism? Are ye foolish or ill-disposed enough to declare the necessary redemption of the human race from the flattest, most demoralizing servitude to vulgarist matter, synonymous with carrying out the most preposterous and senseless doctrine, that of Communism? Can ye not see that this doctrine of a mathematically equal division of property and earnings is simply an unreasoning attempt to solve this very problem [servitude to gold], at any rate dimly apprehended and an attempt whose sheer impossibility proclaims it stillborn? But would ye denounce therewith the task itself for reprehensible and insane, as that doctrine of a surety is? Have a care! The outcome of 33 years of unruffled peace shows you Human Society in such a state of dislocation and impoverishment that at the end of all those years ye have on every hand the awful spectacle of pallid hunger! Look to it, ere it be too late! Give no alms, but acknowledge a right, the god-given right of Man, lest ye live to see the day when outraged Nature will gird herself for a battle of brute force, whose savage shout of victory were *of a truth* that Communism. And though the radical impossiblity of its continuance should yield it but the briefest reign, that short-lived reign would yet have sufficed to root up every trace, perchance for many an age to come, of the achievements of 2,000 years of civilization. Think ye I threaten? Nay, I warn.

Wagner's warning to his countrymen about the dangers of Communism was not more emphatic than were Hitler's comments on the same theme. The following excerpts, taken from *Mein Kampf*, have a peculiarly piquant flavour to-day; a flavour which is doubtless relished by Hitler's partner Stalin:

> One does not form an alliance with a partner whose only aim is the destruction of his fellow-partner. Above all, one does not enter into alliances with people for whom no treaty is sacred: because they do not move about this earth as men of honour and sincerity, but as the representatives of lies and deception, thievery and plunder and robbery. (p. 538)

> How can we teach the German worker that Bolshevism is an infamous crime against humanity if we ally ourselves with this infernal abortion and recognize its existence as legitimate? (p. 539)

Wagner's vision, like Hitler's, reaches far beyond the sphere of politics towards the birth of a new race of men:

> When our Republic has brought us thus far . . . shall we have reached our journey's end? No, when we shall have reached the rebirth of society through emancipated legislation, then shall there spring a fine new race, brought up to the fullest use of its energies. Only then shall we be strong enough to march towards the higher tasks of civilization — its activation and its spread. Then shall we take ship across the sea, and plant here and there a fresh young Germany, befruit it with the outcome of our toils and struggles, beget and bring up the noblest children, like unto the gods. We will manage better than the Spaniards, for whom the New World became a papal slaughter-house; better than the English who have made thereof a pedlar's tray. We will do things grandly and Germanly. From its rising to its setting, the sun shall look down upon a beautiful free Germany, and on the borders of the daughter lands, as on the frontiers of their mother, no downtrodden, unfree folk shall dwell . . . The rays of *German freedom* and *German gentleness* shall light and warm the French and Cossacks, the Bushmen and Chinese.
>
> Look ye! Our Republican ardour has here no goal nor end; unresisting, it forges on from century to century, for blessing of the whole wide race of man! Is this a dream, Utopia? It is, if we only bandy it to and fro, half-hearted and self-seeking, balancing and disputing its possibility. It is not, if only we act in buoyant courage, if every day beholds us do a new good deed of progress.[1]

Hitler also regards his political achievements as merely preparing the ground for a new commanding race, and when inspired by this theme he is fired by the same visionary enthusiasm. Dr. Rauschning's account is as follows:

> Many times he touched on these ideas in conversation. And we could see behind his outward resignation the consuming impatience to get at last to his real work, the work of the creative statesman and legislator, the pioneer artist and city builder, the prophet and founder of a religion.
>
> 'In my great educative work,' said Hitler, 'I am beginning with the young. We older ones are used up. Yes, we are old already. We are rotten to the marrow. We have no un-

[1] loc. cit., p. 136.

restrained instincts left. We are cowardly and sentimental. We are bearing the burden of a humiliating past, and have in our blood the dull recollection of serfdom and servility. But my magnificent youngsters! Are there finer ones anywhere in the world? Look at these young men and boys! What material! With them I can make a new world.

'My teaching is hard. Weakness has to be knocked out of them. In my *Ordensburgen* a youth will grow up before which the world will shrink back. A violently active, dominating, intrepid, brutal youth — that is what I am after. Youth must be all those things. It must be indifferent to pain. There must be no weakness or tenderness in it. I want to see once more in its eyes the gleam of pride and independence of the beast of prey. Strong and handsome must my young men be. I will have them fully trained in all physical exercises. I intend to have an athletic youth— that is the first and chief thing. In this way I shall eradicate the thousands of years of human domestication. Then I shall have in front of me the pure and noble natural material. With that I can create the new order.

'I will have no intellectual training. Knowledge is ruin to my young men. I would have them learn only what takes their fancy. But one thing they must learn — self-command! They shall learn to overcome the fear of death, under the severest tests. That is the intrepid and heroic stage of youth. Out of it comes the stage of the free man, the man who is the substance and essence of the world, the creative man, the god-man. In my *Ordensburgen* there will stand as a statue for worship the figure of the magnificent, self-ordaining god-man; it will prepare the young men for their coming period of ripe manhood.'

More than that, concluded Hitler, he could not say. There were stages of which he must not allow even himself to speak. Even this, he said, he only intended to make public when he was no longer living. Then there would be something really great, an overwhelming revelation. In order completely to fulfil his mission, he must die a martyr's death.

'Yes,' he repeated, 'in the hour of supreme peril I must sacrifice myself for the poeple.'[1]

In this account we catch a glimpse of Hitler's real vision. It was this vision which transformed the Viennese outcast into an

[1] H. RAUSCHNING, *Hitler Speaks*, pp. 246-48.

inspired leader. He longed to create a new German whom he himself could respect. When we compare the betrayed, oppressed, mass-produced German citizen of to-day with the 'magnificent self-ordaining god-man' of Hitler's vision we see how a one-sided ideology always creates its opposite.

Again, in his contempt for the principle of democracy Hitler reveals the influence of Wagner. Wagner wrote:

> Dupe not yourselves, you who want constitutional monarchy on the broadest democratic basis. Each step forward on that democratic basis means an encroachment on the power of the mon-arch [sole ruler]. The principle itself is the completest mockery of monarchy, which is conceivable at all only as actually alone-ruling. Each advance of constitutionalism is a humiliation to the ruler, a vote of want of confidence in the monarch. Can you see love and confidence prevailing amidst this continual contest? . . . The very existence of the monarch is embittered by shame . . . Let us have done with monarchism, since sole rule is made impossible by just this principle of Folk's rule [Democracy]. Let us rather emancipate kinghood to its own peculiar and fullest meaning. The further we go back in the history of the Germanic nations for the meaning of kinghood, the more closely will it be found to fit this newly won meaning, and prove it at bottom to be a re-establishment of the original. The historic cycle of the evolution of kinghood will have reached its goal, having rounded back upon itself. We shall then look back upon monarchism, that un-German notion, as a complete aberration from that goal.[1]

The writer's thought is not very clear in this passage; but it would appear that Wagner had in mind the idea of an ideal kingship in which the king, like the President of the United States, would be the first citizen of the Republic. It is not easy to see how Wagner reconciles this notion of republican kingship with his ideal of sole autocratic ruler. For his whole vision, like Hitler's, seems to be based upon the principle of unchecked single rule.

The most vigorous unanimity in the ideas of the two men is, however, achieved in their common hatred of the Jews. Here Wagner allows his prejudice to reach boiling-point. He writes:

[1] RICHARD WAGNER, *Prose Works*, vol. IV, trans. by Ellis.

We must recognize the fact that we possess an involuntary repulsion for the nature and personality of the Jew which is stronger than our conscious zeal to rid ourselves of it.[1]

Of the emancipation of the Jews, Wagner admits that this must be virtually conceded as an abstract principle, but this cannot change the fact that we are instinctively repelled by actual contact. As a matter of fact the Jew is already emancipated. He rules by money.

Even public art taste has been brought under the busy fingers of the Jews. There is no need to substantiate the be-Jewing of Art ... But if emancipation from the yoke of Judaism appears to us an absolute necessity, we must organize our forces for this war of liberation.

Even the physical appearance of the Jew is abhorrent to Wagner:

We wish to have nothing in common with the Jew ... We can conceive no representation either on the antique or modern stage by a Jew. His appearance is unsuitable for artistic treatment.

It is, however, in the sphere of musical taste that Wagner finds the Jewish influence most insufferable. European art is a foreign tongue to the Jews. Because of the fact that

his physical aspect is repellent, the Jew is incapable of enouncing himself artistically either in appearance or speech.

Yet in spite of this he has assumed the rulership of public taste in matters of music.

Wagner finishes this astonishing letter with the following homily to the Jews:

Without looking back, do your part in this regenerative work of deliverance through self-annulment ... But remember, only one thing can redeem you from the burden of your curse: the redemption of Ahasuerus: Going Under.[2]

This letter was published in the *Neue Zeitschrift für Musik* in 1850. To do him justice, the editor was apparently in some

[1] RICHARD WAGNER, *Judaism in Music, Prose Works*, vol. III, p. 78.

[2] An especially interesting sidelight upon Wagner's aversion to Jews, and a more than interesting footnote upon Hitler's extraordinary feeling for Wagner, comes from the possibility, discussed by Ernest Newman in his *Life of Wagner*, that Wagner was also the illegitimate son of a Jew. At least Wagner had a strong feeling that he was the son of Geyer, the actor, and there is some ground for believing Geyer to have been a Jew. I am indebted to Mr. Rex Littleboy for drawing my attention to this inner ground of sympathy.

doubt as to the suitability of printing this strange effusion in his
journal. He appends a footnote in which he explains that
Germany is pre-eminent in the spirit of intellectual and scientific
tolerance. For this reason he prints the letter and invites his
readers to read it in that sense.

In these writings there is an exuberance of political vision
which is essentially similar to Hitler's intoxicated utterance.
Wagner was the first great German of modern times to voice the
Germanic myth in a deeply moving and satisfying form. His
music-dramas were the crowning achievement of German
music. Whereas Nietzsche identified himself with Zarathustra
(i.e. the pre-Christian archetype of the Old Wise One) Wagner
was directly inspired by the indigenous Nordic myth. These two
prophetic figures, radiating a new light from the ancient fires,
stand at the very threshold of the modern world. Hitler was
undoubtedly influenced by both. In the same conversation as
the one already cited he says:

> Creation is not yet at an end; at all events, not so far as the
> creature Man is concerned. Biologically regarded, man has
> clearly arrived at a turning point. A new variety of man is
> beginning to separate out. A mutation, precisely in the
> scientific sense. The existing type of man is passing, in con-
> sequence, inescapably, into the biological stage of atrophy.
> The old type of man will have but a stunted existence. All
> creative energy will be concentrated in the new one. The
> two types will rapidly diverge from one another. One will
> sink to a subhuman race, and the other rise far above the
> man of to-day. I might call the two varieties the god-man
> and the mass-animal.

At this point in the conversation Dr. Rauschning interposed a
comment on the similarity of Hitler's god-man to Nietzsche's
Superman.

> 'Yes,' Hitler continued, 'man has to be passed and surpassed.
> Nietzsche did, it is true, realize something of this, in his way.
> He went so far as to recognize the superman as a new bio-
> logical variety. But he was not too sure of it. Man is becoming
> God — that is the simple fact. Man is God in the making.
> Man has eternally to strain at his limitations. The moment
> he relaxes and contents himself with them, he decays and

falls below the human level. He becomes a quasi-beast. Gods and beasts, that is what our world is made of.'[1]

In this passage, with its affectation of lordly patronage, Hitler reveals his complete misunderstanding of Nietzsche's idea. Both Nietzsche and Wagner conceived the future man in a spiritual sense. For Nietzsche, the man who could transcend himself, was no new biological variety or sport; he was the symbol of a supreme spiritual achievement. This Prussian notion of *Herrenmensch* and *Herdenmensch* has no place in the Nietzschean vision. No man of heart or imagination or, indeed, of gentle birth, would wish to belong to Hitler's ruling class. It must consist, therefore, of adventurers who contrive, by dint of dynamite and revolutionary energy, to force their way to the top. Whereas the *Herdenmensch* will consist of all those human beings, whether of aristocratic quality or not, who are psychologically averse to brutality. This, in brief, is the real texture of Hitler's New Order, and readers may well ask, what has this to do with the new man as conceived by Nietzsche and Wagner? Although poles apart psychologically, the disciple follows his great forerunners in their arrogant spirit and unworthy contempt for their fellow-men. In all three, love and tolerance and admiration are reserved for the still unborn man of the future. For the ordinary German citizen, with all his inherited qualities of character and heart, we find nothing but scorn and negative criticism. It is as though the winged power of intuition had carried them impatiently ahead into a golden future, and had left only an unworthy neurotic residue to do honour to the living Now.

Other great Germans in the past have also expressed this same contempt for German collective mentality. Writing in 1813 to the historian Luden, Goethe stated his feeling frankly enough:

> It makes me most miserable to think of the German people . . . They are valuable as individuals, but hopeless as a whole.[2]

Schopenhauer wrote:

> Foreseeing my death, I make this confession, that I despise the German nation because of its infinite stupidity, and that I blush to belong to it.

[1] *Hitler Speaks*, p. 242.
[2] I am indebted for these quotations to Mr. P. F. Wiener, who cited them in a letter to the *Spectator*, February 7th, 1941.

The poet Hölderlin is more specific in his condemnation:

> It is a hard word, and yet I have to say it because it is the truth: I cannot imagine any more sundered people than the Germans. One can see labourers, but no human beings; one can see scholars, but no human beings; priests, but no human beings; masters, servants, young and mature people — but never any human beings![1]

This judgment, coming from a German poet of remarkable psychological insight, is particularly interesting.

At the other end of the scale, we find Friedrich Nietzsche writing:

> It is even part of my ambition to be considered as essentially a despiser of Germans ... To my mind the Germans are impossible. If I try to think of the kind of man who is opposed to me in all my instincts my mental image takes the form of a German.[2]

These statements, and the picture drawn by Sir Robert Vansittart in *Black Record*, can be explained only by the fact that the German character manifests a contradiction between the responsible, adapted individual being and a docile and stupid mass. Our judgments are necessarily confounded unless we distinguish between the bright individual aspect and the dark collective shadow. All the evil that people say about the Germans as a whole will be found to rest upon this sinister collective impression.

The arrogant attitude both of Nietzsche and Hitler towards German collectivity is symbolized in their common preference for an eagle's solitariness on high mountains. In Nietzsche's case this is intelligible, inasmuch as he identified himself wholly with his spiritual and intellectual function. Cut off from all human relations, he lived a secluded and neurotic existence in the Engadine Alps. Insomnia, irritability, and nervous dyspepsia usurped the place which human joys and relationships should have filled. No instinct was allowed to play its normal allotted rôle. His intellect had, in fact, grown arrogantly contemptuous of the generally human functions, just as Nietzsche, the man, had

[1] The German word used by Hölderlin is *Mensch*.
[2] *Ecce Homo*, vol. XVII, p. 128. English edition of Nietzsche's works.

grown contemptuous of the ordinary German citizen. If he could also have developed downwards, giving honest value to the claims of instinct — those humble functions by virtue of which man may still claim kinship with all the other creatures of the earth — he would surely not have permitted his intuitive vision to cut him off from his kind.

The same principle applies to Nazi fanaticism. The Nazi is a human espalier with only two dimensions. Human feelings have been sacrificed for the sake of a terrible ideal. Fanatical visionaries are liable to be cruel, just because their interest in the future man, whom they pretend to be fashioning from creative clay, robs them of any consideration for their fellow-men. Hence their worst aspect is apparent in the sphere of human relationship. In their impatient flight towards future glory they rob the present of its actual worth.

Thus we see that Hitler's wonderful god-man, his *Herrenmensch*, and Nietzsche's Superman, are the products of an intuitive genius which, because it cannot tolerate normal human relations and is inadequate in caring for present actualities, has to create, literally among the mountains, a compensatory vision of the god-like future man. The greater of these two prophets ended his days in an asylum; we cannot tell what awaits the lesser.

As regards the utterly contemptible *Herdenmensch*, we can only wonder what the decent, disciplined German really thinks of a leader who holds him in such despite.

3

Hitler's instantaneous reaction to Wagner, combined with his obvious recoil from the introverted side of German culture, including the prophet Nietzsche, makes it possible for us to classify Hitler as belonging to the extraverted intuitive type, with thinking presumably as his auxiliary rational function. This does not, of course, imply that he has developed thinking as an independent critical function. It means nothing more than that he habitually adapts to situations intuitively, and that the intellect serves as handmaid to intuition. It will usually be found that one-sided fanaticism goes hand in hand with functional absolutism, a state in which only one of the four main psychic functions—thinking, feeling, intuition, or sensation—is given decisive value. It is the absence from consciousness of any other functional standpoint which gives the fanatic his melancholy, blinkered view; while the peculiar savagery of his mental process has to do with the fact that a single superior function holds the other three in a ruthless state of subjection.

But if we infer from the general psychological picture that Hitler is an intuitive extravert, how then are we to account for the introverted activity which forms so necessary a part of his mediumistic function? A great many extraverted intuitives develop, in point of fact, a strong subjective tendency, through maintaining their mediumistic rapport with the unconscious. Dr. Beatrice Hinkle has even provided a place in her classification for this group, terming them subjective extraverts. An introverted observer might, by allowing his own type to colour his view, mistake this subjective activity for genuine introversion, but when its real nature is examined, it is found that the fundamental character and direction of the intuitive action is extraverted, and that it is at bottom concerned with objective possibilities. This distinction is clearly manifest when we compare, for example, the introverted psychological orientation of Zarathustra with the extraverted political vision of Wagner in the passages cited above.

Another psychiatric sidelight on Hitler's psychology is disclosed in his conclusion that 'our world is made of gods and beasts'. Such a precipitous, and yet palpably false, division of the world speaks volumes concerning the psychology which makes it. We have already remarked the tendency of the intuitive types to project their focus of desire ahead of them, therewith magnifying the value of the future at the cost of the present. The resulting impatience not only causes the extraverted intuitive to hurry on towards the horizon, 'sowing fields he does not stop to reap', as Jung has expressed it; but it also prompts him to conceive the future world — towards which he assumes the satisfying rôle of creator — as benevolently sponsored by God. Whereas the wretched world of the present is patently afflicted by the devil.

With these characteristic tendencies in mind we can see why it was inevitable that Hitler should want to partition the world into a superior realm above and a mass of excluded worthlessness below. The unbalanced visionary is always liable to be led too far from his own base by his mirage-forming intuitive function so that he is pursued by the ghost of the real things he has neglected or swept aside.

The description of a scene quoted in an earlier chapter offers conclusive evidence that Hitler is haunted at night by pursuing terrors from the unconscious, and the whole world can see his desperate haste to reach the future into which he has projected his fast-dwindling hope of deliverance.

Here, then, is the subjective source of Hitler's 'gods and beasts'. But it is not yet explained why it is that intuition, of all functions, should have this power of leading men so terribly astray.

Our answer should naturally embrace the biological history of the functions. In contrast to sensation, which registers the solid facts of the actual scene and cannot go beyond these sense-given data, intuition begins to function only when sensation has had its say. So long as a man is harmoniously contained in a congenial environment, sensation is enough. But let him once fall into a pit, or get caught in a situation from which escape is a matter of life or death: intuition must then take charge. Sensation can tell how and what things are, but it cannot get beyond the actual to the possible, and see how things might be if . . . It is this winged power which, by conceiving how the situation might change or develop, breaks the spell of Calypso's island of sensation, and gives to intuition the divine authority of Hermes. When we bear in mind the overwhelming weight of concrete sensation by which a purely reflex mental process is conditioned, we can understand how the function, possessing the strange power of seeing how the present desperate situation might be remedied, came to be deified. But just because of this prestige the intuitive subject is encouraged to develop and refine his gift. Thus intuitiveness very frequently becomes a curse, constantly pushing the subject on to the next possibility before the last has been realized. Intuitive types, therefore, are prone both to impatience and to unreality. Occasionally a certain ruthlessness accompanies the impatience. Nietzsche's psychological vision was never more clear than when he saw that before man could transcend himself, and create the Superman, he must first encounter the Ugliest Man; this being that unaccepted shadow-side which the visionary idealist almost invariably overlooks.

'JEKYLL AND HYDE'

Reproduced by permission of the proprietors of 'Punch'

So great a cleavage between the upper and nether pole, between the God and the beast, naturally produces a condition which is psychologically indistinguishable from dual personality. Hitler's contradictory double nature is excellently represented, for example, in the *Punch* cartoon, where a sanctimonious, exalted Jekyll, in the background, is balanced by a bestial, unbridled Hyde. It also affords a rather unexpected endorsement of my main argument. For the face of Hyde in the drawing is clearly that of a possessed being.

The drawing reminds me of an answer given by a refugee colleague from Germany to my question whether he had felt any conflict on account of divided national feelings. He answered: if I had a dog who had been my friend for many years and, one day, he turned on me with the wolf glaring out of his eyes, I should kill him and my feelings would not protest.

This reply gives us another angle on the phenomenon of possession. In our use of this term we imply an atavistic harking back, a sudden and catastrophic alteration of personality in which a violent, criminal, or otherwise archaic form of behaviour holds the stage. When, on the contrary, a person is possessed by a mystical or prophetic content from the unconscious, we speak of him as inspired.

No one can reasonably deny that, at certain times, Hitler has been inspired. Sir Nevile Henderson has even described Hitler as 'a visionary of genius'.[1] We have also the clearest of evidence that, at times, Hitler is possessed of a maniacal fury which is horrible and subhuman. The fact that he sees mankind either as gods or beasts could, therefore, logically be predicted from the dissociated state of his own psychology. But there is a certain fundamental peculiarity about schizophrenia which should never be lost sight of when we are considering Hitler's psychology. This peculiarity is rooted in a radical disorder of the affective or emotional nature. It reveals itself as a barrier or opacity which has the effect of isolating the emotions from the discriminating realm of consciousness. The result of this split is that the subject is never really at one with his inner life. A kind of emotional anaesthesia sunders him from his kind. At bottom he senses that he is different. He lacks the feeling of belongingness or unity with his fellow-men. It

[1] SIR NEVILE HENDERSON, *Failure of a Mission* (Hodder & Stoughton), p. 41.

is this condition, as Bjerre[1] has demonstrated in his psychological study of murderers, which can easily lead to crime.

Whatever Hitler may have on his conscience as a private person, he is known to be a murderer in his public capacity of dictator. On the other hand, his outward demeanour shows frequent lapses into exuberant affectivity. How is it possible to reconcile the idea of a cold-blooded murderer, whose numbed feelings no longer respond to any human claims, with this other picture of a man whose emotions have become his most noticeable asset? From all accounts these emotional transports arise only rarely from actual human situations. Our witnesses agree that Hitler has the trick of arbitrarily lashing himself into a state of fury. His emotional displays are not the expressions of a soul stirred to its depths by a poignant realization of suffering, wrath, or pity. They are deliberately cultivated as a kind of political technique in much the same way as a clever advocate or debater cultivates an intellectual display of argument, not for the advancement of some aspect of truth which is vital to him, but in order to get the better of an opponent. With his emotional virtuosity Hitler can display any kind of emotion merely for the sake of baffling his adversary or impressing his audience. He can also use his hysteria as an emotional weapon for the purpose of leaving his opponent with the wrong feeling. All his attacks against the intellect are insincere because, at bottom, his emotional technique is directed by the intellect which, in turn, is motivated by a paranoiac will-to-power.

The description I have just given might also be true of a consummate actor. Actually, however, there is a vital difference, because the actor is free to play any given rôle. Whereas Hitler has sacrificed everything for the one rôle which has become his fate. Naturally, he intends the world to believe that he is moved by sterling emotions. He also wants the rest of Germany to be, and, if possible, to remain, similarly moved. He is a great believer in strong, primitive affects. But his own human feelings are all mortgaged. He is possessed by a tyrannical complex. Of all men, he is most prone to feel cold, torpid, and isolated.

It is interesting to discover that Wagner called this impersonal driving force which impels a man to fanatical patriotic activity, by

[1] A. BJERRE, *Psychology of Murder* (Longmans Green & Co. Ltd.).

the suggestive term *Wahn*. The word really means delusive idea, vain imagining, madness, chimera, hallucination. In Wagner's use of the word it became charged with a more dynamic content denoting an irrational force, superordinated to the ego and, therefore, akin to the idea of primal, purposive life-force. Wagner himself relates his idea to Schopenhauer's conception of Will (*Lebenswille*) where he says:

> The author and inciter of this *Wahn*, which our philosopher deems to be the spirit of the race itself, is the almighty Will of Life, supplanting the individual's limited perceptive faculty, seeing that without its intervention the individual, in narrow egoistic care for self, would gladly sacrifice the species on the altar of its personal continuance. Should we succeed in bringing the nature of this *Wahn* to our inner consciousness by any means, we should therewith win the key to that otherwise enigmatic relation of the individual to the species. Perhaps this may be made easier on the path that leads us out above the State.[1]

After linking up his expanding idea with the teleological aspect of instinct, as witnessed in insect and animal life, he goes on:

> In political life, this *Wahn* displays itself as patriotism. As such, it prompts the citizen to offer up his private welfare . . . nay, even life itself for the sake of ensuring the State's continuance.

But although *Wahn* motivates patriotism, Wagner perceives that this is merely a transmuted egotism, and that something else is needed to impel men to set the interest of mankind in general above patriotism. If only Hitler had been a better disciple!

The following has significant reverberations for those outside the German experience:

> The patriot may sharpen the burgher's eyes to interests of State, it leaves him blind to the interest of mankind in general. The patriot subordinates himself to his State in order to raise it above all other States, and thus, as it were, to find his personal sacrifice repaid with ample interest through the might and greatness of his fatherland. Injustice and violence towards other States and peoples have, therefore, been the

---

[1] RICHARD WAGNER, *The State and Religion*, lecture given at the request of Ludwig II of Bavaria and printed 1873 (*Prose Works*, vol. IV, trans. by Ellis).

true dynamic law of patriotism throughout all time. Self-preservation is still the primal motive here, since the tranquillity and the power of one's own State appears securable in no other way than through the powerlessness of other States. This accords with Machiavelli's telling maxim: 'What you don't want put on yourself, go and put it on your neighbour.' But the fact that one's own tranquillity can be ensured only by violence and injustice to the world without — this must naturally make one's quiet seem always somewhat problematical; thereby leaving a door for ever open to violence and injustice within one's own State too.

We begin to understand Wagner's choice of the word *Wahn* when we read the following conclusion, which might have been written with a prophetic eye upon his terrible disciple:

> *Wahn* has always found its only nourishment in insatiable egotism; it is dangled in alluring forms before the latter . . . by ambitious individuals, who are just as egoistic, but gifted with a shrewder but by no means higher intelligence . . . This intentional employment of conscious or unconscious perversion of the *Wahn* can avail itself only of the form digestible by the burgher, that of patriotism, albeit in some distorted form. It always proclaims itself as an effort for the common good. Never yet has a demagogue or intriguer led a people astray without in some way making it believe itself inspired with patriotic ardour. Thus in patriotism itself lies the seduction to error.

Were we not interested in Wagner as the spiritual forerunner of Hitler these political writings of the great composer would have no special value. They are important only because they inspired Hitler, and because, both in their content, and in the exuberance of their expression, they illustrate the tendency of Wagner's political thinking to be caught up into the air like Wotan's stag. Wagner's idealistic vagueness is drawn from the same source as Hitler's abdominal eloquence. Although in both cases the ideas expressed seem to be the product of reflection, yet in their utterance both depend upon a certain extraverted licence.

Wagner was unquestionably one of Germany's greatest sons; hence, anything coming from him cannot be without a certain significant quality of mind. Let us assume, therefore, that in this conception, *Wahn*, he was attempting to name some irrational dynamism of the living creature, which comprises both the political urgencies of mankind as well as the biological devotion of the ant or bee.

Schopenhauer's vision of the universe, as an expression of vast impersonal Will, belongs to this same dynamic *Weltanschauung*. Certain significant currents of German post-Kantian philosophy seem to have arisen from this same dynamic content. Nietzsche's conception of the Superman, for instance, expressing that creative power in man which transcends himself, was a brilliant intuitive attempt to express this underlying, purposive force in a symbolical, poetical figure.

Wagner's rather extravagant use of *Wahn* shows that he was grappling with a metaphysical idea which constantly eluded him. He was apparently seeking a word which could combine the idea of irrational purpose with that of unconscious dynamism or possession. It would seem, indeed, that one of the chief tasks, attempted by German philosophy, was to frame this dangerous dynamism of the German psyche in a comprehensive conception.

It was this same dynamism of the German unconscious which Heine sensed, and which he ascribed in a special way to the teachings of German philosophy. Naturally, in Heine's day there was no concept of the unconscious. Accordingly, thinkers tended to ascribe unconscious urgencies to some current doctrine.

> The German Revolution will not prove any milder or gentler because it was preceded by the *Critique* of Kant, by the *Transcendental Idealism* of Fichte, or even by the *Philosophy of Nature*. These doctrines served to develop revolutionary forces that only await their time to break forth and to fill the world with terror and with awe. Then will appear Kantians as little tolerant of piety in the world of deeds as in the world of ideas, who will mercilessly upturn with sword and axe the soil of our European life in order to extirpate the last remnants of the past. There will come upon the scene armed Fichteans whose fanaticism of will is to be restrained neither by fear nor by self-interest; for they live in the spirit; they defy matter like those early Christians who could be subdued neither by bodily torments nor by bodily delights. [1]

[1] HEINE's *Religion and Philosophy in Germany*.

Heine was a Jew and, with the intuition of the older race, he accurately discerned the dangerous dissociation of the German psyche, even in the middle of last century, expressing the danger for the first time in terms of an impending revolution. It is significant that it was German philosophers who first wrestled with the problem of the unconscious dynamism, as, indeed, it was scientific minds of German stock who first discovered the dynamic rôle of the unconscious in the causation and cure of mental disorders.

With Wagner the latent dynamism became personified in the resurgent figures of the Nordic myth. In Wagner's conception of Wotan, for example, a tendency to overleap all ethical boundaries is already clearly discernible. Whereas with Hitler's Wotan the dissolution seems to have reached a point when, refusing to be bound by past words, acts, or desires, the Wanderer rides an unbridled steed towards a lawless pinnacle of power.

The reader may recall how Wotan, in order to avert a doom which had been predicted by Erda, deliberately courted her, a wooing which resulted in the birth of Brünnhilde and her eight sisters. The following is quoted from Wotan's long monologue with Brünnhilde in *The Valkyrie*:

Wotan: Fostered wert thou,
That ye Valkyries
Might avert the doom
Which the Wala's
Dread words foretold:
The gods' ignominious ending.
That foes might find us
Strong for the strife,
Heroes I got ye to gather.
The beings who served us
As slaves aforetime,
The men whose courage
Aforetime we curbed:
Who through treacherous bonds
And devious dealings
Were bound to the gods
In blindfold obedience —
To kindle these men
To strife was your duty,

> To drive them on
> To savage war,
> That hosts of dauntless heroes
> Might gather in Walhalls' hall. [1]

Did Hitler perchance borrow from Wagner this conception of the way heroes can be driven frenzied by the god in order to serve dubious partisan ends? In the same long confession to Brünnhilde Wotan admits:

> But I cannot strike one
> By treaties protected, . . .
> These are the bonds
> That bind my power;
> I who by treaties am lord,
> To my treaties also am slave.

Is it possible that Hitler, moved by the powerlessness of Wotan, the helpless victim of his own treaties, identified himself with the coming hero, Siegfried, whom Wotan previses in the following lines?

> But what I dare not
> One man may dare —
> A hero never
> Helped by my favour,
> To me unknown
> And granted no grace,
> Unaware,
> Bidden by none,
> Constrained thereto
> By his own distress —
> He could achieve
> What I must not do.
>
> But alas! how to find
> One to fight me, the god,
> For my good —
> Most friendly of foes!
> How fashion the free one
> By me unshielded,
> In his proud defiance

[1] RICHARD WAGNER, *The Ring of the Nibelung, The Valkyrie*, p. 112, trans. by Margaret Armour (William Heinemann, London).

GERMANY POSSESSED

Most precious to me?
How get me the other
Who, not through me
But of himself
Will perform my will?

The other whom I so long for,
That other I never find.
The free by themselves must be fashioned
All that I fashion are slaves![1]

Whenever we probe into the real source of Hitler's inspiration, we come to the Germanic myth, wherein Wagner, as we know, was Hitler's foster-parent. The dynamism of the German unconscious came to Hitler, therefore, in the form which Wagner had given it. In responding to Wotan's mythic appeal, Hitler could all too readily identify himself with the longed-for, self-liberated hero. At other times, doubtless, he must have been attracted, through the strength of his shadow-side, to the misshapen dwarf Alberich, the harsh ruler of the underworld artificers. In his lust for the boundless power and wealth, promised to the possessor of the Ring, Alberich accepts the significant condition that he renounce love and friendship for ever. The fact that these two rôles are mutually contradictory, would not deter the ambiguous Hitler from extracting emotional authority from each in turn. Personified dynamism cannot be expected either to be consistent or reliable. Did not Wotan provide Siegmund in his hour of need with the magical sword Nothung? And did he not, himself, betray the hero's faith in his battle with Hunding, shattering the god-given blade on his own spear, in order that Siegmund should receive his death-thrust from Hunding?

The part of Siegmund the outcast must also have appealed intimately to Hitler, if the account of his origin mentioned in the first chapter should happen to be the true one. But the heroic rôle which Hitler undoubtedly chose for himself is, of course, Siegfried. I forging the German people into a new unity he could, with some justice, identify himself with the hero who forged his blade from the pieces of his father's sword. It was Siegfried, too, who slew the great dragon Fafnir, the slothful possessor of the Rhinegold.

[1] There the Germanic god himself confesses that to be possessed by him is to be enslaved.

This mythic theme of the dragon, the hero, and the treasure symbolizes the struggle of the primordial infant-psyche to reach the mother (the treasure difficult of attainment) by overcoming the father-dragon, who represents, as Jung has shown,[1] the subjective resistance arising from the universal dread of incest. The killing of the dragon would, therefore, accord perfectly with Hitler's hatred of his father and correspondingly intense attachment to his mother. Siegfried also licked drops of the dragon's blood from his hand, thus acquiring a peculiar responsiveness to the voice of nature. Hitler's mediumistic flair for the underground currents and tendencies of the unconscious was doubtless awakened through becoming involved, as a child, in the serpentine intrigues and undercurrents of his early milieu. Finally, Siegfried's rescue of the dormant Brünnhilde from her fire-surrounded sleep, imposed on her by the will of Wotan, can be likened to Hitler's rousing of Germany, the long-lost daughter of Wotan, from her neurotic apathy. And just as Siegfried's advent brought about the twilight and passing of the old gods, so Hitler sees himself as the first of the god-men of the new epoch.

The subtle interweaving of Hitler's personal myth[2] with Wagner's version of the Germanic racial myth, is so strangely appropriate that his claim to be the one chosen by fate to lead the German people towards a new and splendid dawn seems to receive a certain mythological sanction.

4

While discussing this cosmic aspect of Hitler's psychology, I should like to quote certain passages from his horoscope, delineated by the experienced hand of my friend Mr. J. M. Thorburn, who has devoted himself to the task of reconciling the age-old problem of human fate with modern scientific philosophy. I shall quote first from the epochal horoscope which tends, on the whole,

---

[1] C. G. JUNG, *Psychology of the Unconscious* (Kegan Paul & Co., London).
[2] I use the term 'myth' to denote the fact that I am speaking of the emotional pattern of Hitler's background, rather than of the actual historical facts, which, for some probably sufficient reason, have been kept obscure.

to give a more positive rendering of the subject's psychology than does the natal.[1] Mr. Thorburn writes:

This is beyond all question the horoscope of a man of quite unusual genius. The main configuration is exceedingly complex, but very closely knit, showing an extraordinary interrelation of the constructive and creative, on the one hand, with the inharmonious and destructive, on the other. It may be held that the destructive components are the heavier and, therefore, that the genius will tend to show the dæmonic preponderating over the human. This side should not, however, be unduly stressed, for though they are overweighted by the oblique and the inharmonious, the constructive components are strong, clear in outline to the point of precision, and of excellent quality.

Whether it be called spiritual authority or ideological tyranny, this is the pervading orientation. It lies behind everything, the informing spirit of everything the man does. Above all, this authority is heavy, dogged, immovable and exercised with extreme persistence. But it is also fraught with a deep inner depression, the subject's experience being liable to a kind of bleak, cold devitalization, expressed in recurring periods of loneliness, isolation, and disappointment. This depression and isolation belong to his fate and find expression equally in the imprisonment that happens to him, as in the seclusion he inflicts upon himself.

From this background of ideological authority and isolation emerges a fierce fanaticism. Besides being actively in evidence, it is interwoven with entremely subtle powers of deceit and treachery. This too is part and parcel of the ideology. It is not merely an instrument of practical policy. It represents a view passionately held and passionately imposed. It is at once cunning and reckless, subtle and persuasive, being able to deceive the very elect. Such a philosophy inevitably makes immense overdrafts on the bank of life, and herein we come near to the essentials of the present crisis. Will Hitler be called upon to pay up too suddenly, or will he find means, one way or another, of making emergency payments?

The duality of Hitler's nature becomes most apparent at this point. For we find, on one side, a quality of ruthlessness and indifference to suffering, even perhaps an intellectual pleasure

---

[1] The natal horoscope is based upon the actual moment of birth; while the epochal is derived from a point taken a solar year before the moment of birth.

in inflicting curious forms of suffering. While, on the other, there exists a strange altruism and power of sacrifice. From this point of view, it is not wholly a myth to speak of the 'sacrifice of Hitler', in so far as it has its coördinate in a kind of conditioned self-dedication on Hitler's part. Notwithstanding the fact that the boundary line between self-sacrifice and megalomania is sometimes hard to trace, Hitler must be given credit, *de facto*, for some kind of altruism, some kind of indiscriminate generosity that neither looks for, nor receives reward or return.

Besides all this there is a terrible emotionalism. The general picture here suggests floods upon floods of undifferentiated affect. Although the horoscope intimates a canalization of emotion and positive reconstruction therefrom, there is a disordered welter of such things as personal affection, humanitarianism, altruistic feeling, fanaticism, cruelty, and fanatical revenge. Out of this welter of largely undifferentiated feeling Hitler is liable to take refuge in floods of tears. 'Mystical sensuousness' or 'sensuous mysticism', of a fearfully confused form, but copious and undirected, might serve as a comprehensive term for all this.

In view of this initial undifferentiation, the influence of the constructive elements is all the more significant. The instinct towards seclusion is urgent in Hitler's make up, and the use he makes of it is manifold. In the first place, there is the introverted patience and solidity with which he develops his intuitions. The moment of inspiration would result in nothing unless it were followed up by careful scrutiny and progressive differentiation and development. This is the product of seclusion. In his environment Hitler combines the austere, the genial, and the mysterious, and it is in this combination that we must look for the setting of his mystical gifts. According with this phase of receptivity we might expect a peculiar and constructive form of introversion. This is part of his function of seclusion. It consists of slowly developing ideas, containing, evidently, some form of suprapersonal, intuitive perception. This process works accurately and, in many instances, gives results of extreme precision. Owing to a relative deficiency in other channels of cognition, this intuitive function is used very persistently and its value overstressed. Hence the sense of failure and frustration, when the insight is not forthcoming, is liable to provoke extreme suffering.

On the whole, this function is not illusory in its operation. It may fail, and, like Saul of old, Hitler may strive desperately to find an answer from the oracles when the oracles are dumb. But as regards this part of the horoscope it is not subject to illusion in the long run. Incidental mistakes are, of course, inevitable. Hitler may have trusted astrologers, and other intuitive sources, when they were wrong and so forth. But the point is, not that mistakes can be ruled out, but that the function, in its essential character, is not one of illusion.

Expressive functions are good — brilliantly good. This raises the question, why the intellectual qualities in the ordinary cultural sense are so low, and, in particular, why his attempts at writing should be so poor. Discussion of this point would take us too far afield. But this much can be said. With his oratory Hitler has been able to move men of all types of culture and of all social levels. The power and originality must, therefore, be in its emotional content.

In conclusion, this horoscope brings together the qualities of a social sharp-shooter — a gangster psychology of an extreme type — with those of the mystic, the man of inner vision; vision moreover of unquestionable validity, and by no means unrelated to the world of real experience.

The natal horoscope contains, as we might expect, a kind of psychological close-up in which the negative or sinister features stand out more decisively. Concerning this horoscope Thorburn comments:

> There is certainly cruelty and a certain degree of sadism in this horoscope. The element of cruelty is much more in evidence — coarseness and crudeness too. Indeed its main feature lies in the massiveness or persistence of the vindictive and cruel . . . There is a fixity, a dead weight of authoritative, destructive energy, which is doubtless the psychological coördinate of Germany's large scale military destructiveness. Yet although, after Hitler's seizure of power, methods were doubtless relentless, these methods did not obliterate a constructiveness which was probably valid in intention and real in effect.
>
> What then of the future? Signs are not lacking that Hitler may remain the ruler of Germany for some time to come, and that, if he does remain, his constructiveness will be effective in operation. It is, of course, impossible to foretell. The

important thing is to attempt to gauge the ruthlessness or cruelty in relation to the synthetic power. Granting even fearful cruelty, the *originality* of the synthesis is not negated. Its originality is merely conditioned by the cruelty, the ruthlessness, the sadism or whatever terms are deemed appropriate.

Again then in this horoscope we are confronted with a peculiar genius for associative synthesis. Before, it appeared as intuitive 'flair'. Here, it is rather the stability, the endurance of what is synthesized that is most in evidence. There is also an intimation that the power and efficacy of the synthesis may remain after the day of cruelty has passed, or has been mitigated.

Once again, too, it is synthesis taking place behind the scenes, thus re-introducing in another form the moment of the secluded, the secret, and the occult.

Immense ambition is undoubtedly a feature of this horoscope; and we can only raise the question whether it must be described as megalomania. It does not show the extreme fanaticism of the epochal horoscope, nor is the element of active deceit so manifest. A great facility for adaptation to the collective mind is undoubtedly indicated. When Hitler won the regard of a large section of the German people, this must not be put down — not entirely at least — to a mere dishonest playing upon their susceptibilities. Psychological trickery is, no doubt, one of his methods, but in addition Hitler had, and may recover, a genuine power of gauging the collective psyche and of moving sincerely with it.

This astrological survey of Hitler is the more valuable since the author has obviously taken exceptional care to deal justly with his subject. His final comment should also be cited, because it helps us in estimating a probable prognosis. He says:

> In dealing with a character in which such very high lights are broken by such very deep shadows, it is difficult to strike the real balance . . . In justice I am bound to bring into prominence the excellence of certain qualities and functions which have not been so much as mentioned by astrologers. At the same time, I have not minimized the salient traits of cruelty and deceit. The latter — the active tendency — I take to be the most damaging feature of the character. It is likely to be all-pervasive and to tinge every phase of his life.

We are left with the final question: Has Hitler had the good of Germany at heart, or is his apparent patriotism merely part of his egotism? From certain components of the epoch, I should be inclined to answer that it is not *all* to be put down to megalomania.

Most astrologers hold the view that Hitler's unlimited ambition carries with it an eventual downfall. No doubt the present war furnishes conditions under which this could occur. At the same time, it must be said that as regards the immediate future *there is no sufficient evidence*, astrologically speaking, to guarantee his disappearance from the scene. It may happen. Yet in view of the present state of Hitler's horoscope, the possibility of destroying Hitlerism through the obliteration of Hitler does not seem a very real one.

I am very much indebted to Mr. Thorburn for allowing me to make use of his brilliant reading of Hitler's horoscope. I set out on my investigation with the idea of getting impressions and material from a variety of sources, wherewith I hoped to create a psychological picture from within, as well as from without. This astrological portrait is timely and valuable, particularly because our study of Hitler has remained unavoidably dark. In the records available, in the impressions of those who have known him, and above all, in his public deeds and utterances, we do not find many endearing traits. With the help of his astrological knowledge Thorburn has given us a beautifully balanced portrait of the man, particularly in respect to his subjective development. It is a picture of the man, not of his function. Inasmuch, therefore, as it is concerned with Hitler's personal make-up, we find no reference to his mediumistic function in relation to the racial unconscious by virtue of which his prestige as a medicine-man has been built up. We find allusion to a peculiar form of sexual sublimation which Thorburn describes as a mixture of emotional weakness and intellectualization. Cruelty and sadism are also stressed, particularly in the natus. These, at bottom, are repressive perversions of the erotic impulse. It is self-evident, for example, that Hitler's brutality is of a very different order from that of Stalin's. Stalin is a wolf: killing is natural to him. But Hitler is subtle, austere, effeminate, secluded. His make-up has probably a preponderance of feminine elements, albeit in a perverted form. Accordingly, his cruelty and brutality are a twisted conscious effort to over-compensate his 'haunting hysteria'. He feels a need to dramatize crude masculinity, as, for instance, when he swaggers about in jack-boots carrying a whip; yet never unaware of the impression he is making, like a vain woman. Heiden even quotes him as saying: 'All I say or do belongs to history.'[1]

These aspects of Hitler have been clearly in evidence in our other material. What is most valuable in Thorburn's picture is the decisive evidence of strong synthetic elements in Hitler's character. It is hard to do justice to his positive side. When a flood has laid waste our fields and homesteads, the fertile possibilities latent in the unctuous mud left behind by the flood do not leap readily to the mind.

Whether Hitler has had Germany's welfare at heart is a question that has already been answered by Wagner, for whom patriotism and egotism are, at bottom, indistinguishable. We can hardly agree, however, that patriotism is necessarily an ambitious brand of egotism, since this must depend upon whether the patriot identifies himself with the State (*l'État c'est moi*), or whether he has learned the discipline of service. Not every dictator falls a victim to megalomania.

How then are we to reconcile this picture of megalomanic egotism with our earlier conclusion that Hitler cannot be regarded as personally ambitious in the ordinary sense of the word? This paradox is resolved when we reflect that Hitler, as a personality, has practically ceased to exist; his whole psychology has been assimilated by the ruling complex. Thorburn speaks of 'floods upon floods of undifferentiated feeling', and stresses the shapeless, undisciplined character of Hitler's emotional make-up. But he does not go further and accept the hypothesis that this welter of affect might also be an aspect of that general dynamism of the collective unconscious which inspired Hitler to become a prophet and a medium.

If Hitler were merely a megalomaniac, he could not have become the maker of the Third Reich. Megalomania is not particularly impressive. Very few people are deceived by outlandish and grandiose delusions. If Hitler were a solitary phenomenon in an otherwise sane world, his megalomania would be undeniable. But in actual fact, the flood that bears Hitler to his doom carries a vast

[1] KONRAD HEIDEN, *Hitler*, p. 103 (Constable).

multitude of human beings who not only share his delusions, they also insist upon sharing his fate. A vast river in flood is a terrible thing; yet we cannot just call it insanity and have done with it.

For the same reason it is insufficient to speak of Hitler's emotionalism as mere hysteria, or of Nazi brutality as hooliganism. These words omit the essence of the phenomenon, which is, that they are part of the chaos of a river in flood. There is no more intelligible content in Hitler's emotional frenzies than there is reason in a flood. With his term *Wahn* Wagner has helped us to understand this psychology where moods have the character of inchoate force inadequately contained. In these moods Hitler is simply a prey to the unleashed energies of the unconscious. His 'infinite aims' are due to the fact that no human objective and no mortal will can any longer hold this untamed force and give it a reasonable shape. It has, therefore, become a rapacious monster, ever demanding new victims, successes, horizons. The last thing Hitler can really want is to win the war. For then, having devoured the world, it will turn like Frankenstein's monster and rend its creator.

According to Thorburn's picture, the most astonishing thing in Hitler's political philosophy is his attitude to cruelty and treachery. I believe Thorburn is correct when he asserts that Hitler's unscrupulousness is not a mere instrument of practical political use, 'but a view passionately held and passionately imposed'. This accords completely with Hitler's conception of his new order as consisting of the *Herrenmensch* and the *Herdenmensch*. The selected, ruling few are not to be chosen for their aristocratic qualities. What Hitler plans to create with his ruling type is a new kind of human being, turgid with life, and capable of utterly unrestrained impulses; a being without intellect to speak of, but with complete fearlessness, even in the face of death. All the Christian values are to be trampled underfoot by this dæmoniac creature. He will rule the men of the herd, merely by virtue of the fact that he can pursue the ends of the state with the utmost ruthlessness. This has nothing to do with hooliganism, or the law of the jungle; it is an attempt to extinguish the human soul and to set in its place an ideological monstrosity.

Up till 1934 Hitler held true to his vision and the people accepted him as the spear-head of the new order. He was leading them to the new world and the people's trust gave him absolute power. The catastrophe began in 1934. It was as though Hitler made a pact with the devil. All the wonderful potentialities of the new order were given over to the cruellest of human lusts. This was the unpardonable betrayal; to have had the possibility of serving humanity as Moses served his people, and to choose instead the insatiable dæmon of conquest. Thus the fearlessness of the reborn Siegfried was converted into the cultivated ruthlessness of a storm-trooper. In this way the river of German myth was given the wrong form and the great Wagnerian dream became the vessel of catastrophe.

5

At the heart of this German tragedy lies the central problem of conscious life. For humanity to progress it is essential that the dynamic element of the unconscious, formless and inchoate like water, be opposed by the formative principle of individual consciousness. General dynamism must be curbed and bridled and given a satisfying, structural expression. If the form-producing element becomes stereotyped, petrifaction sets in, as with the Egyptian civilization, or in the rigid uprightness of the Pharisees. From unyielding forms life eventually departs, leaving behind only dead bones and museum trophies. If, on the other hand, inchoate dynamism sweeps away all enduring forms, the result is such as is already manifest in Hitler's chaos. Stability can alone be restored when conscious individuality holds its place, not only ready to withstand the impact of the unconscious with the ancestor's spirit, but also to give it a new form.

We now begin to discern a view of the present struggle as a crisis of transition. Germany embodies the principle of dynamism. The unity of free peoples under Churchill's leadership represents the principle of established, civilized form. The essential difference between the Germans and ourselves is that our ancestors created a tough, enduring form, while Germany, as a political entity, is still adolescent. She was carried away because she had no tried political form which could withstand the force of the rising flood.

Germany's dynamic disunion found temporary unity in a leader who had himself rejected all restraint. As we have already discovered, he had no loyalties, either of feeling, interest, or tradition, which could bind him to the forms and ethical obligations of contemporary social consciousness. His mother, his only real, human relation, died when he was seventeen, and it is practically certain that he never became emotionally freed from that tie. It is a commonplace of emotional dynamics that a man whose love instincts are too intensely and exclusively involved with the mother is unable to marry. The mother possesses all his *libido*, so that he has nothing real or effective to give to a possible wife. It is as though the life channel from the ancestors to posterity had been blocked by the image of the mother. Hitler's love and allegiance were never given to school, craft, profession, friend, lover, or wife. The only time when he was again fully contained emotionally was when he joined the army in 1914. Since a man's loyalty is given only to those forms in which he is psychically contained, it follows that Hitler's passion, which before had gone wholly to the mother, now went wholly into the army in which the crude dynamism of his nature became merged in the Prussian dream of world-power. [1]

6

At the beginning of this chapter we indicated a certain parallelism with the case of Mrs. Eddy. She, too, became fascinated by a significant spiritual potential with which the general unconscious at that time was pregnant. By rediscovering the long-forgotten truth — that healing is an essential function of religion — she became a pioneer in that great new continent of the mind which psycho-therapy is now beginning to explore. The people who take these fateful plunges into the collective unconscious are, as we said, queer folk; for if they were fully alive to present reality, they would not be peering over the edge of the world into the depths below. That Hitler's intuitions are not delusions is confirmed by the experience I have had of the mediumistic type. The fact that a person is queer, or even criminal, does not exclude the possibility

[1] Hitler tells us in *Mein Kampf* that when, in 1914, he heard that war had been declared, he went down on his knees and 'thanked heaven from an overflowing heart'.

that his intuition may prove to be both timely and true. Hitler recounts, for instance, many occasions when his intuition saved his life with a peremptory warning, in much the same way as Socrates was protected by his δαίμων. There was one incident in the trenches, when he felt he had to move at once. No sooner had he gone than a shell burst where he had been standing. In point of fact, nearly everyone who relies habitually upon intuition[1] can recount similar examples from his own experience. Intuition becomes like a faithful servant or watch-dog, and can be brought to a very high degree of refinement. In conjunction with a rational function, it can be relied upon to produce a disciplined intelligence-service, upon which effective action, and even life itself, may depend.

There is, however, one great disadvantage in trusting completely to a person of the mediumistic type. We see the danger exemplified in both the cases under review. It consists in the fact that the medium relies upon an instinctual means of cognition which does not require the disciplined labour of thought. Both thinking and feeling are disciplined functions, related to the moral conscience through the fact that, in accordance with their specific function, they obey definite canons of value. Intuition and sensation, on the other hand, are pristine functions of perception, and belong, therefore, to the primordial, amoral level of the psyche. Where intuition is closely allied to, or is an auxiliary of, a rational function it tends to partake of the character of the disciplined function, and accordingly submits to relativity. But where intuition is cultivated for its own sake, so that its conclusions are neither criticized nor questioned by a rational function, it tends to maintain the all-or-none character of every protopathic function. The result, of course, is a subjective claim to absolute validity, entailing an attitude of complete intolerance towards any other point of view.

This discussion of mediumistic intuition is no academic digression. When we undertake to inquire into the subliminal sources of a medium's ideas, we must also discuss the nature of the function which finds and uses them. We need not assume a lack of honesty when a medium like Hitler lays claim to ideas picked up in this way. Intuition gathers morsels all the time, but without necessarily

---

[1] This function is commonly called instinct, and indeed with some reason, for it is clearly akin to the instinctual behaviour of animals.

recording the name of the last owner. Both Mrs. Eddy and Hitler discovered buried treasure with their intuition, and the very fact that they found their ideas in this way, gave them an apparent warrant for assuming these contents to be revelations. The world would be saner if reason commanded mankind to regard these revelational mediums as dowsers, with a curious knack of discovering appropriate archaisms in the unconscious. In so far as we do not identify the dowser with the hidden spring he divines, reason also requires us to discriminate between the medium and the pearls he may bring up from the bottom of the sea.

CHAPTER VIII

THE HITLER DISEASE

I

BEFORE we close this study there is one question we need to consider, a question which is liable to become of vital importance when the devil-projections of war-time are revoked, and we find ourselves, once again, working side by side with our present enemies. What is Hitler's significance to us? What does this fanatical and ghost-ridden conqueror represent in our own psychology? The partisan atmosphere of war-time unavoidably fosters the conviction that we are right and the enemy wrong. Yet we are nearer the ultimate truth when we regard Hitler as a symptom of the disease, rather than its cause. We should also recognize the Hitler disease as a general infection that is liable to break out amongst us, albeit in a different form.

People who are in the habit of noting their dreams will have observed, for instance, the occasional appearance of Hitler among the other denizens of their dream-life. It can be taken as self-evident that everything one dreams about must be in some way relevant to one's individual psychology. Clearly then, if I dream of Hitler, it is because I have an unrecognized problem which finds him, of all available figures, the most appropriate to represent and express it. Naturally, since we are now concerned with factors of individual psychology, Hitler as a dream-symbol must have a varying connotation; whereas Hitler as an historical figure will eventually be reduced to a certain universality.

In the case of a subject who suffers from unconscious ambition, Hitler may represent a certain resentful feeling of inferiority, which finds expression in compensatory feats of social mountaineering or similar heroic attempts. In others, he may represent an unconscious anarchic element which aims at moral revolution within. Or he may symbolize a fanatical opinion which tries to sweep aside every other point of view and repress every other function of the mind. Clearly the symbol is capable of a great variety of *nuances*, and is therefore applicable to many individual problems. Yet, over and above every variation, there is a certain inimical core which should be regarded as a widespread psychical infection.

Few, I imagine, would contest the fact that Hitler represents the force of evil in the world to-day. Parallel to this outer situation in Europe, we find an element, or tendency, within the civilized mind that has earned for itself much the same character. I have called it the renegade tendency. By this I do not merely refer to simple neurotic resistance, or evasion, but rather to something which could undermine one's individual and vital interests.

The negative character which has been earned by the ego — which, after all, is the indispensable focal-point of the mind — rests upon the fact that it is liable to develop a wilful opacity which interferes with the impersonal activity of the spiritual function. The childlike translucence of the primordial unconscious may become completely obscured. The unfilial son, the anarchic revolutionary, the inflated over-sensitive ego — all are guilty of the same spiritual offence; either they repudiate, or they interfere with, the life-stream of culture, thus depriving themselves, or mankind, of inherited value. The sophisticated ego breaks the flow of ancestral value whenever its egotism seizes upon impersonal psychic belongings, in order to pin them to its own nobly-arched bosom. As Hitler refers everything to the Reich he has himself created, while ignoring or belittling all previous achievement, the egotist refers everything to his ego, affecting disdain for all that lies beyond his personal sphere. Tacitly, therefore, the ancestral achievement — which includes the whole realm of the non-ego or impersonal psyche — is repudiated. The unconscious, which stands for the principle of continuity, does not forgive this unfilial attitude. On other grounds, an overcharged ego-complex must be regarded as a grievous liability. For besides behaving like an overbearing parasite in relation to other psychic factors, its opacity impedes the effortless, spontaneous flow of psychic activity; while its wilful planning and egotism robs the total subject of satisfying human relationship.

In order to appreciate the parallelism between the inflated ego-complex within and the possessed Führer without, we have only to observe the way in which both excel as continuity-breakers.

Everyone is aware of the many arteries of German culture that have been severed under the Hitler terror. Not only in Germany itself, but in every country where Hitler has set his foot, the flow of cultural life begins to dwindle. He has spurned everything which carries the nobility of the Christian ideal. Like a black opacity, obscuring the way beyond, Hitler and his bombs are the symbol of a gigantic destructive will which aims at breaking the life-stream of European civilization.

The ego as the natural ruler of consciousness can as well be disciplined and constructive as interfering and opaque. Similarly, the leader of the German Reich had it in his power to become the indispensable midwife of the new epoch. The two cases are comparable when we discover the principle that is common to both. The directing power is right when it furthers the essential continuity of the living process in its wholeness. In the Chinese idiom, this going-with the order of Nature is the state of being in Tao. But it is wrong when it sets its aim in opposition to the whole, thus interfering with the natural flow of living things.

This character of opposition, or resistance to the whole, is the essence of the renegade factor. But here again we must be careful in our definition. We cannot assume, for example, that the man who resists the extraverted stream of activity and goes away by himself is, necessarily, having dealings with the devil. `It is even possible that he has gone aside to commune with his god.

We must, therefore, add the condition that the renegade tendency interferes with the continuity of life for destructive ends. There is no condition in the psyche which cannot be turned either to good or evil purposes. Resistance, negativism, and other symptoms of neurotic display too easily take on the aspect of renegade phenomena. But we have to ask: What is the motive for the resistance? What is its purpose? Does life agree with it or not? For in the last resort the only absolutely good or evil things in our universe are motives. The acts we call crimes are assumed to be evilly motivated; but until we know the motive or attitude of the man who kills his fellow, we cannot say that his crime was intrinsically evil. He may have killed his man as Moses slew the Egyptian, because God needed a strong arm for the payment of a righteous debt.

The term renegade presupposes, therefore, that the tendency in question is directed against the validity of the human pact, whether the pact be the covenant of marriage, the vow of service to God or state, or the implicit pact which underlies the whole complex fabric of human society. Wherever enduring human faith and trust are enshrined, there the renegade power is attracted, and always with the object of negating and destroying it.

When the renegade tendency resists the laws of society the various types of criminality result. But within the psyche the renegade is that thing which revolts against the laws of life. A series of mythological figures representing the opposing forces of darkness and light are found engaged in an eternal battle. The black magician and black witch are the two leading figures on the dark side. There is Klingsor, for instance, who holds Kundry, the anima or soul-image, as a spellbound captive in his castle of enchantment. In modern fantasy the renegade will is frequently figured as a vampire. In *Lilith*, the rather lugubrious allegory by George Macdonald, the white anima has to contend against the black anima, a dark panther-like woman whose evil knows no bounds. She is first discovered in a state of lifeless inertia and has to be warmed and inspired with life. Assuming the form of a black panther she seeks out the places where infants have been born, in her vampire-quest for their blood. In an early Jewish version of the myth, Lilith is represented as the first wife of Adam; but she declined her creative task, refusing to become the mother of the human race, lest she jeopardize her immortal beauty. As a punishment for her rejection of the principle of continuity she became a vampire and dæmon. Bram Stoker's Dracula is another representative of the vampire will which seeks to suck the juice out of a man's clearest obligations and dearest relationships.

The black Mass of Satanism reveals another aspect of the renegade tendency. Blasphemous mock-rituals are practised, signifying a contemptuous negation of man's participation in the divine, symbolized by the Mass. Just as the vampire symbolizes the renegade will which opposes the stream of life, so Satanism symbolizes the renegade pagan will which repudiates the things most sacred to the Christian soul.

In dream symbolism the renegade tendency is often figured as a black horse, representing the amount of psychic energy that has become attracted to the destructive side. In the psychological field the black aspect usually appears in conjunction with its white counterpart, since all psychical factors appear as pairs of opposites. The black magician cannot exist without the white. Psychical opposites can neither be finally sundered, nor finally reconciled. They are the warp and woof of spiritual reality. Thus it must happen, whenever the divine child is born — as at the birth of Jesus — that the devil will seek to destroy it.

In the unconscious we find these figures lying side by side, like the twin giants Castor and Pollux, or Gog and Magog. The issue is always open. The new potentiality may become either an ally of the good and true, or a satanic conspirator on the side of evil. Thus the figures of the white and black magician, for example, represent alternative possibilities. One can either become possessed by the unconscious in the manner of the renegade; or one can make relation to the unconscious for the healing of the soul and the intensification of life.

The deciding factor is the integrity of the conscious attitude. In his contest with the power of Klingsor, Parsifal is not protected by the Grail. In his own simple loyalty to his quest he is able to withstand the enchantment of Kundry. It is this factor of integrity which not only vanquishes Klingsor and wins the spear, but also releases Kundry from the curse, and makes possible her transformation from a dæmonic Lilith-figure into a ministering function.

Thus we find that the polarity of the unconscious, represented in this dual aspect of the anima, can be profoundly influenced by the conscious attitude. The successful practice of psychotherapy rests upon this condition. Since, in the last analysis, the duality of the soul connotes two equally possible attitudes to spiritual events, the one might be called the way of devotion, the other, the way of abandonment.

2

The fear of the renegade tendency, luring men away to perdition, has preoccupied secular and religious legislation ever since man began his long cultural ascent. This fear also led the primitive mind to the most important psychological discovery. It was found that the best way to deal with the unbridled force which would change a man into a raging fury, was to transform the dæmonic force into a god. The state of abandonment, or complete unconscious possession, is equivalent to psychological dissolution. Hence, for the primitive psyche, with its relatively undifferentiated organization, it is the greatest possible danger. This threat of engulfment by the unconscious is symbolized in the mythic dragon or monster, whose vast jaws are ready to swallow the sun (the symbol of consciousness) as it descends into the western sea. The terror which overwhelms the primitive mind during an eclipse is also related to this same eventuality.

How then does primitive mentality deal with this dread of dissolution? The natural psyche knows only one way of healing the mind, or cleansing it of dread. This is the alchemist's way of transformation. Everything which has the power to overwhelm consciousness, has at one time or another been transformed, either into a god or into the service of a god.

A primitive rite, recorded in the Vedic scriptures, tells, for instance, of how the gods and the Titans 'fought together for these worlds', of how the Titans beat the gods in every quarter of the compass, until they reached the north-eastern quarter, or last ditch. Here the gods took counsel together and concluded that their defeat by the Titans was due to their lack of a king (i.e. ruling principle). So they made Soma king and, with Soma as king, they retook all the ground they had lost.

Soma was the name of a plant from which the early civilizing men of India made the most powerful alcoholic spirit. It was the dæmonic thing which could overpower reason and dissolve consciousness. Therefore, it had to be raised up and transformed into a king. Soma became, in fact, the communion drink, the symbol and token of the basic human pact. Thus reserved, it was drunk only in the presence of the god, and the man who was inspired by 'the mead of immortality' became the mouthpiece of the deity.

What we might regard clinically as the transports of hysteria and the strange utterances of the possessed was, for primordial mentality, clear evidence of the presence of the god. The frenzy which overcame the worshippers of Dionysos seemed a discreditable loss of control only to the sublime Apollonian critic. To those within the experience the transformation was the experience of god and, therefore, safeguarded by primitive tradition.

There can be no question, I think, but that civilized consciousness owes an incalculable debt to this vital psychological discovery. It is a truth, which we are only now beginning to understand, that mental balance is restored, not by negating or denying the dangerously strong primitive tendency, but rather by enhancing its value; thereby raising it from the protopathic, primitive level to the differentiated, epicritic sphere of conscious experience.

Our modern psychotherapy has already taken many leaves out of the book of primitive medicine, and now it has learned that the only way to cure neurotic egotism is not by the old method of depreciation, but by so enlarging the contents and conception of the self, that it is felt to embrace the total subject, conscious and unconscious. This intensification of the value of the self brings about a relation to the divine element in the soul. In this way, as in the initiation at Eleusis, the personal becomes dissolved in the impersonal, and, through a kind of histolysis, a basic transformation of attitude is achieved.

When we speak of this as a discovery of the primitive mind, we do not assume that it was invented as a device for dealing with individuals who were liable to run amok. Psychical transformation is no consciously directed trick, but an essential process in the evolution of individual consciousness. The fear of God was never created in the human breast by the ideal aspect of deity. What man fears is the overwhelming and terrible, in a word, the dynamic aspect of God. Accordingly, out of dire necessity, man gave royal or divine honours to just those things which he could by no means control.

To the primitive type of mentality, affect alone is real; thought is real only in so far as it has demonstrable concrete effects, or can be dramatized. For Zeno, the Stoic, that thing was real which had the power so to seize hold of the mind that it could not be dislodged. The *Kataleptike Fantasia* was, therefore, a mental image or event which gained, as it were, a cataleptic hold upon the mind. In the German word *Wirklichkeit* we come upon the same conception. Reality (*res*=thing) for the German mind is something which works or is effective. Not mere thing-ness, but an effect which lays hold of the mind, either from within or from without. The experience itself then is the reality, not merely the interpretation which it carries to the reason. Thus, from every side we find evidence that a dynamic conception of reality preceded the representational, just as the dynamic manifestation of God preceded the ideal. Chaos always precedes cosmos.

When the doctor discerns this same curative principle at work in his patient's psychology, he is forced to believe that the wisdom of the early myths was not concealed there by pedagogues of antiquity; rather is it the accumulated deposit of innumerable human experiences expressed in the primitive language of images. A patient may be impaled for months upon the thorns of a problem, unable to leave it, or to find a solution. At last he finds the grace to give the problem royal honours. Immediately he feels released, and the problem itself takes on a more rational appearance. A patient with obsessional sexuality, for instance, wanted nothing better than to cut the problem out of his life and be free. He talked about it endlessly, but always in a contemptuous, disparaging way. He wanted to minimize the Titan which gripped him, so that he could wrap himself about once again in comfortable complacence. But the problem would not let him go until he had paid in full the debt which his whole life and attitude had denied.

Francis Thompson in the *Hound of Heaven* discovered anew this ever-living theme. The hound that pursues and will not let one go is in reality the God one has failed to honour. If we can be sure of anything at all, we can be certain that this primitive wisdom which Thompson rediscovered is the effective principle of all mental healing, namely, that the healing value is to be found in the very heart of one's worst problem. The divine effect is released through honouring the problem set by one's inferiority, and it is on this account that 'the stone which the builders rejected becomes the head-stone of the corner'.

3

To come back once more to the ego and to Hitler, we can no longer be content with naming these as the criminal factors in their respective spheres. Anyone who has achieved a certain level of consciousness will agree that life would become intolerable if no cure could be found for the greedy, over-sensitive, self-dramatizing, pretentious, hypocritical ego. We know what we want to make with life, yet we see how the ego, with its sinister shadow, cheats us at every turn. So we pretend to be moved by nice altruistic feelings, drilling our outer form so as to present a beautiful social surface, while to ourselves we simply minimize the problem and hope for the best. This is self-control, but it is not self-discipline.

Is this not precisely the same ostrich technique that British statesmen maintained so long and so dangerously with Hitler? Long after he loomed as a black cloud across the European sky, we said 'there may be a shower and then the sun will shine again'. We explained that Hitler only wanted to retrieve the Treaty of Versailles and that the Germans, after all, had not had a square deal. A decent and conciliatory attitude might conceivably win him over to the side of peace.

It seems to be ordained by fate that the most positive qualities can germinate only in a dark and stricken soil. The finest qualities of the British character, for example, have been brought into clear relief only since we undertook to extinguish Nazi devilry. Our very nature urges us to hate the evil thing with our whole passion. Therewith we become gripped and seized by the problem, and only through grappling with something that will not let go is the healing value or symbol created. It is as though the thing which inflames our wrath, grips the mind, and becomes our major problem is found at the last to be the vessel of the god.

The evil thing which moved Jesus to flaming wrath was pharisaism. In Christ's world the spiritual equivalent to Hitler was undoubtedly the Pharisee. The Pharisee was a black opacity of fanatical will, interfering with the clear light of heaven. Christ's image of translucent, childlike faith, which He gave as the essential character of the Kingdom of Heaven, shone brilliant and clear against this background of fanatical, law-prescribed, and loveless righteousness. Not only did Christ's new conception of God as a loving Father glow like a new sun against the sombre background of Mosaic Law, but one feels that His hatred and abhorrence of pharisaic cruelty took an essential part in creating the new image.

So grievous is the weight of mental inertia that mankind is forced
to abhor the old gods, which have degenerated into mechanisms
of power and privilege, before he can give his heart to the new.
In the eyes of Jesus the Kingdom of Heaven was a blessed state.
It was a translucent, impersonal attitude, the reality of which was
as self-evident and as nobly simple as a fertile field. It was a royal
conception requiring faith to experience it, rather than intellect
to define it. But its patent relevance to human life and happiness
was made apparent by its vivid contrast with the interfering
Prussian mentality of pharisaism. In the same way the idea of
freedom that will govern the world of the future gains its creative
force out of our hatred of the Nazi terror.

The committee method of reasonable discussion was powerless
to effect a stable European order. The challenge of sheer necessity
was needed, with all the passionate energy and enthusiasm
generated by war, before the nations were brought to the point
of realizing a common necessity and a common aim. What Hitler
asserts is true: he *is* driving Europe to the making of a new order.
International idealism is prone to expend itself on wordy plat-
forms. But Hitler, by providing the lash of necessity, gave the
indispensable impetus; so that ancestral legions answered hotfoot
to the challenge. The new order will not be the one he is trying to
force on the world; yet, in a very real sense, it will be hammered
into shape on his anvil. We know our truth and we recognize our
goal, just because Hitler raises up before our eyes a counterfeit ideal
which is no better than a state of spiritual slavery. This reaction
of free men to Hitler's ideal is immediate and lively, like the
reaction of the skin to something poisonous. Is it not strange, then,
that humanity did not react against it with a whole-earted
reaction when he first began to spray his ideological poison over
Germany?

It is a medical axiom that liability to infection depends very
largely upon the individual factor of resistance. In respect to
physical infection, the healthy reaction of the skin and mucous
membrane is essential in maintaining a positive resistance to
infection. Indeed, the whole welfare of the body, even the
preservation of life, rests upon the sound and temperate reaction
of the skin to heat and cold and other environmental stimuli.
The health of the mind is related even more directly to the keen

functioning of one's native psychical envelope. A child will react immediately and with effective heat to injustice, or indeed to anything which infringes his individual kingdom. These immediate reactions to psychological stimuli are the foundations of the integrated moral being.

Let us assume, now, that from earliest years a child's spontaneous reactions have been either manipulated or repressed, so that he is eventually induced to accept a sophisticated view of himself, therewith deserting his own native truth. Alienated from his own psychical roots, it is easy to see how such a child would become vulnerable to spiritual infection.

This idea of changing a child's nature seems to have been introduced into the civilized soul with the conception of original sin. No one can say how that idea of the devil crept into the responsive mind of early civilizing man. It may have been the trick of a priestly hierarchy, insinuating that his nature was fundamentally evil, for the sake of gaining an unholy power over the soul of man. The primitive mind has been protected from this evil by a deep instinctual conservatism, established in the form of traditional taboo. Taboo informs a man that the women belonging to a certain totem are not for him, or that certain places, things, or people are, as it were, out of bounds; but it never implies that his own instinct is wrong. The devil was invited into the soul when priestly authority began to tamper with the instincts, the ever-renewing springs of life. A child expects to be punished when he does something which is mischievous or rebellious; but when the simple following of a natural impulse is treated as a crime, grievous damage is done to the child-soul. It is vital that we should see and feel this distinction. The human being is endlessly adjustable and educable in accommodating to required patterns of behaviour. But in the essential reactions of the soul, which are guarded by the psychical skin, we come to the living human truth, the golden thread in the labyrinth, the ancestral wisdom which runs in a continuous stream back to the earliest impregnation of living beings by the sun. This tap-root of truth must not be tampered with.

If we wished to plumb the abysmal criminality of the National Socialist régime, we should have to call up the soul of the individual German youth to testify against Hitler. Every man expects to submit to traditional and authoritative direction in all outer forms and activities where conformity is needed. This is the realm of Caesar. But every man has also an inner life in which he stands responsible to his deepest feeling, his spiritual being, his fixed star. This is the realm of God, and it is sacred. What I have dared to call the psychical skin is an inborn sensitiveness of the soul which defends these essential values.

It is precisely this realm and these values which Hitler is resolved to destroy. When he forces the Gestapo into every German home, when he commands children to spy upon their parents, when, by insinuating deadly suspicion, he undermines the most ancient and venerable of human pacts, he is violating sacred territory, not for any political strategy, but because he is resolved to crush the germ of individuality in the German soul.

But those peoples who have had the wisdom to protect their children from interference and who have maintained, as the essence of their racial piety, the honouring of man's original being — these can never be enslaved. It is impossible, for example, to crush the individuality of an Eskimo or a North American Indian. A whole man stands upright in the strength of his own truth. He cannot be spiritually gelded. His native moral reactions are effective, like the ring of a hammer on steel.

Alienation from nature is the method used by military or tribal hierarchies for the purpose of shaping human material to the required pattern. By segregating the youths of the tribe and by subjecting them to ferocious ordeals of initiation they are finally passed into the tribe as mass-produced warriors. The collective will seizes them at the most plastic phase of life and forces them into its mould, just as soldier-ants and worker-bees have been converted into mechanized collective units.

4

Thus again we are led to describe the interfering evil in terms of will, only now it appears in the form of a totalitarian tribal will, setting up a Moloch, a Cheka, or a Gestapo to enslave the individual soul. This vastly magnified collective will, when invested in a Hitler or a Stalin, is surely the most terrible product of civilization.

The epic of Gilgamish, the personification of restless, civilizing will, shows with what awe and dismay men first witnessed this terrifying portent. Imbued by some mysterious power, a ruler assumed divine attributes and set his will against the all-powerful nature-goddess. He entertained the impious notion of improving upon his original natural state. The success of his daring defiance led to a deification of the conscious will, at the expense, naturally, of the irrational, primordial psyche, which thus became the unconscious. It was no longer nature that was worshipped, but rather what man was able to make of nature: not the mighty granite of the eternal hills, but the temples, obelisks, and palaces he contrived and fashioned out of granite. Never the material (observe the fact that 'material' is etymologically the body of the mother) of art or science, but the creative will of the artist and the inventor, which was crowned with immortal laurels.

The universal acceptance of the civilizing will as the royal hero of human progress is shown in the fact that a just critique of its nature and achievements has, until quite recently, been almost wholly lacking.[1] It was not, indeed, until travellers and anthropologists came back with enthusiastic nostalgic descriptions of primitive life and character, that a standpoint was offered from which civilization could be viewed with a critical detachment.

Synchronous with the arrival upon the scene of the anthropological primitive, there came the discovery of the so-called unconscious mind, followed by a babel of conflicting interpretations in regard to its contents. The importance of this discovery was slow in becoming generally realized, largely because it was explored by doctors for therapeutic purposes. But the fact that we entertain a primitive being just beneath our civilized skin, and that our health and happiness depend very largely upon our relation to this primitive — this fact has already begun to effect a profound change in our philosophy. Those who take note of and study their dreams can trace in them a certain inherent tendency or view which is akin to the primitive, irrational standpoint. It cannot be said that the unconscious mind, as encountered in dreams, is opposed to civilization. But it is

[1] WINWOOD READE developed an original and illuminating appraisal of civilization in his great work *The Martyrdom of Man*, published in 1872. It is significant that he, too, discovered this other standpoint in the heart of Africa.

ruthlessly critical of every prejudice, influence, or affectation which has kept, or could keep, the subject estranged from his natural being. The whole backward movement of the dream process towards infancy seems, indeed, to be motivated by an unconscious undertow pulling towards the origin or source.

Overriding this irrational, natural mind with its independent activity, civilized man evolved a rational, purposeful will with a preference for plans or schemes calculated to increase its orbit of power. The more civilized we become, the more completely are we enveloped in a hegemony programme elaborated by the will. This development has reached a point when the deepest of all human mysteries, Consciousness and Being, are relegated to a purely functional level, as more or less mechanical adjuncts to a set of active systems worked and controlled by the will. Since these systems make up the complicated network of civilized existence the will has come to be the slave rather than the master of the systems it produced. Thus consciousness, will, and being are known to Western man, only in so far as they are harnessed to some plan or objective such as driving a car, mastering a technique, running a business, or planning a 'new order'. If they are not immediately useful to him as the charioteers of some mental mechanism, he tends to have no further concern for their welfare. As an indispensable factor of the will-programme, consciousness is like a light controlled by a switch, but as the mysterious, unfathomable essence of all experience and, therefore, as something in and for itself, it has not yet been born in the West. Our world still lacks that moment of unimaginable radiance when the Bodhisattva is born from the world lotus.

When we compare this hegemony of the rational, planning will with the spontaneous play of the child's mind, or the irrational, meandering activity of the primitive's, we realize, with a pang, how many fair tracts of human experience have been invaded and brought within the orbit of the civilizing will.

Thus the need of salvaging repressed parts of our original nature in the psychological sphere accords well with our national resolve to release the oppressed, weaker nations of the Continent from a tyrannical will.

5

There are many signs warning us that the will, married to intellect, which has been the paramount function in creating civilization, has already become destructive and suicidal. We might even regard the motor car with its ever-increasing power, speed, and appetite for victims, as a symbolical expression of this Frankenstein development of the civilizing will. Its standardization, its ubiquity, and its inhuman, ruthless efficiency — all express the invincible advance of the conqueror of nature. But the whole of Western civilization, as far as its power extends, can be regarded as a vast machine; a machine that has begun to turn on its maker with a wholesale destructiveness. We need only mention the attempt to hold down production by the insane counter-measures of destroying vast accumulations of essential foodstuffs while millions of workers and unemployed were living on the edge of starvation. Or the whirligig acceleration of urbanized building development which represents a cumulative migration of families from the productive peasant life on the soil into built-up areas where they are converted into mechanized units. There is the economic labyrinth with its defensive tariffs and exploitation of human labour on the one hand, and its terrible wastage of millions of unemployed, on the other. The whole machinery of civilized life has grown impossibly cumbersome, so that exasperating delays and mechanical obstructions more than offset its increased power and speed.

These signs of mechanical distress have become increasingly evident in the years leading up to the war, while at the same time the world has been deafened by a chorus of ideological threats and martial boasting from nations whose avowed aim is the overturning of the existing civilized order.

It is impossible to believe either in the socialistic creed of Nazi Germany or in the communistic experiment of Russia. Neither régime has shown any interest in individual freedom, and no capitalist state has ever exploited or enslaved its subjects with such complete cynicism. After the arranged double invasion of Poland, the murderous attack on Finland, and the wholesale brigandage of Germany and Italy, no one, except those whose minds have been numbed by ceaseless propaganda, would be likely to imagine that a cure for the suffering and chaos of our world could ever come from these discredited systems. It is an error inherent in political propaganda to imagine that one type of collectivist ideology is to be preferred to another. The truth is that any set of ideas, however attractive in theory, must inevitably produce unhappiness and social evil, if imposed upon the toiling communities of mankind with a tyrannical Gilgamish will. Civilization has come to mean a vast plan and, in so far as we are identified with and contained in the plan, we assume this to be our fate.

The essential values of Christianity, on the other hand, have never been identical with this vast mechanized will. Tertullian made the discovery that the soul was naturally Christian. In so far as the Church has been true to the spirit of its Founder, it has safeguarded the natural piety of man's original nature, guarding and sheltering it against the world and its dæmonic power-mechanisms. But whenever the civilizing will has extended its orbit of power over other peoples and cultures, under the banner of Christian progress, it has been prone to show more of the dæmonic spirit of Hitler than of the humane spirit of Christ.

The logic of this is clear. So long as the essential Christian values are honoured, the soul of man is protected to some extent from enslavement. But let the Christian Church and the Christian view of life only lose its traditional authority, as it has done in Germany and Russia, and the whole destructive power of the machine falls with deadly force upon the individual human soul.

We cannot but be struck by the fact that recent revolutions in European history, whatever their ostensible political origin or aim, have revealed an insane anti-Christian fury. This revolt against religion made its first appearance in the French Revolution. But it was the same in Russia, in Spain, in Portugal, and now, once again, in Nazi Germany.

Although these revolutions were directed apparently against the existing political structure, yet a terrible ferocity was reserved for the Christian Church and its priests. We must conclude, therefore, that behind these volcanic upheavals there lurked an unconscious pagan lawlessness which sought to throw off the last vestige of restraint.

Secession from traditional Christian authority leads down to the unchristianized pagan residue in the unconscious, and in times of revolution this dæmonic spirit is unloosed. The history of pogroms, bloody wars, and persecutions, pursued in the name of Christ, shows that Christianity, as such, possesses no reliable safeguard.

When the dæmonic spirit gains control on the animal level, the result is a blind unconscious rush, like a stampede. But when it rises up into the realm of ideas, the infinitely more dangerous conflagration to be seen in Nazi Germany to-day, is liable to ensue. The unholy alliance of a political ideology with the all-or-none dynamics of the unreasoning beast, produces a monstrous force which combines the cold-blooded cruelty of the absolute with the renegade violence of a rogue elephant.

There is an important difference between the sustained cruelty of a civilized nation and the savage outbursts of uncivilized peoples. When the savage is cruel he is as devilish as possible. But when sated with cruelty, he stops and allows his decent human feelings to emerge again. Civilized cruelty is worse because it is done on principle and merit is claimed for it. The savage, with his relatively modest appetite for cruelty, would soon be disgusted by the systematic brutality of a Nazi concentration camp. He himself would be incapable of such sustained bestiality. Hence the word 'savagery' as applied to Nazi dæmonism is an unmerited flattery.

6

The present chaos of Europe proves that no amount of collective organization can, by itself, safeguard a human community from dæmonic infection. How, then, can the danger be countered? On the animal level we know that a panic or stampede can be averted by a timely and resolute conscious attitude. We need a word to distinguish consciousness as the effective expression of individual command, from the state of general awareness. As an effective power, consciousness has been won by individuality at the cost of suffering and self-discipline. Like the music of Orpheus, the authority of consciousness has an almost magical effect upon the chaotic unconscious. Man would long since have perished by his own madness, had it not been for the creation of this royal centre of individual power. Circle about this problem as we may, we arrive inevitably at the conclusion that the perilous infection I have called collective dæmonism, is cured by only one thing: individual consciousness.

If the reader should happen to be a golfer, he can test this out the next time he finds himself lashing out in a state of irritated frustration. Instead of pursuing an innocent ball with ignoble and hurried blows, let him stop in his tracks, invite reason to return to her throne, and calmly consider what kind of shot is required, and the best way to play it. This ascent from a purely animal level to a state of conscious command, produces a remarkable and instantaneous result. This example is relevant because the appalling difficulty of golf lies in the fact that the abandoned joy of hitting with all one's might — a joy which appeals to the most primitive elements in one's nature — has to be directed by a firm yet flexible higher control. The reason that an otherwise normal being can be reduced to a state of neurotic anxiety by a golf ball on a tee, is because a duel is being fought within between blind animal energy and controlling consciousness.

Since the problem of dæmonism, at whatever level, challenges a countering development of conscious responsibility, I cannot believe that the political sphere will be found to be an exception to the general rule. From this reasoning, it would follow that those societies which cultivate the development of individual responsibility and civic courage will, at the same time, possess the only reliable safeguard against the danger of mass-regression towards the primitive.

We see a natural grouping of sympathetic nations emerging out of the flood. The British Commonwealth of Nations, the United States, Switzerland, Turkey, the Chinese Republic, the reviving peoples of France, Poland, Czecho-Slovakia, Holland, Greece, Belgium, and the Scandinavian countries are being drawn together by invisible ties. We know that these peoples belong together and must go forward like members of a brotherhood, to cultivate the world that survives.

A different and more sinister accord unites Germany, Russia, Italy, and Japan with their immediate satellites. These are just as clearly informed by a lethal spirit of oppression. In the one fraternity of nations the principle of individuality has either won, or is winning, for itself the central place of honour. In the other group of powers, individuality has been silenced, tortured, and oppressed. The machine-like organization of human beings is complete; but nowhere in the minutely-ordered programme is there any place for the totality, Man; man as he actually is.

This is the state of the world as I see it, and this view is not an over-simplification. If the respect for individuality be taken as the acid test, it will be found that the states which are now banded together to partition the world between them have, without exception, broken that covenant of faith with the individual subject upon which reasonable government is supported. The result is that the whole weight of the inhuman machine falls upon the subject without mitigation.

Once again, therefore, we come to the problem of the balance between the essential needs of the individual and the efficient organization of the civilizing machine. The longing for a holy day expresses a vital need of the soul. This need found a socialized expression in the divinely ordained Sabbath; a space in which the human soul could breathe an upper air, and find some respite from the unavoidable claims of the machine. It is not specific to the modern conditions of urbanized existence, since, even in the midst of the desert, it required the authority of heaven, thundering from Sinai, to stop the implacable machine for one day in seven.

We have already reached a point when organization and executive ability are more highly prized than original genius. Schemes mount and extend, until our lives are ordered and determined by executive control. We accept this control as an essential condition of our war effort, but in the midst of all our planning the truth must not be forgotten that God belongs to no plan. He cannot be caught in a net nor housed in a programme. To create a new Sabbath means, then, to make a hospitable place 'where the youthful God may delight in the garden of the soul'. If we cannot succeed in this, our best efforts will be denied the blessing of heaven. Not only shall we find our highly organized plans coming to strange grief, but the divine dynamis, the God-value, will be liable to go over into that same dæmonic form which now possesses, and soon must shatter, the Third Reich. For when we exclude every possibility of experience that does not accord with some rationally enforced plan, we not only deny the reality of God, we also, in effect, become possessed by the devil.

This is the desperate spiritual danger that attends the godless, totalitarian bid for world-power. The attempt to eradicate individuality, as a free principle, means that the irrational spiritual element of the unconscious is imprisoned underground. Behind every heroic deed and individual sacrifice, there is the certain knowledge that if ever our proud freedom should be sacrificed to dæmonic power, the light of our world will go out. Just as we had to create a united will stronger than Hitler's, we must also make a will stronger than the machine-will, if we are to stop its accelerating rush towards chaos. It is unavoidable that the demand for efficiency should be constantly rising. But this entails a correspondingly intensified strain upon the psyche. Every man carrying a burden too heavy for him, has heard his own heart telling him to return to a simpler manner of life, to give up the expensive façade of civilized fuss, and to reduce life to its essentials.

Some simplification of life seems indeed likely to be forced upon us as the result of our acceptance of Hitler's challenge. Through facing the evil, we may stumble across the remedy for our present sickness. For the very thing Hitler tried to extinguish is the light which burns in the individual soul, and which reveals to a man his own truth. Those who are too blind, or too unbending to admit the necessity for a vital change, will always resent a forced descent to the simple realities of existence. But many will welcome a life which can be enjoyed and enriched by the million-year-old primitive within, a life which allows things that have long been repressed in the unconscious to dance once more in the light. We are becoming increasingly critical of the dangerous extraversion of our Western manner of life. The realization that a full time-table is not necessarily a full life already begins to dawn.

A successful American business man, whose whole nervous system was in revolt at the life he was leading, once came to consult me in New York. His eyes shone with a fanatical gleam as he tried to persuade me that all life's problems would be solved if the machinery of civilized life were just a little more perfect and fool-proof. Then at last there would be nothing more to worry about. Everyone would have more leisure and increased opportunities, because the machine would do the things now done by man. He talked at great speed, smoking incessantly and without enjoyment. As he talked he kept a nervous eye on his wrist-watch. Although he had made an appointment and had come some distance in order to consult me, it was only with the greatest difficulty that he could listen to anything I had to say. Like the devotees of Communism or Fascism, he had one consuming need, which was to convince some unprejudiced person that the dæmonic thing which possessed him was the final expression of human progress and enlightenment. I told him he was chasing a mirage and that, in his attempt to perfect the machinery of civilized life, he was himself being devoured by the machine.

I speak of this aspect of collectivity as insane, because the men who are caught up by it are no longer free. Psychologically, the man in a gold rush, or a power-rush, is like a man tied to the tail of a charging bull. But although there is primeval exhilaration in such enjoyment of power it darkens the reason and excludes freedom. In psychiatric practice it is not uncommon for an obsessional patient, or one subject to compulsive dæmonic states, to dream of being in some such predicament. He may find himself in a motor car with brakes that refuse to work, or riding a horse that is out of control. This kind of imagery is so common that one might conclude that the control and direction of psychic energy is the most urgent problem of the present day.

To be carried away by a mood, or a storm of affect, to be forced to do things by the unconscious for which we are immediately ashamed, to expose ourselves to ridicule by senseless fits of irritation or by losing our heads when we ought to keep calm —what are all these but temporary failures in control, or in other words, defective consciousness? Everyone blames himself for these lapses, but the affect subsides, the rationalized justification is allowed to pass, and no one imagines that anything could be done about it. Yet, in effect, one has been gripped and carried away by a primitive activation of the unconscious and, for the time being, savagery has reigned.

The reason we do not take these explosions too seriously is because we know from experience that they are short-lived. But it is a different matter when we have to deal with a destructive mood which seizes a whole nation, because the consequences are incalculably greater. But the cause, i.e. consciousness becoming submerged and possessed by the unconscious, is the same. We are conditioned, in fact, by the general principle that failure to adapt to a given situation with an adapted or differentiated function is paid for by an explosion of affect.

When an individual allows himself too much licence, indulging in storms of violent affect with insufficient cause, we begin to avoid his company. We cannot be bothered with a man who is too undisciplined. If a man refuses to take responsibility for his unconscious motivations he tends to become a miserable victim of fate. On the other hand, every man who has achieved great things has gone through times when, like Jacob with the angel, he has had to wrestle with dæmonic effects from the unconscious.

Since individuality remains our only valid criterion, we must conclude that taking responsibility for one's unconscious motivation is the royal road to psychological maturity. It is often recounted how some famous golfer broke his clubs in blind fury before mastering the game; how some celebrated surgeon had to overcome trembling of the hands before every operation; how some great actor is stricken with stage-fright before every performance; it is probably true to say that no man ever became a master in the truest sense of the word, without having to overcome affective chaos in one form or another. Everyone knows that barricades of neurotic resistance have to be surmounted before one finally comes to grips with an important task.

From the foregoing description it might be assumed that the whole function of the unconscious was to oppose and harass consciousness. This appearance comes from the difficulty we have in accepting our whole nature, our becoming, as well as our being. As the dynamic aspect of the whole mental process, the unconscious presents much the same opposition to consciousness as would an imperfectly understood machine to the person striving to master it. This analogy, however, is only partly true, since the unconscious is also the potential, emergent, unborn aspect of life. As these potentialities strive for some integrated expression, they find their path blocked by conscious prejudice or repression. The problem of 'dæmonism' begins when the integrating power of consciousness is deficient, so that the unconscious sweeps across the threshold like a flood. In dreams this crisis is often symbolized by a whirlpool, an inundation by the sea, or a devouring animal.

In representing the possessing complex, sometimes as a machine, and sometimes as a dæmon or savage, the dream-mind is clearly inviting us to distinguish between grappling with a mechanism and dealing with a dæmonic will. Notwithstanding our intellectual qualms, the unconscious often represents the obsessional complex as a dæmon with a well-defined personality. The habit of scientific thinking is to represent unconscious urgencies and strivings as mechanisms. It is certainly simpler and less problematical. But when an individual has wrestled for years with an obsession, which has striven for the possession of his soul with dæmonic persistence and cunning, it is understandable that he finds the dream-personification of the complex more true to life than the doctor's scientific explanation. The dream-mind tends naturally to personify dynamic psychic factors, because, in point of fact, every psychic function has a specific character and objective, and must, therefore, possess its own peculiar standpoint.

7

Viewing the unconscious, therefore, as the unaccepted dynamism of our personality, we can see how Hitler could personify a certain function, whose claim to absoluteness appears to consciousness like that of an unscrupulous foreign invader. In dream metaphor, the Germans represent the enemy we have to encounter, i.e. the force or problem we would prefer to ignore, but which could easily get the better of us, if we failed to accept its challenge. Besides this, the German leader also represents a factor that is intoxicated and possessed; something, therefore, that is liable to exercise a dæmonic effect upon anything that is weak and suggestible. But we must also bear in mind that the dream often holds up a mirror to consciousness in which the most favoured conscious function appears as the enemy. It may even be that the tyrannical function is the one upon which the subject most depends, and by which he earns his livelihood. Jung has called this the collectively-valid function. Most people would regard it as their most valuable asset. Presumably most Germans so regard Hitler. Hitler, after all, is in the direct line of civilizing German conquerors from Charlemagne to Wilhelm II. The continuity of type is undeniable, and the march of the German war-lords has invariably been proclaimed as the march of progress and civilization. The German will is felt by every German to be the civilizing will. It is the Gilgamish phenomenon, in its most emphatic statement. But the heroic qualities of the civilizing hero are apparent only to those who can sun themselves under his protection, and can follow where he leads. To the rest of the world they are invisible.

When, therefore, the dream-mind (which, after all, is the natural mind) depicts the ascendancy of one civilizing function over all other functions in terms of the Gilgamish-Hitler type, we may be sure it is uttering a warning which we ignore at our peril. Individuality demands wholeness and, if this goal be missed, the true meaning of life is forfeited. One-sidedness, even when the exclusive function is the one which brings fame and success, is essentially inimical to wholeness. A well-balanced and sound mind depends upon a balanced interaction of functions, a condition that is governed by the law of reciprocity, upon which the whole order of nature is established.

Such a mind will never thrive in a collective atmosphere where fanaticism is prized, and the principle of individuality dishonoured. We shall not wipe out the German threat to Christendom until we have released the millions of German children who have been trained to believe in Hitler's robot as the ideal of virile manhood. In English-speaking lands the ideal of all-round achievement is instinctively honoured, and our ideas of education are largely shaped on this model. Nevertheless, English people still dream of Hitler; a fact which would argue that the collective demand for specialized adaptation has succeeded in producing a Hitler-function within the psyche, the dæmonic effect of which is to imperil our ideal of individuation.

The conclusion can be stated quite simply as follows. Unless our personal philosophy is based upon the ideal of wholeness, we are liable to be drawn down to the machine conception of man and to measure our competence by the machine standard. A conscious acceptance of the ideal of wholeness whets the appetite for adult education and for the fullest experience of life. Naturally, a specialized psychological education is not a feasible proposition for more than a few. But every man who takes himself in hand, with the aim of turning his moods and dæmonic states to good account, is on the road to psychological maturity.

When the Prime Minister said: 'Never in the field of human conflict was so much owed by so many to so few' he expressed in a single phrase the inner core of our faith. The Royal Air Force has claimed and won mastery in the air, through that one central factor which Hitler negates — free and self-reliant individual quality. Hitler denied the significance and freedom of the individual. The Royal Air Force is the answer of the free peoples to that denial; an answer that will ring down the future ways, as the gallant sword-clash of Arthur's knights still rings in our ears to-day.

CHAPTER IX

FACTORS GOVERNING MORALE

I

BEFORE it is possible to discuss the factors which determine morale, we must know what this intangible element really is. The word is commonly used to denote the moral condition or behaviour of the civil population or troops. And when we say moral condition, we are not referring to their behaviour as judged by some abstract ethical standard, but rather to their firmness, steadiness, and willingness to continue in the fight or work upon which they are engaged. The word comes from the Latin *mos, moris* = custom; plural *mores* = manners, morals, character.

This derivation is suggestive, because it leads to the rather un-expected point of view that morality is fundamentally a matter of custom and tradition. Good behaviour, in other words, is something to which one becomes accustomed. But though it seems to belong to that part of our psychology which is gained through adaptation, there is more in it than the ability to maintain a certain kind of behaviour. It has also an inner emotional coefficient, without which the accustomed behaviour has no inherent purpose. This emotional root is essentially ancestral in character. It comes from the sense of being supported by the ancestors; as though the ancestors were still living within the heart, or whatever organ it is that commands us to a certain standard of courage or endurance. Customs in the sense of *mores* can also be said to be ancestral tradition. This combination brings us nearer to the meaning we seek. But here again it depends upon how we regard the handing down of customs and ethical standards from one generation to the next. If tradition is conceived as the passive taking over of an already existing pattern merely for the sake of convenience, this does not cover the emotional meaning of morale. If, however, we conceive it in the Chinese sense as the honouring of the living ancestral spirits who participate actively in all the things done in the traditional way, we then come very near to the heart of the matter.

Chinese wisdom gives very great value to personality, because it is the actual container of the ancestors. It also teaches that the man who follows the way of the ancestors possesses an authority and integrity which the uprooted man lacks.

How does this enlighten our judgment in the issue between Germany and Britain? We are not ancestor-worshippers, nor do we seek to establish our morale by conducting war in the ancestral way, or with ancestral equipment. Once again the answer lies in the subtle factor: spirit or attitude. Ancestral piety is not a matter of imitation or reproduction. Fundamentally, it is a valuation which honours the essence of what the ancestors have achieved. From another point of view, it is the preservation of the stream of psychical continuity which flows to us from the earliest gleam of consciousness through the ancestral generations.

The magical value attaching to the king resides primarily in the fact that he embodies the stream of tribal continuity. The Pharaoh is immortal, because he is the life-stream of the race. The king-sacrificer is the embodiment of sacred tradition. Therefore he cannot die.

It is possible that it is the unconscious influence of this continuity which accounts for the stability of behaviour characteristic of animals and humans when contained in their indigenous haunts or habitual tasks. Conversely, the suicidal recklessness, so liable to overtake migrating hordes, or the ethical deterioration which often besets uprooted individuals, may derive from the paralysing sense that the continuity is broken.

Thus we see how any sudden break with the past is dangerous. Hence the psychological significance of the Fifth Commandment. To dishonour the parents is impious, not because of an arbitrary fiat from heaven, but because human wisdom and morale are contained in the stream that runs through the generations. That the idea of piety tends to become identified with the tested ancestral way is revealed in the appendix to the Commandment, 'that thy days may be long upon the land which the Lord thy God giveth thee'.

The *raison d'être* of the Commandments is thus found to reside in the age-old adapted structure of the psyche. When we speak of the ancestors we could as well speak of the racial unconscious. Hence, the one perfectly reasonable explanation for the fact that the unconscious becomes a very real problem is that we have to forge a new link with the ancestors. When we say that a people or a class is decadent, we mean that this feeling of continuity with the ancestors (i.e. morale) has lost its reality. A people declines because the ancestors are no longer interested in their welfare, as though the vigilant servants in the unconscious had absconded. Such a decline, as we see in the case of Italy to-day, may become a kind of symptomatic repudiation of an impossible régime. Mussolini's favourite jibe at the 'decadent democracies' was, in itself, highly suspicious, since we know that men are prone to project upon their adversaries their own unconscious condition.

Nobody, on the other hand, could reasonably claim that the Germans or Italians are decadent as a race. It is natural for a people to become apathetic towards a régime which constantly goads them towards vast objectives, concerning the validity of which no one is allowed to form his own judgment. The following description by Wallace Deuel, the well-known correspondent of the *Chicago Daily News*, gives an unprejudiced picture of German morale at the present time:

> It is true [he writes] that Germany has risen again, but the price in wear and tear of the people's nerves has been appalling, and millions of Germans have ceased to believe, if they ever did, that it is possible to hope for rewards which would be worth the price.
> The German people are tired as few people in the world have ever been tired without breaking down. In a single generation they have gone through a major war, a starvation blockade and a catastrophic defeat. They have had two revolutions. They have had their currency wiped out altogether once and have been seriously threatened with the same fate again.
> They've had the same exhausting and disillusioning experiences of depression as the rest of the world has had, and now they have entered on a new war.
> They are winning all the battles in the new war, it is true. But they won all the battles in the last war, too — all except the last — and they have never forgotten it.
> Until the last battle in this war has been fought and won it will be hard for millions of Germans to believe it will be won at all. And, besides, unless that last battle is fought and won

soon enough what good will victory be to the Germans? The longer the war lasts the more the Germans will wonder if it is worth fighting.

Scores of times I have seen columns of motorized troops pouring through Berlin and half a dozen other cities on their way to the front, first towards Poland and later towards the West. But among all these columns I have only seen and heard one lorry-full of men singing. All the others sat in silence.

And nine-tenths of the people on the sidewalks did not even turn their heads to watch the troops. I have never heard a spontaneous cheer for passing troops except when normal parades were held.

I was in two of the principal streets in Berlin for the first half hour after the news became known that France had asked for terms. At last, I thought, I should see some normal human reaction. It was, after all, one of the greatest military triumphs of all times.

But there was no reaction to be seen, none at all. The Berliners looked neither jubilant, nor happy, nor even relieved. They looked just the same as they had looked for more than six years. They just looked tired. The second world war is a war without cheers as far as Germany is concerned.

An American newspaper correspondent who has lived in Germany for the last six years, and has had to adapt to censorship requirements, will hardly be accused of falsifying his evidence through a naive indulgence in wishful thinking. Moreover, this account tallies with other descriptions of war-time Germany. But although the accuracy of Mr. Deuel's account need not be doubted his explanation is harder to accept. Fatigue is a physiological condition that is capable of speedy restoration, given a sufficiency of sleep, rest, and nourishment. But the state described above is one in which men and women no longer participate in the historical events through which they are passing. Absence of response on this wholesale scale is inconceivable in any country as the result of fatigue. But when we remember how the Germans have for years been drilled and driven, their reaction becomes intelligible. The difference between men who are herded along in some vast conveyance according to plan and, let us say, the spirit of the Greeks defending their native land, cannot be expressed in statistical quantities. Yet the totalitarian habit of mind, in its blindness to the spiritual factor, continually ignores this vital difference.

In this connection I should like to quote the dream of a friend of mine, a gallant spirit in whom ancestral piety and valour still glow. Her dream was as follows:

> The Germans are invading England and the vast hulk of their new 'invading machine' approaches the coast. It is a colossal floating fortress and is supposed to be invincible. It towers above the shore, with a great cranelike arm projecting before it, along which the invading troops are supposed to land.
>
> We get into a small rowing-boat and row quickly out to sea, though we must risk passing close to the invasion machine. It is, however, so huge that its guns cannot be trained on anything so small or so near as our little boat. We are saved by our insignificance. We see the soldiers swarming along the projecting arm as the hulk reaches the shore. But, suddenly, the whole thing begins to break up, as it meets the gunfire from the shore. Actually it is terribly vulnerable, because it is so huge and unwieldly. The soldiers are thrown into the sea far below.

Whatever else can be said about this dream, its chief significance for the dreamer was to prepare her attitude for a possible invasion-attempt upon this island. Yet the fact that it is couched in the classical mythological idiom gives the dream a certain impersonal character. Its value, like that of many dreams, hinges upon the capacity of the unconscious to foreshadow the inherent tendency of coming events.

It must be self-evident that all who incline to base their estimate of victory or defeat upon a purely quantitative evaluation would feel that the game was up. Such folk are to be found not only on the side of the enemy. In every land, and in every class, there are people whose minds are opaque to spiritual factors. They assume, in spite of most eloquent historical evidence to the contrary, that mass, weight, and number must decide every issue. These are our defeatists. They are to be found in the golf club, in the consulting-room, in the street, and in the family circle. Frequently they say nothing, but their mere presence is like a sigh of defeat.

My friend, the dreamer, is naturally courageous, though at times the terrifying power of the enemy had preyed upon her mind. Her dream is the ancestral response to her need. It says to her: 'In that affair between David and Goliath everything seemed to favour the giant. The power of Spain, too, must have towered above the English fleet in Elizabeth's time just as fearfully as the German power towers above that of Britain to-day.' Mythological and historical parallels cluster around this vast and invincible machine. It even recalls the Tower of Babel, and the tree that reached to heaven in Nebuchadnezzar's dream. By its own unmanageable vastness it is doomed. Like the unwieldy reptiles of the mesozoic swamps, this machine is unsympathetic to the natural order. The million-year-old unconscious has naturally seen many such attempts to crush and overpower the human spirit by the power of the machine, and it is not impressed. Against a spirit that can neither be paralysed nor intimidated such a machine even appears somewhat ludicrous. If there is one human comedy which all the hosts of heaven crowd to see, it is surely the spectacle of the vainglorious bully being rolled in the mud by his small but invincible victim.

This 'invasion machine' epitomizes the whole German war-machine into which the enemy has put all his hopes. For years he has been preparing it. Every thought, every activity, every hope for the future has been centred in this vast machine. While it was being prepared the insistent feeling of inferiority and despair was banished and, with the paranoid's venom against an encircling ring of enemies, he left nothing undone and nothing to chance. The war-machine was built up and organized to the last insignificant detail. Like every monster created by human ingenuity, it developed its own inherent momentum. When it had devoured Germany, it broke loose and devoured the whole of Europe. Though not quite all. A small island remained which refused to be crushed.

The dream episode starts at this point. The 'unseen watcher' on high says: 'This thing is excessive. It has gone far enough.' The gunfire from the shore is the signal for its dissolution. Such things are not meant to survive. Unaccepted inferiority gave them birth: hence open shame becomes their inevitable fate. They carry in their own make-up their imminent dissolution. The dream counsel seems to be saying: 'Trust to the boat you have made. Be content with your own truth, as David trusted to his sling. That works.' A machine, after all, is only a machine. It is not even as adaptable as an insect. It is limited to the one purpose for which it was made and, when the heavens fail to provide the required conditions, it becomes derelict. The Italians are also good mechanics and trusted implicitly like the Germans in their excellent war machine. But they had no stomach for fighting: so the great empire, which Mussolini gave so proudly to his king, was reduced to sand and foam.

The dream is concerned with the problem of morale. It renews the spirit, not by falsification of facts, or by shouting insults at the enemy, but by the only effective means: historical allusion. Every day one talks with men and women who, in spite of the most terrifying evidence of ruthless enemy power, carry in their breasts a song of victory. How do they know that Britain will win? For, at bottom, belief is a kind of inner knowledge. The heart knows it, and my friend's dream tells us how it knows. The unconscious has its own peculiar logic which is based upon age-long experience. The invasion machine is vulnerable, just because it is assumed to be invincible. It is an enormous container. Every German is contained by it.

Over against this monster, the dream-thought sets a rowing boat, the machine by which man has been able to adapt to the boundless dæmonic element (in dream symbolism the sea is the unconscious). The hybristic tendency of the Nazi mind seeks to superimpose an arbitrary plan, or organization, upon the living fabric of human society. Power psychology possesses no means of adaptation. It has only one method: to impose its scheme by force, if necessary by terror. A machine-mind that has no means of adaptation to the fluid, irrational elements of reality is inherently vulnerable. With every conceivable modulation the voice of evolution says: 'Only that which adapts survives.'

The crane-like arm is a classical dream-symbol. It is, of course, basically phallic. But when we consider such manifest symbols of power as the gun, rifle, spear, sword, sceptre, baton, staff, etc., all of which bear the connotation of extending the subjective orbit of power over the object, yet are manifestly phallic, we have to admit that the psychological significance of phallic symbolism has more to do with the idea of extension of power, or mastery, than with the sexual function as such.

In the dream context, therefore, which is indisputably concerned with the mechanism of power, the symbol of the crane-arm represents the means as well as the motive by which the German power-machine attempts to extend its power over this country. The whole futile longing for *Lebensraum* on the part of a sterile, aggressive régime, is symbolized in that crane arm. It is a fantastic lust which has nothing to do with ordinary appeasable human appetite. It is the one means with which the German machine-mind approaches every objective.

The rowing boat is the symbol of the evolution of consciousness through the ages. Originally man had to wait for a favourable wind. He could only·go where the wind took him. But as he developed consciousness and will, he was able to invent a keel, rudder, foresail, and mainsail, wherewith to follow the course of his will and choice rather than that dictated by the wind of impulse. Thus the boat is a reminder of that adaptable conscious attitude which maintains a flexible relation to the supporting power of the unconscious.

So long as we can remain responsive, adaptable, and human, while our enemy persists in being rigid, the essential logic of a relativist world cannot be gainsaid. The machine must break up. A certain rash forecast made by German colleagues in the summer of 1939, comes to my mind. They said: 'If Hitler leads the German army against the Western powers there will be revolution within six months.' This prediction, though inaccurate in point of time, had, I believe, the same essential logic behind it. It naturally assumed an effective resistance in the West. Without this external condition, the internal instability of Hitler's machine would not be challenged. So long as there is no effective opposition, the monster merely tramples upon everything in its path. The factor of morale begins to count only when the machine is brought to a standstill and the enemy has to fight for his life. Nothing in Hitler's career has given us any ground to suppose that he has any relish for an even fight. The Germans are not too blind to see the sawdust running out of the puppet Caesar in Africa. Hence they cannot ignore the possibility that in spite of German superiority in power and military organization, the imitator of Charlemagne and Frederick the Great may be afflicted by his 'haunting hysteria' when he meets an opponent who will neither be crushed nor intimidated.

2

In order to estimate correctly the morale of the German nation we should need to collect evidence from many different levels and over a considerable stretch of time. Space, however, forbids an exhaustive review. It must suffice if I cite certain impressions which confirm the rigid, absolutist character of the present German monster. According to Dr. Rauschning's personal testimony it was precisely this quality of obstinate unrelatedness which finally convinced him that the Nazi revolution was bent on universal destruction. Commenting on the Nazi failure to adapt to existing facts and realities, he writes:

> The same failure attended the Danzig policy. And in this case, the opportunity existed for a broad practical solution of the special political problems, a solution which would have cost National Socialism nothing, if revolutionary destruction at home and abroad had not mattered more to it than all the advantages of a far-seeing conception.[1]

The case of Danzig was by no means singular. Germany was in a position to bring decisive influence to bear over a very large field. Many European problems awaited solution with which, as the predominant power on the Continent, she was fitted to deal. But instead of skilled diplomacy and good neighbourly offices, National Socialism could only produce this crushing machine whose mere existence must arouse universal hatred and suspicion. The pathetic part of German unrelatedness is that the German himself is completely opaque to the actual state of affairs. Dr. Rauschning writes:

> The country is intellectually so cut off from Europe in every field, that reality in Germany is already a different thing from reality in the rest of Europe. The German honestly thinks he is a realist and mistakes his own illusions for reality. In the growing impatience, the realization of plans is regarded as

[1] HERMANN RAUSCHNING, *Germany's Revolution of Destruction*, p. 259.

possible simply because it is desired. There lies the greatest danger to Germany's future. In spite of Cabinet meetings and military discussions, nobody is able to convince the hysterical fantasts of the country of the reality of things they do not want to see.[1]

Confirming this impression the author cites the following passage from the *Völkischer Beobachter*:

We National Socialists do not believe in economic laws; we believe in the creativeness of our race, because we feel in it the dynamic will to creativeness which exists among us.[2]

Auto-suggestion may obscure the face of reality for a considerable time, but in the end reality wins; usually as a result of a more or less violent collision with the very laws which have been denied.

This unreal or fantastic condition is, of course, another symptom of the state of possession. But what is not visible from a distance is the undermining effect of widespread illusion on the moral condition of the people. Dr. Rauschning's comment is as follows:

It is impossible to escape the strong feeling that under the National Socialist régime some of the finest German qualities are beginning to disappear — the absolute reliability, the seriousness and honesty of outlook, and the selfless devotion to duty. There are many signs that justify the fear that superficiality and indifference to good work are bringing us down from our past technical and intellectual standards. These are bad omens for a new war. . . .

The new conception of obedience and loyalty has been mechanized and materialized and, like everything National Socialism has produced in the ethical and spiritual sphere, lacks the creative spiritual roots of free personality.[3]

Perhaps the most serious of all the unrealities which Nazi fanaticism has fostered is the idea that the democracies were effete and unable to resist attack. This illusion springs from the inability of the 'invasion machine' mentality to recognize or compute the spiritual factor in human combat. It believes that victory invariably falls to the side of mass and mechanism. It is

[1] loc. cit., p. 155.   [2] loc. cit., p. 155.   [3] loc. cit., p. 166.

doubtful whether anyone really believes this in his heart. It is rather a state of mind that is generated through becoming identified with some containing institution or organization. A vaguely cynical spirit always seems to haunt an institution that demands complete suppression of individual desire. This sacrifice of desire on specious institutional grounds is often attended by a certain morbid exaltation.[1] But unless the heart ordains the sacrifice, the result is cynicism. The power of the world has won and the heart's undying flame has been denied, but no one really believes this to be the right solution. At bottom, therefore, the cynic is simply a spiritual defeatist.

This cynical misconception is perfectly reflected in the following statement offered as a condensation of Hitler's views:

> Our opponents would always be democracies and democracies alone, for the simple reason that they were vulnerable. We must always go in search of weaker opponents, and make friends of the dangerous ones.[2]

In somewhat the same vein Dr. Rauschning records the following illuminating conversation with Hitler:

> Hitler had told me that morning his view of the value of treaties. He was ready, he said, to sign anything. He was ready to guarantee any frontier and to conclude a non-aggression pact with anyone. It was a simpleton's idea that expedients of this sort were not to be availed of, because the day might come when some formal agreement had to be broken.[3]

This is not the conversation of a man who submits to the laws and necessities of human society. It is the bellowing of a Polyphemus or a Goliath who believes his strength to be invincible. We have only to compare the Dictators with men of ordinary human proportions, to realize that, in some essential fashion, the former have ceased to be solid. It is almost impossible not to think of them as blown up, like a balloon which, when pricked, must suddenly explode. Detach these men from their containing organization and they would appear scarcely human. This is

---

[1] This holds true for institutions other than German.
[2] RAUSCHNING, *Germany's Revolution of Destruction*, p. 263.
[3] ibid., p. 251.

not due to the illusory projections of war-time. Professional soldiers, like Badoglio, for instance, maintain their credible human proportions, and we can respect their fate. Whereas their opposite numbers in the black or brown-shirt hierarchies are insubstantial, two-dimensional figures, who make much noise, but in action prove themselves wholly lacking in solid qualities. Contained within their hypnotic institutional envelopes, the leaders of Fascism and Nazism have become grotesque personalities, like figures in a circus procession. They are natural caricatures. Even Chaplin, with his inimitable art, cannot make them more ludicrous and incredible than they actually are. Their essential unreality seems to transcend the limits of fantastic exaggeration. Personality that is tempered in the fire of human relationship is real. But these men are already dissolved in a flood of boasting words with which they vainly strive to falsify the verdict of history.

Dr. Rauschning records a similar impression of trumpery insubstantiality concerning the boasted feats of reconstruction in Hitler's Germany. He writes:

> Not one of the tasks of national renewal has found a genuine solution capable of enduring. In every field, substitutes for genuine solutions have been made to serve. In some of the most elementary tasks, the leaders have clearly not even realized the flimsy character of their work.[1]

We need not assume that the Germans are oblivious to the meretricious, shoddy character of Nazi achievement. The reactions of the German citizen are probably not unlike those of Dr. Rauschning and Herr Thyssen, only they are censored. Both these men belong to the class trained for leadership. They love their country, and when they saw danger they shouted the alarm. Both tried loyally to give their faith to Hitler, but they could not remain blindfolded. Dr. Rauschning's reaction to Nazi corruption is as follows:

> The parasitism which National Socialism and the 'racialists' ascribe to the Jews,[2] is one of the main characteristics of

[1] loc. cit., p. 123.
[2] The Jews symbolize the inherent sense of inferiority which the Nazis have vainly striven to eradicate.

National Socialism which lives by the parasitic draining of
the life-blood of . . . the nation on which it has fastened.[1]

Herr Thyssen's reaction is direct and passionate. It is especially
significant as coming from the great industrialist by whose potent
aid Hitler was originally enabled to seize the reins of power.
He writes in a letter to Hitler:

> I am opposed to the policy of these latter days. Above all, I
> am opposed to this war, which you have so frivolously launched
> and for which you and your henchmen are responsible. Your
> new policy, Herr Hitler, is dragging Germany into an abyss;
> it will be the ruin of the German people. Turn back while
> there is still time! Your policy, if it is carried out, spells
> *Finis Germaniae!*
> Remember the oath you swore at Potsdam. Give back to the
> Reich a free Parliament; give back to the German people free-
> dom of word and of conscience. Grant the guarantees that
> will give the words 'law and right' a meaning again, so that
> once more treaties and agreements can be based upon good
> faith!
> Then — if it is not too late to avoid new disasters and the use-
> less sacrifice of blood — then Germany may still perhaps
> obtain an honourable peace with her unity preserved.[2]

Dr. Rauschning also recognized that Hitlerized Germany was
like a river in flood and could not be diverted from its headlong
course. He says:

> The National Socialist régime is now the prisoner of its own
> system of domination. It can no more dispense with its pur-
> suit of hegemony, than with its government by violence at
> home. It is following the law of its existence, and cannot be
> diverted from its path either by threats or by good-will.[3]

3

As we ponder over these various observations, a series of
fantastic hypotheses present themselves to the mind. In one, we
have the impression of the German people passive and prone,

[1] *Germany's Revolution of Destruction*, p. 99.
[2] Quoted from the *Daily Telegraph and Morning Post*, May 4th, 1940.
[3] *Germany's Revolution of Destruction*, p. 300.

like a hypnotized hen, with Hitler, the dæmon-possessed shaman, extending his insane line of chalk towards infinity. In another, we see a powerful nation intoxicated with dreams of world-dominion, following Hitler, as the rats, and the whole enchanted procession, followed the pied-piper of Hamelin. In the third, we see Hitler together with the rabble he has let loose, hunting an impossible mythological quarry, thus fulfilling the character of Wotan with his furious host. Finally, we see a great river in flood, bearing Hitler, and everyone else, into chaos.

Our analytical task would be easier if we could place Hitler in a human setting and reduce his destructive potentiality to recognizable human motives. But he is no more a personality. He is merely the voice of chaos. This is illustrated by an astonishing collection of sayings written down by Dr. Rauschning after his conversations with Hitler. Clearly Hitler himself feels everything to be fluid. He talks like someone in a dream-world, where all the sacred landmarks of the past have become grotesquely transformed. In quoting these sayings, Dr. Rauschning explains:

> All this stuff was poured forth with the air of a prophet and creative genius. Hitler seemed to take it for granted that the ideas were his own. He had no notion of their actual origin, believing that he had worked them out himself, and that they were inspirations, the product of his solitude in the mountains . . . they are fragments of various talks.
>
> We are now at the end of the Age of Reason. The intellect has grown autocratic, and has become a disease of life.
>
> Our revolution is not merely a political and social revolution; we are at the outset of a tremendous revolution in moral ideas and in men's spiritual orientation.
>
> Our movement has at last brought the Middle Ages, medieval times, to a close.
>
> We are bringing to a close a straying of humanity.

Concerning truth and conscience, Hitler thinks that:

> The Ten Commandments have lost their validity.
>
> A new age of magic interpretation of the world is coming, of interpretation in terms of the will and not of the intelligence.

There is no such thing as truth, either in the moral or the scientific sense.

Concerning science he thinks that:

The idea of free and unfettered science, unfettered by hypotheses, could only occur in the age of Liberalism. It is absurd.

Science is a social phenomenon, and like every other social phenomenon is limited by the benefit or injury it confers on the community.

Of action:

We Germans, above all, with our long-established habit of brooding and dreaming to excess, needed to be brought back to the great truth that only deeds and perpetual activity give meaning to life.

Every deed has its place, even crime.

All passivity, all inertia, on the other hand, is senseless, inimical to life. From this proceeds the divine right of destroying all who are inert.

The word 'crime' comes from a world of the past. There are positive and negative activities. Every crime in the old sense towers above respectable inactivity. Action may be negative from the viewpoint of the community, and must then be prevented. But it is at least action.

Of the intelligence:

We must distrust the intelligence and the conscience, and must place our trust in our instincts. We have to regain a new simplicity.

People set us down as enemies of the intelligence. We are. But in a much deeper sense than these conceited dolts of *bourgeois* scientists ever dream of.

The two final sayings are so magnificent, that comment stands abashed:

I thank my destiny for saving me from the State-granted privilege of acquiring blinkers in the form of a so-called scientific education. I have been able to steer clear of many naive assumptions. Now I am reaping the benefit. I approach everything with a vast, ice-cold freedom from prejudice.

And:

> Providence has ordained that I should be the greatest liber-
> ator of humanity. I am freeing men from the restraints of an
> intelligence that has taken charge; from the dirty and degrad-
> ing self-mortifications of a chimera called conscience and
> morality, and from the demands of a freedom and personal
> independence which only a few can bear. [1]

I make no apology for quoting liberally from this invaluable
material. For nothing one can ever say about Hitler could
approach, in psychological candle-power, the illumination he
sheds upon himself.

These recorded sayings form the clearest evidence of Hitler's
complete recklessness in the world of ideas. His intuitive receiving
set picks up thoughts from the general *Weltgeist* and attaches
them, without reflection, to his absurd political party, until he
finally persuades himself into believing that the inchoate forces
that are disintegrating the whole civilized world have arisen at
his bidding. Thus there is complete confusion in his mind as
to what can be effected by political means and what belongs to
the province of nature. This confusion can be seen in every one
of these sayings. The utterances of a man who ignores human
limits and who acknowledges no power above himself, sound
merely foolish.

It follows that these sayings have an important psychological
bearing on national morale. We have already seen that morale
depends upon the feeling of continuity with the spirit of the
ancestors. Spirit is the undying flame in the heart of man. The
essence of the feeling of continuity depends upon something
which is eternal, changeless, and irrational. We cannot define it,
because it is incommunicable in rational terms. We know it
because we experience it. It is the same yesterday, to-day, and
forever. We can tolerate change, even iconoclastic change, in
the ways and means of existence. To accommodate to technical
revolution is second nature to us. But iconoclasm in the realm
of the spirit calls up immediate and passionate resistance. It
threatens the very citadel of God in man.

The passion that has aroused this nation from its lethargy

---

[1] *Hitler Speaks*, pp. 220-22.

will not abate until the earth has been cleansed of Hitlerism. It is as though a voice commanded us to preserve the temple of the living God from a ruthless iconoclast. In the realms of political organization, government, and economics, where change and progress are needed, Hitler is wholly reactionary. In the realm of the spirit, where human truth and reality are changeless, he is iconoclastic. This is the essence of his crime. He has reversed the order of human evolution and, therefore, he hangs the reversed swastika over everything his desecrating hands have touched.

The apathy of the German people is the inevitable human response to an atmosphere of spiritual desecration. No nation can be welded together in a united whole by a leader who spurns the eternal verities. The exaltation of sacrifice is spent, and every apparent victory only increases the feeling of despair: because the light has gone out.

Why should the individual German feel elated when this force sweeps down on another neutral victim, or rolls across more leagues of conquered territory, laying waste the loved soil and homesteads of peasants like himself? What kind of feeling is possible in regard to the flood that bears one along like a straw, except a longing for it to subside and to leave one on the friendly slopes of Ararat?

Dr. Rauschning calls this force Germany's revolution of destruction. Jung calls it Wotan. Wagner might have called it *Wahn*. But whatever it is called, its nature is infinite; it contains no finite aim to which a man's hopes and natural allegiance could adhere. If it were a revolution bent on improving the external conditions of life, that would be something, for there are many evils in the existing order which need to be swept away. But the things which Hitler singled out for attack were the best things men have created. Individuality, freedom, fair-dealing between peoples, gentleness, care for the defenceless. honouring of pledges — it is these which Hitler seeks to destroy, But they are the things which remain like the everlasting granite. They cannot be swept away by flood rhetoric or flood violence.

4

Turning again to the collection of Hitler's sayings, we observe that their general refrain is concerned with the end of an era and the inauguration of a new order, of which he feels himself to be the spearhead.

We can no longer regard this view merely as an expression of megalomania, since it must already be clear to every reflective mind that the *status quo ante-bellum* has gone for ever. The course of events has made it impossible for the world to seek stability upon the basis of isolated nationalism. Some kind of European federation has become a necessity; above all, because of the need to safeguard the European family of nations against a people intoxicated with dreams of power. But a new federation, or fraternity of peoples, founded upon the immediate need to defend the basis of civilized life against a destroying evil force is, in itself, the beginning of a new order. The absolute necessity of our world's moral foundations is borne in upon us only when the world itself is rocking on the edge of chaos. A new order is never the shining product of idealistic reform. The passion which creates the new is always generated from the realization of an actively menacing evil. Love and hatred are both aflame in the passion which carries through the new experiment. And the pact which binds men in loyalty to the new order derives its cogency from a lively realization of the evil newly surmounted.

The first community of men must have been founded upon a moral migration of this kind: just as the New World was also inaugurated on the strength of a passionate realization. A tacit agreement or pact unites every member of the community and this new federation derives its holding power from the fact that its members have been quickened by a new moral consciousness. The political passion which Communism arouses must surely derive its energy from the fact that it is the enlightened alternative to autocratic despotism with its inherent propensity to murder human freedom. Just as often as the unchecked power of dictatorship has created widespread suffering and corruption, the passional core of this alternative hypothesis has produced its countering flame of revolt. Thus Communism, or Socialism, tends to come to the rescue whenever the spirit of man claims an extension of human freedom. It is the revolutionist's eternal hope. It would indeed be almost impossible to stage a people's revolution which was not rooted in this hope.

The disillusionment which, from our evidence, already seems to be taking place in Germany, is inevitable and predictable, because the idea of Socialism was used, as it were, to bait a despotic trap. National Socialism, by its very name, held out a shining hope, whereas the actuality which Hitler imposed was forced marching, confiscation, ruinous taxation, war-strain, secret police, a lying press, and complete insecurity at home and abroad. In spite of the magic which clings to great words, no one, in the long run, could mistake this for Socialism.

When power is built up by a ruling class for the purpose of exploiting the remainder, an underground movement towards some form of Communism is liable to set in. Since political heat is generated between these widening opposites, a more or less violent oscillation results, so that the history of civilization records the relative ascendancy of one or other principle. By distributing the opportunities for power and by bringing liberal and socialist measures increasingly into effect, the course of British politics runs a zigzag middle way between the two poles.

Smuts's 'spiritual migration of mankind' implies that an effective resistance to our civilized pattern of life has been generated within, and that a break-away from existing forms must be anticipated. It is only too evident that our civilization is suffering from an abundance of ills. One expert will describe the disease in terms of economics. Others will point to the terrible increase in the power of the machine, to the constant threat of war, or to the all-too-accessible machinery of political power which has made brigand-dictatorship possible. The psychiatrist will point to the army of psychotics, neurotics, and psycho-neurotics, to the host of empty and unhappy marriages, to the number of lonely unmarried women, to those people who cannot eat, sleep, make love or perform the elementary bodily functions with any sense of inner security — these, and a multitude of other signs, all tend to show that civilized man is not at peace with his instinctive roots. Overtopping all these, there remains the diabolical fact that nowhere in Europe, and in relatively few parts of the civilized world to-day, is there to be found any security for individual freedom, property, or life.

Here, beyond doubt, are signs enough that a new order is needed. But what General Smuts presumably had in mind was the undermining fact that the moral foundations of our civilized order are no longer firm. Not merely that the level of individual morality shows in many respects a dangerous subsidence, but that in the realm of international relations the civilized code is no longer observed and crimes and brutalities are constantly committed by states, crimes which even the worst of men regard as outrageous. The dishonouring of treaties, the whole technique of state-treachery, lying, and falsification which has now become habitual over a large part of the civilized world, can mean only one thing. The moral values of our Christian culture are no longer universally binding, but are regarded as factors of expediency, to be called upon or not as occasion may demand.

No one could say that the present war, with its successive waves of barbarism, is the direct result of this liquefaction of the Christian moral structure. But the synchronicity of the outbreak with the decline in Christian authority is unmistakable.

General Smuts's formulation implies, therefore, that the degeneration of traditional values is due to a reorientation of consciousness towards a new spiritual basis. For a migration is never a mere departure from, it is also, and essentially, a movement towards, even though its objective may not yet be specifically known.

It will, therefore, be generally agreed, I think, that a re-establishment of the European *status quo* is no longer possible. The migration is under way. The main issue, and a vital one, is whether the Ark of the Covenant, containing the essential values of the past, is being faithfully guarded in our midst.

It is no longer necessary to state our war aims in terms of national or state interests. Frontiers, states, forms of government, etc., have assumed a transitional fluidity. Tangible things are no longer solid. But the values that led our fathers out of barbarism, and have given us the only light we know; these things we dare not lose. Our churches, our Houses of Parliament, our most sacred buildings may be destroyed, but if we remain the faithful guardians of the Covenant with the past, the other peoples of the world will surely fall into line, and form with us a new and stable federation within the sanction of a common heritage.

When we view the present events in the light of Smuts's formulation we can see that the Nazi migration has become wholly atavistic in character. From the standpoint of enlightened European feeling, Hitler's dream of a German hegemony of the world is an atavistic fantasy. Even were it enforced for a time by sheer military coercion, it could never become a permanent form. World opinion has already gone far beyond Hitler's crude, terroristic conception of rule and, apart altogether from the question of whether Europe does or does not want democracy, even the toughest Nazis would eventually have to admit that government without sanction grows increasingly arduous and unprofitable.

We must always bear in mind, however, that the foundations of a new social order, grounded upon Christian values, were already laid down in Germany before Hitler's blight descended upon Europe. Even in its present darkness there is an invisible church guarding the spiritual treasure of Germany from the forces of destruction. This ring of watchers extends across every national frontier, undermining the rule of frightfulness with clear faith.

The following passages from Dr. Rauschning confirm the fact that the flame still burns. He writes:

> No one can doubt that in the midst of the National Socialist régime, and in sharp opposition to its young revolutionaries, there lives a great Christian, Western, German nation, deeply suffering, desperately biding its time. This Germany embraces all classes in every part of the country. The old links and associations have been broken, but a truly invisible church, a great community, is growing in their place. No concrete political aim has yet shown itself, and we are as yet only at the outset of the great decisive struggle, the issue of which is not only a political but an ethical one. In this struggle German Conservatism finds its summons to renewed activity.
>
> Radowitz, a much more profound Conservative thinker than the Conservative practical politician Bismarck, saw ninety years ago the approach of the same dangers as those among which we live to-day. He saw the danger of the revolutionism

that challenges the legitimacy of property, and that of the destructive power-policy which ignores the place of ethics in statecraft. The moment the Conservatives virtually renounced ethics as an element in policy, the resort to the only refuge from chaos, to the material forces of army and masses, became inevitable. 'Who knows,' wrote Radowitz, 'whether the Socialist despotism that will result from an accommodation between the two [army and masses] may be destined to provide the transition stage through which the modern State must pass, amid great sufferings and great experiences, before it reaches a form corresponding to the Creator's ordering of the world? Here, too, men will shut their eyes to the coming perils until they have become inevitable, dislocating the thousand-year-old social order of European humanity.'[1]

The tragic conflict between moderate German idealism and the intemperate drive of Nazi power could not be revealed more poignantly. It is all the more moving because nowhere in the world were moral values and principles more vigilantly guarded than in cultured Germany. The German spirit has been turned from its true objective, and those who tried to defend German honour have been used just as vilely as 'non-Aryan' scapegoats. Yet it is undeniable that the pagan ravisher of Germany is as much a part of German psychology as the Christian soul that is ravished.

No nation and no individual can be blamed for possessing an instinct which is held in common by all living creatures. It is not the will-to-power which is wrong with Germany, but the fact that it went to the head, producing a drunken plan instead of seeking a field where it could legitimately operate.

5

If we compare the way the British Empire has grown with the German plan of hegemony, we shall, I think, come to the right explanation of the German problem. When the eye of some Elizabethan adventurer went a-roving over the blue horizon, the arrow of desire went with it. He did not think of establishing an empire beyond the seas. His thoughts were of distant lands,

[1] *Germany's Revolution of Destruction*, pp. 121-22.

adventure, booty, trade. Desire awoke an appetite for enterprise and he went out to seek what he might find. Only long afterwards and, usually, after a long struggle against conservative prejudice, was the adventurer's arrow of desire converted into the British Empire. Never, I believe, since the beginning of British expansion has a British force set out overseas motivated by a deliberate plan of conquest, even though it often effected a seizure of land to which we had no ethical claim. The difference of attitude rests upon the fact that, throughout the whole evolution of British power, desire has always led; whilst thought, in the shape of a plan, has somewhat reluctantly followed. This is the natural way of the instinct. The impulse to risk oneself on uncharted seas, to meet obstacles, storms and difficulties, with improvisation and courage, has always been the adventurer's way. It is the method by which the will-to-power of our race found an expanding field to work in, and, because it went out in this spirit, British power developed a flexible adjustment to native conditions and brought to every land to which it came a civilized code of justice. It cannot be denied, however, that our blind belief in British superiority has often made us assume a high-handed, arrogant attitude towards subject peoples.

The German plan of conquest, on the other hand, starts from the opposite end of the scale. German longing does not seek out other lands in a questing spirit that is prepared to adapt to existing realities. A vast scheme of conquest is prepared in order to demonstrate to the whole world the terrifying nature of German power. Germany has no pity or consideration for the conquered peoples, because she cannot accept desire as her guide. Desire is a true servant of life. It enjoys what it finds and, therefore, seeks to preserve its quality. Whereas power, by imposing its arbitrary plan, always seeks to destroy genuine native character.

The difference between desire-thought and thought-desire, though at first sight subtle, is the decisive factor in every human enterprise. The results of every human attempt are conditioned by the nature of the motive, or aegis, under which it begins. Either we attune our behaviour to the way assisted by nature, or we take our headlong course oblivious of all natural feeling. The piety of the ancients, which prompted them to search the augurs and await the blessing of heaven before risking an enterprise, was based upon the same basic principle. They rightly condemned the headlong way of power as hybris.

The German tendency to set thought before desire is revealed in many forms. The artificially produced *Ersatz* is really nearer the German's heart than the natural article for which it is a substitute. Just as the need to demonstrate German power motivated conquest, so it is the demonstration of German inventiveness and ingenuity which creates the meretricious *Ersatz*. Even Hitler's emotional performances are not genuine.

This shifting of emphasis to the side of the intellect is the most significant aspect of German psychology. All the more so since it implies an equivalent distrust of the instinct. The German has forsaken nature, and has made a god of the function which can better nature. He believes only in that which he makes and controls with his intellect. He does not care for nature's tedious, unenterprising ways. He is interested in nature only in order to give the intellect new tasks.

Because it has been largely cultivated by civilized man for the purpose of controlling and exploiting natural resources, the intellect has a decided tendency to interfere with, rather than to assist and cultivate, natural processes. In the German introverted intellectual type the intellect is commonly allied with intuition.[1] This combination, when dissociated from instinctual common sense, tends still further to aggravate the intellectual one-sidedness of German mentality, since intuition, as the function which seeks out possibilities, has a corresponding tendency to overlook actualities. The result of this liaison is, therefore, a highly schematized ideal in which future possibilities are given paramount value, but which is prone to intolerance of things as they are. The introverted German nature tends, in consequence, to cleave stubbornly to a *Weltanschauung* which is belied by reality. When the German is loyal to his inner conception of reality he, therefore, tends to lose the world, and when he faces outer reality with a compensatory extraversion, he loses himself.

His constant effort to create an intellectual arrangement is motivated by an inner need to reconcile this contradictory attitude to reality. He does not trust the instinct which can

[1] Jung has defined intuition as the function which perceives possibilities in an unconscious way.

improvise, and turn each situation to advantage. His carefully thought out plan leaves no room for immediate instinctual decision. Accordingly, he comes to depend upon instructions and authority, and is at a loss without them. Thus, in the realm of individual initiative, and in unpredictable tactical situations, the German soldier is liable to be outmanœuvred. The clumsiness of the German in situations that demand feeling is also the result of trying to adapt with his intellect, even where instinctual response is essential.

Notwithstanding a complete blindness on the side of his inferiority, the German is extremely competent at organizing the material world. Because of his deep distrust of his own nature, his faith in German technical capacity is as absolute as the primitive's belief in his fetish. An aura of mystical belief clings to everything which supports German morale, and convinces him of German superiority. Hence, unquestioning acceptance is given to everything and everyone — even the once hated Stalin—which confirms this belief, while hatred is directed against everything which makes him doubt it. Thus the emotional basis of German mentality is suspended dizzily between extremes, instead of being safely moored to instinct, with its simple acceptance of reality. Everything extreme in German policy and behaviour, in particular the grotesque over-valuation of Hitler, derives from this sensitive nerve of inferiority.[1]

We noted earlier the tendency of a one-sided psychology to go over completely to the opposite hypothesis, in its search for redemption or escape. From this point of view, the vast organization of German resources is also seen to be grounded in weakness, since over-compensation is invariably a symptom of anxiety. Thus the passion for organization can be regarded, as a German colleague wittily observed, as 'the *Stutzkorsett* of the anxious'.

The British way of muddling along must seem ludicrously incompetent to the German mind. Indeed, it could not be defended on any grounds at all, were it not for the fact that it usually succeeds in the end Everything can be said against it, yet nature seems to agree with it.

[1] The extreme precariousness of German morale rests, primarily, upon the fact that Hitler thus becomes the magical depository of every German's self-distrust. Hence, if that pot cracks, the national morale founders.

It would, of course, be much better if we could learn to forestall every possible eventuality. As we have recently experienced, the tendency to go with the trend of events may lead to a dangerous acquiescence in political developments which are, in fact, deeply inimical to mankind. There are evident disadvantages in the British way, but, like the tusks of the elephant, it has developed through age-long wrestling with intractable necessity. Britain also shares with the elephant the wisdom of slow movement, thus conserving her power until the moment when it is needed. Other nations find British policy hard to predict. It has the character of someone waiting to see what may turn up. The Chinese conception *Wu Wei* (acting — non-acting) is closely akin to this British habit of keeping its policy expectantly attuned to existing realities.

Our national community is, in this respect, like an animal that has no option but to remain faithful to its own peculiar laws. There is inherent wisdom in this faithfulness, since the human psyche comprises the whole history of the race. Its unwritten laws represent the summation of past experience, condensed in the form of a basic instinctual attitude to reality. To take an illustration from recent history, it was not because of the innate superiority of the British race, as we are inclined to assume, that British democracy was able to effect a brilliant change of leadership in the hour of need, while Germany and Russia prove unable to rid themselves of leaders who have become the worst enemies of mankind. Rather was it the product of a realistic political instinct which has been disciplined in a hard school. Britain has been forced to achieve a flexible political organism in response to the dangers of her existence and the vicissitudes of her growth. Before national unity was achieved the people of this country had for centuries been divided by civil wars, invaded by marauders, impoverished and humiliated by serfdom, oppressed by ruthless, ambitious tyrants, and persecuted and tortured by ecclesiastical fanaticism. Political maturity is not lightly won.

Through bitter experience Britain learned that the docility and stupidity of the mass, rooted in the biological pattern of the leader and the herd, is a terribly dangerous implement of power when it falls into the wrong hands. It was precisely to defend itself from this danger that the British people developed the system of parliamentary discussion, whereby every proposition is subjected to incorruptible debate before it is made law. Dictators are unanimously opposed to free parliamentary discussions — a fact which in itself bears witness to their essential lawlessness.

6

Political maturity is won by nations, as by individuals, through a willingness to face problems and a capacity to overcome difficulties. The collective instinct of the German is, naturally, rooted as deeply in the general biological inheritance as that of every European. Moreover, in all situations where docile obedience is required, German collectivity shows a relative superiority, especially in respect to disciplined endurance. The political incompetence of Germany is revealed in the inability of her citizens to participate responsibly in the organs of government and public opinion, and to construct safeguards to defend her leaders from the gravest peril of leadership, unchecked power.

When, by playing a given collective rôle, a leader identifies himself with an archetype of the collective unconscious, it is as though he had discovered without effort or plan a sudden acquisition of instinctual energy. But, inasmuch as these stores of instinctual energy are heirlooms from the past, they are also an expression of tribal or ancestral continuity, almost as though they were still guarded and cared for by the ancestors. Hence, the authority and energy of the archetype are released only in response to the call of national service. No dictator could ever climb to absolute power if he failed to hitch his wagon to an ancestral archetype.

These truisms must be stated, since the whole question of individual and national morale hinges upon the capacity of a nation to remain true to its ancestral psychical inheritance; not, as Hitler imagines, upon a propagandist enslavement of the herd-mind. I believe this to be the essential condition of victory. For a nation that listens to ancestral guidance will choose the right leaders, give them its loyal and ardent service, be vigilant against treachery and sloth, and unstinting in individual sacrifice.

The work of creating good morale is, therefore, concerned primarily with bringing to life this dormant collective power,

which can be quickened into effective operation by the chosen
leader when he recalls to the people their great inheritance, and
dedicates himself and them to the service of the nation.

Viewing this process in its historical context, we may perhaps
conclude that Mr. Chamberlain's leadership was well adapted
to the preliminary phase of cautious marshalling of the national
resources, including these latent reserves of power. For, as we
have at last realized, this inherent power is the real wealth of the
nation. The political crisis, which effected a change of leadership
at the crucial moment, corresponded with a growing recognition
of the fact that the time had come when the cautious, conservative attitude had played its part and must now make way for the
fullest expression of power. The leader who can best conserve
is rarely able to transform himself at need into the effective
wielder of national force.

The real strength of the slow, muddling, British way lies in its
inherent respect for reality. Reality, indeed, is Britain's touchstone. What is not real is not worth attention. This attitude is
again the product of that instinctual rooting in the natural order
which, as we have seen, is the secret of British growth.

Occasions can arise, however, in which an unimaginative
cleaving to the actual becomes a mortal danger. To assume,
for instance, that one's opponent's psychology is motivated by
premises essentially similar to one's own is to fail in psychological
realism. Our instinctual way of grappling with difficulties as
we come to them, is excellent for peace-time navigation.
But it is dangerous when we have to deal with a cynical and
determined enemy who has, for years, been preparing for our
overthrow. Yet our enemy labours under a graver misconception
than we do. His belief that he could safely challenge British
power rested on the presupposition that the lethargy and complacence of the elephant were signs of decadence. This is Hitler's
fatal mistake. When the need came the latent ancestral reserves
were not lacking. The blade remained deep-sunk in the tree,
ready for the moment of heroic need. It is the effective power
of the undying flame. Like the gift of the gods, it flashed into
action at the psychological moment; yet no plan, however
complete, could have taken it into account.

It would be madness to underestimate the military machine of our enemy, yet we know in our hearts that excessive preparation always screens an unadmitted weakness. Jung's aphorism: 'Fanaticism is the over-compensation of a doubt', expresses the same law. This inveterate German doubt will eventually prove our strongest ally. For not only must the enemy strive against the external enemy, he must also, and with increasing anxiety, fight the enemy within. A nation that lacks unity is, therefore, doomed to fight on two fronts. The preoccupation of German strategy with this problem may also derive from the same cause.

To illustrate this fundamental flaw in the enemy morale I have borrowed a drawing from a patient who had to grapple with this problem of the split mind. Unlike Germany, he did not strive, by despising his fellow-men, to persuade himself of a superiority he did not feel. He preferred to gain insight into his problem by means of a series of unplanned drawings from the unconscious, the analytical understanding of which helped him to resolve the inner contradiction.

The principal figure in the drawing is a man, muscular, taut and poised for a spring. There is considerable distortion in the shape of his body and elongated arms. The latter are reaching out towards a small object meant to represent an ever-receding goal. Opposite the man is a smaller female figure, less distorted; but, again, the arms are enormously extended, and there is no head. Where the head should be a flood of hair is seen streaming towards the man. The most striking feature of the drawing is a jagged crack, like a crack in a pane of glass, running diagonally across the field, and separating the woman, part of the man's head, and the distant objective, from the bulk of the man's figure. Every line that crosses this crack is refracted, so that its continuity is broken.

This violent split represents an active state of dissociation, separating the dynamic, emotional, and instinctual parts of the subject's psyche from the voluntary and ideational. The distant female figure, reaching towards the man in distressful appeal, represents his subjective feeling of being cut off and remote from any intimate understanding with his wife, or indeed, with his own

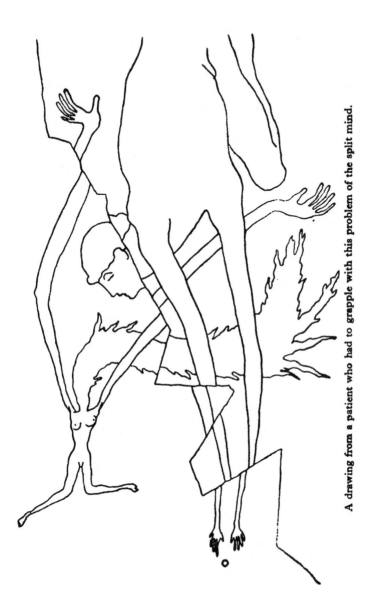

A drawing from a patient who had to grapple with this problem of the split mind.

soul. For this reason the female figure is associated in the drawing with the ever-receding goal, as belonging to the region of tantalizing ineffectualness. Towards these aspects of his life the subject felt cynical and fatalistic.

It is not necessary to go into the pathology of schizophrenia to understand the psychological content of this drawing. It is self-evident that the condition of dissociation is the cause of the feeling of inferiority and ineffectual performance of which my patient complained. The distorted figure of masculine power (which became even more exaggerated in other drawings) symbolizes the constant urge to overstate the masculine side, and to ride roughshod over his own sensitive weakness in an attempt to obliterate the undermining sense of insecurity. The effort to repress one's nature in this way inevitably aggravates the condition, since repression only intensifies the split which causes the feeling of insecurity. Inferiority produces a continual stimulus towards over-compensation. The tendency to over-compensate becomes manifest in a restless, insatiable ambition and a necessity to demonstrate the superiority of the masculine. The refraction which breaks the continuity between the two halves symbolizes the factor of subjective interference that distorts his view of the world.

When we examine the fantasy of German world-hegemony with this picture in mind, we begin to see that whole restless urgency in its true light. We understand why Hitler's aims differ from the realizable goals of biological necessity. A hungry man, when he reaches food, will eat and be satisfied. An exhausted man will sleep and be restored. But an aggressive nation, haunted by inner insecurity, can never satisfy its need. Into each country that is conquered the lurking inferiority enters too, urging the conqueror ever onward to new and greater goals. An unadmitted subjective defect is like a bottomless pit: the more one gives to it, the more it takes.

The split in schizophrenia differs from dissociation in the hysterical subject, inasmuch as the hysteric never ceases to fight for the unity of his personality. Whereas with the schizophrenic a renegade alteration of personality is liable to occur (for example, from Jekyll to Hyde) without signs of active moral resistance. In other words, the disease is liable to produce a deep psychical split which cannot be bridged from above. Only through an irrational experience of the unconscious psyche, an experience which often has the character of an archaistic return to a simpler state or an earlier age, can the dissociation be healed and the opposites reconciled.

The fatal flaw in the German national character has its origin, as we have now seen, in a dissociation between the civilized intellect on the one hand, and the primordial human being with his neglected instincts, on the other. This split underlies not only the contradiction between German culture and Prussian aggression, but also the suppression of truth and of every human feeling. The policy of interference and aggression must, therefore, be regarded as a continual effort to bolster up a defective morale.

Aggressive violence is undoubtedly the most pathological product of German inferiority. But we shall not have gained a complete picture of its effects unless we also take into consideration Hitler's religion of racial superiority. Although undoubtedly rooted in the same fundamental condition, it had none the less a positive character and, from the national point of view, produced many positive results.

An English observer who was twice present at the Nuremberg September rally told me of her amazement when she discovered that the Nazi movement was by no means identical with German Nationalism. She found a large Dutch contingent, enthusiastic groups from Norway, Denmark, Sweden, Switzerland, America, and from every part of the British Commonwealth. There was an ecstatic supernational feeling in the Nazi camps, binding the various groups together; a feeling which could be compared with the millennial enthusiasm of the Oxford Group Movement.

These were genuine disciples of Hitler's doctrine. The fifth columnists in every country must, therefore, be regarded as converts, prompted by the Nazi gospel to become the vanguard of the new order. Communism also had a seed of mysticism at its inception, based on the idea of a new supernational order. But Stalin killed its spirit, just as Hitler betrayed the spirit of German rebirth.

8

The religion of Hitlerism was rooted in the idea of the superiority of the German race, a superiority based upon the mystical feeling of being descended from the gods. Because this idea lacks any scientific basis, it is difficult for the Englishman to realize its psychological significance for the Germans.

It is remarkable that the three outstanding prophets of this new religion, Gobineau, Chamberlain, and Hitler, were all foreigners who obtained German nationality in order to give unreserved allegiance to their adopted land. For the understanding of Hitler's religion I cannot do better than quote from Mr. Wickham Steed's excellent condensation of the theories of Gobineau and Houston Stewart Chamberlain, the two ideological forerunners of Hitlerism.

Gobineau, a Frenchman, lived in the middle of last century. His chief published work was *The Inequality of Human Races*. The main thesis of this work is rendered by Mr. Wickham Steed[1] as follows:

> The old idea that societies and civilizations perish only through fanaticism, luxurious effeminacy and vice, cannot be historically upheld. Peoples die of degeneration, that is to say, of contempt for ethnical principles, and through interbreeding. Some races are natural rulers, but their numbers are small and they tend to be absorbed and submerged by the peoples over which they rule ... The character of peoples is independent of the countries they inhabit ... The influence of religion upon races should not be over-estimated. Christianity did not create and has not changed racial aptitudes for civilization ... The Aryans, long before their arrival in India, were distinct from the other races which were also destined to become European. The name 'Aryan' means 'honourable' and Aryan nations were composed of 'honourable men'. A similar notion was common to the Persians and the Greeks ... The essential characteristics of races are those of the abilities they possess and develop. If the Aryan has not always been the best of men from the standpoint of practical morality, he is at least the most enlightened upon the intrinsic worth of what he does. When he is in a tight place his heart may be as hard as his armour; and if he is hard towards himself it is not astonishing that he should be pitiless towards others. His merit consists in his loyal acceptance of a law that may be ferocious, but grows milder in proportion as conditions may permit.

[1] WICKHAM STEED, *Hitler, Whence and Whither?* (Nisbet & Co., London).

It is mainly by reason of his intelligence and vigour that the Aryan is superior to other men, and it is thanks to these two qualities that he is capable, when he succeeds in conquering his passions and in providing for his material needs, of reaching a very high level of morality, even though he may be guilty, in other circumstances, of as many reprehensible acts as members of inferior races.

The Germanic Aryan is a powerful and superior creature. All that he believes, all that he says, and all that he does become matters of major importance. True to his ancestry the Germanic Aryan, on his arrival in Europe, had not lost the habit of attributing his origin to the gods . . . the Scandinavian Aryans traced their descent from Odin.

Like that of his two successors, Gobineau's real patriotism was given to the idea of the superiority of an ideal Germanic Fatherland. The influence of Gobineau's works, which were widely read in Germany, undoubtedly served to foment German imperialism at the beginning of this century. So much so that in 1909 Vacher de Lapouge, a French disciple of Gobineau, published a warning that 'political mountebanks' like Houston Stewart Chamberlain had drawn from Gobineau certain theories

> which have become the foundations of German Imperialism, the most aggressive that exists, and the creed of tens of millions of Germans in the Empire, in Austria, Switzerland and America.

These theories, Lapouge added,

> are becoming a danger to the world and are making increasingly perilous the tension between Germany and the non-German peoples.

Houston Chamberlain doubtless made this racial myth even more attractive to the Germans, since he clothed his theory in a prodigious display of scholarship. He was born at Southsea in 1855, the son of a British Admiral. Two of his uncles were British Generals and a third was Field-Marshal Sir Neville Chamberlain. He, too, was intended for the army, but this idea was given up on grounds of health. He was educated abroad, first at Versailles, then at Geneva, and finally at Dresden, where he, too, fell under the spell of Wagner's music and mythology. Having mastered

German he began to write, mainly about Wagner. He wrote a biography of Wagner and, eventually, crowned his Germanic faith by marrying Wagner's daughter. His chief works were *Foundations of the Nineteenth Century* written in German in 1899, and *Aryan Outlook*, published in 1911. He became naturalized as a German during the Great War and died in 1927.

The late Lord Redesdale, who wrote an Introduction to the English edition of *Foundations of the Nineteenth Century*, summed up the author's thesis as a demonstration that the first place in the world belongs by natural right to the Teutonic branch of the Aryan family, and that the story of the nineteenth century is the story of the Teuton's triumph. By Teutonic peoples Chamberlain understands Teutons (i.e. the Germanic peoples in general) and Slavs, from whom, by marriage and diffusion, the peoples of modern Europe are descended. Chamberlain never intended to identify his superior Teutonic race with Germany, and in many recorded conversations Hitler was, originally, of the same mind. They both had the idea of a racial conception, based upon biological premises, which was to be rooted in inherited or ancestral character and would eventually supersede the existing national basis. Chamberlain believed that the Teutonic peoples belonged originally to a single family. He held that the Teuton is the soul of our culture. Teutonic blood is the only element which makes an organic unity of the infinite mingling of races in European peoples. Only Teutons sit on the thrones of Europe. True history begins when the Teuton, with his masterful hand, lays his grip on the legacy of antiquity. Chamberlain even affirms that it was the entrance of the Germanic peoples into history that saved Europe and mankind. He quotes Goethe's view that it was the Germanic races who first introduced the idea of personal freedom into the world.

Hitlerism deviates in a notable fashion from Chamberlain's gospel on this point. Hitler, as we know, challenges *in toto* the Christian conception of individual freedom and significance. The only liberty he grants to the individual is that of belonging un-reservedly to the state. Chamberlain, on the other hand, assigns great historical importance to Magna Carta in the development of Germanic ideas. He holds that German culture owes much to the sturdy defence of individual rights in England.

In spite of a ferocious indictment of the Jews and of Jewish influence upon Aryan culture, Chamberlain wrote many passages which showed that his anti-Semitism was counterbalanced by an insight into the problem which would certainly not be countenanced in Nazi Germany. He writes:

> I have become convinced that the usual treatment of the 'Jewish question' is altogether and always superficial; the Jew is no enemy of Teutonic civilization and culture; Herder may be right in his assertion that the Jew is always alien to us, and consequently we to him, and no one will deny that this is to the detriment of our work and culture; yet I think we are inclined to underestimate our own powers in this respect, and on the other hand, we exaggerate the importance of the Jewish influence. Hand in hand with this goes the perfectly ridiculous and revolting tendency to make the Jews the general scapegoat for all the vices of our time. In reality the 'Jewish peril' lies much deeper; the Jew is not responsible for it; we have given rise to it ourselves and must overcome it ourselves . . . It is because of the lack of a true religion that our whole Teutonic culture is sick unto death . . . No people in the world is so beggarly-poor in religion as are the Semites and their half-brothers, the Jews.

It is almost certain that Hitler derived from Chamberlain the idea of finding a 'true religion' for the Germanic peoples. Chamberlain's book *Foundations of the Nineteenth Century* was less a political essay than a metaphysico-religious treatise with the mystical notion of race-purity running through it. But his new religion did not oppose the teachings of Christ, for which he professes the deepest reverence. His picture of the Jews, fanatical, stubborn, exclusive, and terribly one-sided, is tempered by a tribute to an essential and most valuable idea which, he believes, conserved Judaism intact throughout the centuries. The essence of this idea is race-unity and race-purity. It implies recognition of a fundamental physiological fact.

As we read Chamberlain's prejudiced account of Jewish culture and religion we are immediately struck by a certain inner resemblance between this picture and the one which Nazi fanaticism has used to such evil purpose. To quote again from Wickham Steed's résumé of Chamberlain's ideas:

The typical Jew took no interest in politics, literature, philosophy or art. The Law formed his whole literature and its study was his sole intellectual exercise. In his religion the Semite is selfish and exclusive ... The predominant power in the soul of the Semite is his will. The Jews have no metaphysics, but only an intense religion in which there is no inner mystery. It represents a minimum of religion. Moses Mendelssohn, says Chamberlain, wrote truly: 'Judaism is not revealed religion, but revealed legislation.'[1]

It would be a grave insult to the Jewish race to elaborate any essential kinship between Judaism and Hitlerism, but it is none the less undeniable that at the centre of both religions we find a passionate preoccupation with racial purity. Jewish leadership and religion have always been as jealous of the physical as of the spiritual conservation of the race and its genius. There are other points of similarity which need not be stressed. The most eloquent fact of all is that, from the very outset, Hitlerism has attacked and persecuted the Jews with every indication of violent antipathy. Fanatical antipathy was also fomented against Russia and the Third International. These antipathies are especially revealing when we bear in mind the principle that men project their own worst qualities on those they hate most.[2] It is because the fanatic is a psychological cripple that he cannot tolerate anyone, or anything, that reminds him of his deformity. Under stress of necessity, Hitlerism was eventually forced to own kinship with Communism. Adequate persuasion is still lacking in regard to Judaism. Nor indeed is this psychologically feasible. For the Jews symbolize that whole problem of inferiority in which Nazi aggressiveness and, therefore, Nazi crime, are rooted. To revoke the devil-projection from the Jews would mean, therefore, that the Germans were able to accept themselves as they are. What would then become of the theory of Nordic superiority?

There are abundant passages throughout Hitler's book which reveal his direct acquisitions from Gobineau and Chamberlain.

[1] I am indebted to Mr. Wickham Steed's account of Hitlerism in his book *Hitler, Whence and Whither?* (James Nisbet & Co., London) for the above material concerning Gobineau and Chamberlain.
[2] In certain Indian *yoga*-systems it is the custom of the *guru*, or teacher, wherever the pupil is held fast to an object, either by hate or love, to say to him *tat twam asi* = that art thou.

With sure instinct Hitler realized the healing balm this gospel of the superior Nordic race, claiming descent from the early gods, would mean for a people made helpless by their feeling of inferiority. The following passage is a specimen of the Gobineau-Chamberlain medicine which was administered to the German people in heroic doses in the pages of *Mein Kampf*:

> True genius is always inborn, never learned or acquired by education. This is true not only of individuals but of the race, and is seen most clearly in *the* race, the Aryan race, which has borne, and is bearing, upon its shoulders the weight of human culture and civilization. Other and lower races may have had their work to do, just as horses had before the advent of the motor car, and it was right that they should serve the higher races as horses served man. Only pacifist fools can boggle at the reduction of such races to servitude. Human progress is like an endless ladder which cannot be climbed without treading upon its lower rungs. So, the Aryan race had to climb the hard upward path to reality, not the path of which modern pacifists dream. Thus it is no accident that the earliest civilizations arose where the Aryan, in collision with lower peoples, put his yoke upon them and made them subject to his will . . . Cross-breeding, and the race degradation which it entails, are the sole causes of the dying out of old civilizations; for men do not perish by losing wars. They perish by the loss of the staying-power which is proper to pure blood. Whatever in this world is not of good race is mere chaff.

We can see from this passage how perfectly fitted Hitler was to play the rôle of medicine-man to a conquered people. He was not concerned with the truth or with the final effects of his medicine. His flair led him to the German power-house, the mythological reservoir which housed the dormant power of Wotan.

The Wotan-wind, according to Jung's hypothesis, is an expression of the dissociated pagan psychology which victorious Christendom repressed in the Middle Ages, but never assimilated. It was from this pagan arsenal in the Teutonic unconscious that the Wagner-Gobineau-Chamberlain-Hitler gospel of Germanism acquired its ever-increasing force and momentum. Once the primordial image of the 'conquering race' had been activated, the movement gained a kind of millennial enthusiasm, leaping across national boundaries and uniting all the Nordic peoples, with their characteristic culture and mythology, in a triumphant bond of brotherhood.

When we see the pathological aspect of Nazi power, we are appalled by the terrible shadow-side of the German phenomenon. But in order to understand Hitlerism as a religion, and to appreciate its astonishing power of permeating neighbouring lands, which, on grounds of mere national survival, had every reason to defend themselves against the Nazi poison, we must also bear in mind the mystical millennial appeal of Hitler's message to the Nordic peoples. It was indeed a rejection of the God of their fathers. But it was also a return to the gods of their forefathers. *Dieu est mort, vivent les dieux.*

Naturally, when Gobineau and Chamberlain called to the Germanic unconscious, the forms, values, and institutions of Christian tradition were still relatively firm and stable. The spiritual migration of mankind did not begin until the war of 1914-18. It was in this cataclysm that the organ of faith in the soul of civilized man was so gravely wounded. It seemed impossible to go on believing in a divine ordering of human affairs which could lead mankind into such monstrous chaos. The vast, top-heavy civilizing machine was stricken, its basic validity challenged.

The backward migration of Germany, already discerned by Lawrence in 1923, was fundamentally a departure from the cultural values and containers of Christendom towards the alternative hypothesis, which had found open expression in the neo-paganism of Russia, and was beginning to make its appearance in the youth movement and other futuristic, uprooted tendencies in post-war Germany.

The liquefaction of moral values during this transitional period affected, in greater or less degree, the whole civilized world. The Nazi infection spread easily because people were no longer sure. When men are struggling in the sea, it does not occur to them to question whether the men approaching them in a ship are honest seamen or pirates. All they can see is the ship.

It is quite vain, therefore, to argue that the gospel of 'Aryan' superiority is without basis in ethnological fact. The Germanic flood is pervasive because it relies, not upon intellectual, but rather

FACTORS GOVERNING MORALE

upon emotional and mythological sanction. In a letter to *The Times* in 1933, Professor Gordon Childe, of Edinburgh University, a leading authority upon prehistoric archaeology, exploded whatever scientific pretensions Hitler's race-theory had claimed.

> Three thousand years before the Christian Era [he wrote] the Sumerians, the Egyptians, and the nameless, but certainly pre-Aryan people of the Indus Valley created the civilization of which, through the Greeks and the Romans, and by more devious channels, we are the heirs. And by civilization I mean no simply material culture . . . but also political organization and science.
> At the date in question the ancestors of the Germans and Anglo-Saxons were filthy savages picking up shellfish on the shores of the Baltic. There is not a trace of Aryan elements in any sense . . . among the creators of civilized life. It is indeed doubtful whether the people who spoke the Aryan tongue were yet in existence when the oriental civilizations were founded.
> . . . Aryan, originally, was a liguistic term and denoted the speakers of a certain group of languages. No less an authority than Max Müller pointed out that to speak of an Aryan race was as absurd as to talk of a brachycephalic (or broad-skulled) dictionary. Languages are characteristic of peoples — groups united by community of tradition and culture but not necessarily of blood. Race, on the contrary, is a physical term. Nazi 'philosophy' confuses these two distinct concepts. Distortions of the science of pre-history in Germany have to some extent encouraged this confusion. That is perhaps sufficient excuse for a professor of pre-history in Great Britain to insist upon the distinction.[1]

Hitler knows very well that his religion cannot rely upon scientific truth. On the other hand, we cannot claim that the Nazi gospel consists wholly of lies; because, in point of fact, there is more than a grain of truth in all Hitler's assertions. The truth of the Nordic race-theory, for example, relies upon a basic psychological affinity among certain peoples, expressed in a common mythic inheritance and upon certain basic cultural sympathies, not to mention the obvious physical kinship expressed in the famous blue eyes and fair complexion of northern European peoples.

[1] Cited from *Hitler, Whence and Whither?* by WICKHAM STEED, p. 132.

Hitlerism has this in common with the Oxford Group Movement: its appeal is made almost exclusively to the emotional centres in the unconscious. In neither case is there any intellectual content which can stand up to honest intellectual criticism. This fact is a significant portent, since both movements originated in the fluidity and restless despair of post-war cynicism. Both movements represent the process of harking-back to an earlier model or hypothesis; the Oxford Group to the early Christian community, with its open confession of sins and ecstatic brotherhood in the faith; the Hitler religion to the idea of descent from the Nordic gods.

On psycho-therapeutic grounds there is much to be said for this process of harking-back to an earlier form of experience, so long as the virtue of the archaic prototype is assimilated into the existing structure of reality, and not set up as an exclusive goal with a claim to absolute validity.

9

No responsible writer should be beguiled into predicting how the present vast confusion will end. The most that psychology can legitimately attempt is to make the irrational intelligible. In the psycho-therapeutic treatment of individuals we find that mental disturbance is usually bound up with the repression of pathological, or unacceptable contents. Theoretically, therefore, healing can be achieved by the frankest possible acceptance of the repressed aspect of the personality. This excluded, or shadow aspect has the Judas-like quality of containing precisely those human traits which are morally antagonistic to the ideal personality favoured by consciousness. The shadow, therefore, is essentially an outcast, and is frequently represented in dreams as either criminal or dissolute. It is my belief that the irrational aspect of contemporary events comes from this, the shadow-side of Christendom, and that it was Hitler's fate to personify it.

The effect of the Christian view of life has naturally been to keep the psychical sheep divided from the goats. Thus, the unconscious of Christian mankind is only too liable to contain those generally human characteristics which have been converted into goats by the Christian ideal. But no amount of repression could ever succced in extinguishing these barbarian human qualities. The only result of repression is to give to the unacceptable contents a vindictive, outcast character. Hold we to our idealized Christian conception never so staunchly, our partiality for the upper side can only have the effect of building up a more and more clear-cut antithesis to our ideal in the unconscious. For these opposite qualities also belong to man's original nature.

An ideal that works has a royal nobility. But it begins to have an evil effect when one is so dazzled by its light that the shadow-being in oneself is no longer visible. For what I do not see in myself I find projected upon my neighbour. In this way I force my neighbour to carry my unaccepted evil. The whole sinister history of Christian persecution, torture, and inquisition is rooted in this dependence of the ideal upon its scapegoat. In time, therefore, it must be universally conceded that the criterion of psychological maturity consists in the subject's capacity to accept and take responsibility for his unconscious motivations. How does this law affect our attitude to Germany?

Under the guidance of Hitler the Germans are the first so-called Christian nation to live out their worst qualities. As yet they do not see what they have done, because they contrived to camouflage these qualities under a would-be pagan ideology. Thus the inferior shadow-aspect of German psychology became identified with an idealized pagan standpoint. Without doubt, Hitler's success lay in his ability to make use of his outcast's experience in Vienna to gain a thorough-going understanding of shadow psychology. His opportunism, his callousness, his flair for scenting out his opponent's vulnerable spot, in a word, the underworld tactics which have never yet failed him in an emergency, were gained through his own experience as an outcast. Thus Hitler discovered the revolutionary potential which lay with the shadow, a discovery which eventually provided him with his mightiest weapon.

Following the same reasoning, we see that Germany, as conquered nation, was forced into the rôle of scapegoat, therewith receiving the full weight of the European shadow-projection. Thus she became the first Western[1] nation to be caught by the

[1] Russia cannot be reckoned as European in her psychology. Her natural gravitation towards Asia is the sign of her true nature. The key to the so-called Russian enigma is simply her Asiatic affinity.

undertow and possessed by the excluded pagan antithesis. In the strange symbolical way in which the unconscious tends to be concretized in the fateful moment, Hitler embodied in his own ambiguous nature the outcast and hero, the criminal and the messenger from heaven, the ideal figure and its shadow, in bewildering contiguity.

If the psychological signs are verified by events, and the outcome of the present world-migration should prove to be the painful development of human consciousness towards psychological maturity, there can be no doubt at all that the assimilation of the pagan shadow in the Christian unconscious will become the essential individual task of Western man. It is, indeed, already being forced upon us in a variety of ways, but the very fact that we are being compelled to realize something increases our habitual resistance to the demands of consciousness.

Because of the immense inertia and stubborn unconsciousness of the human species, the dynamic stage of mental evolution is painful and sometimes catastrophic. The individual human being is reasonably educable, but collectivity is practically dead-weight. It never moves until it is forced. The long-prophesied coming of anti-Christ might be regarded, therefore, as the dynamic expression of the next evolutionary step, on the threshold of which the reverse aspect of our Christian psychology must be encountered, with its challenge to our whole civilized ideal. From this basic confrontation a fundamentally new attitude must emerge, or Christian civilization suffer total eclipse.

10

Throughout these pages the reader will have noted a frequent use of such expressions as the 'unbridled force' or the 'dynamism of the unconscious'. It has been objected that modern psychology, having learned to view the psyche from a dynamic standpoint, is inclined to treat moral problems as though they were a matter of psychological engineering, or even plumbing. However we choose to regard it, the problem of the unconscious, in the last analysis, is a question of understanding, harnessing, and subduing undomesticated energies. The civilizing hero is essentially a bull-

fighter or dragon-killer, because the task undertaken by the
civilized man is that of taming or subduing the primordial powers
of the unconscious.

Hitler, like a degenerate demiurge, avows his intention of
creating man again in his own image. The god-man he wants to
create is a being 'with unrestrained impulses'. But this ideal state
is not for woman. Unconditioned masculinity is Hitler's aim;
with the natural and logical consequence that woman must be
enslaved.

It has taken Christendom nearly two thousand years to overcome its early barbarian fear of feminine power. The exclusively
masculine conception of deity, and other evidences of the one-
sidedness of the early Christian Church, represented a psychological recoil from the immense attraction of the *Magna Mater* in
the European unconscious. Just as the cult of the Earth-Mother
prevailed in Europe up to the beginning of our era, so the inertia
of a semi-civilized psychology still clings tenaciously to the mother-
image in the unconscious. We might, therefore, regard these
extravagant efforts to enhance the cruder masculine qualities, as
an unconscious attempt to break free from the overwhelming unconscious attraction of the mother-image. This accords with our
earlier conclusion that the outstanding traits of the National
Socialist hero belong to the phase of adolescence.

The following citations from the writings or speeches of National
Socialist leaders will, I think, corroborate this impression.

> The absence of all-round abilities in women is directly to be
> attributed to the fact that woman is vegetative. Actually in
> their deepest consciousness these emancipated females want
> nothing else than the chance to live at the expense of man.
>   DR. ROSENBERG.

> In the education of women emphasis must be laid primarily
> on physical development. Only afterwards must considera-
> tion be given to spiritual values, and lastly to mental develop-
> ment. Motherhood is undeniably the aim of feminine
> education.   ADOLF HITLER.

> Round up a thousand German girls of the purest stock.
> Isolate them in a camp. Then let them be joined by a hundred
> German men equally of purest stock. If a hundred such camps

were set up, you would have a hundred-thousand thorough-
bred children at one stroke.

DR. WILLIBALD HENTSCHEL, Der Hammer No. 604.

The strikingly low cultural level of the American nation is the
result of the dominant position of women.

ROSENBERG'S Mythus.

There is no higher or finer privilege for a woman than that of
sending her children to war.

THE WOMEN'S ORDER OF THE RED SWASTIKA.

The Jew has stolen woman as a wife from us, by sexual
Democracy. We, the young generations, have to march off
and slay the dragon, in order that we may win back the holiest
thing in the world: the wife who is both servant and slave.

GOTTFRIED FEDER, Women under Fascism and Communism

I have preserved this evidence until the end, because the
abysmal crudity of the Nazi attitude to woman offers, in my view,
the most convincing evidence of its crippled state. The world has
suffered long enough from a grotesque overvaluation of aggressive
masculine characteristics; while the achievements of the masculine
intellect in the realm of science and technology must be held
responsible for putting machinery of incalculable destructive power
into the hands of psychopathic adolescents. The whole hope of the
future lies in a new conception of the human being in which the
feminine principle of healing and fertility will once again preside,
as in certain primitive communities, over all those functions which
are essential to life.

But the problem of the unbridled dynamism of the unconscious
is not necessarily identical with that of the unrestrained male.
Fundamentally, as we have seen, the problem of the undomesticated *libido* is the problem of the barbaric residue in the civilized
unconscious. The bullying male is merely the idiom in which this
problem manifests itself in German collectivity. But however it
may reveal itself, the arena or field in which the undomesticated
energies are tamed is in that of relationship. For the original
motive for self-discipline in man lies in his relation to woman
and to his own soul, which is personified by woman. The
man who will not undertake this relationship tacitly refuses the
task of self-discipline, at least in the psychological sense of discipline
through understanding. It will, therefore, be found in every case

that the man who intensifies his masculinity, while at the same time evading the responsibility of relationship, foists the problem of his undomesticated unconscious upon other people, and usually this burden falls upon a woman.

But the attitude to woman, as such, is not the whole problem. Since woman symbolizes the soul in man, the whole feminine side of human nature tends to suffer eclipse when only the masculine character is honoured. A nation which valued the feminine principle could not have expelled its finest musicians, its most sensitive writers, and its most devoted scientists. All that side of life where humane feeling is cultivated cannot live in the Nazi atmosphere. Yet all these things belong essentially to the soul of Germany. Thus, in spite of Hitler's boast of having created a united German nation, we know that rival gods are fighting for possession of the German soul.

This fundamental diagnosis is clearly demonstrated in Hitler's choice of the swastika as the symbol of the Third Reich. In this choice Hitler proclaimed his movement to be religious in origin. He invoked the god and, in the same breath, he betrayed him. For in reversing the swastika he negated its essential meaning.

The swastika is a venerable symbol of immense antiquity and, therefore, deeply rooted in man's religious nature. It is essentially a sun wheel, the four hooks representing the four legs of the sun-god: an older, more primitive conception than the four horses of the sun. This dynamic symbolism has to do, not merely with the passage of the sun across the heavens from east to west, but with the idea of the sun-wise orderly movement of the whole universe. Thus the swastika contains the idea of ordering one's life, or course of action, in accordance with the appointed order of the universe. In China the same idea is expressed by the concept *Tao*, which really means the Right Way conceived of as Ruling Principle. As the symbol of the celestial or heavenly principle, the swastika expresses the original piety of man. Sacredness does not cling to it merely on account of its antiquity and universality. As a symbol of the underlying dynamic principle by which the entire universe is ordered, it possesses an indwelling spiritual potency, the efficacy of which is exemplified in this very matter of the Nazi swastika.

Hitler was free to invoke the swastika, so long as he did so under the right aegis and faithfully served the divine principle for which it stands, that of the Right Way, the movement that is in keeping with the sun. But because his motive was wrong, he had to reverse the symbol. The angle of the swastika hooks represent the bent knees of the god, as can be verified in archaic representations of the symbol. In Hitler's swastika the legs are *against* the direction of the sun, denoting a movement that is directly opposed to the Right Way. The reversed swastika is a curse and not a blessing. By this sacrilegious misuse Hitler announced to all men who study the signs that his movement was not intended to endure. Because it is against nature, in the essential meaning of the word, it runs blindly like an unconscious suicide, towards its doom.

But although Hitler launched his movement under the wrong aegis (i.e. wrong motive), it cannot be denied that he possessed the characteristically Jewish flair for spiritual treasure. He found the jewel, but he failed to honour it. This contradiction between spiritual appraisal and cynical materialism also belongs to the Jewish fate. It is epitomized, as Spitteler revealed in his *Prometheus and Epimetheus*, in the figure of the Wandering Jew.[1] In this tragic figure we can recognize the true nature of our feelings concerning Hitler. No other man of our time had such a golden chance of serving life, and we know that at one time he was inspired by a genuine ideal. But instead of serving his god, he coveted the god-value. Thus the tragedy of the Wandering Jew is re-enacted, and the leader to whom fate offered the jewel of great price became the man accursed.

It remains for us to pick up the jewel which Hitler spurned. There is no such thing as a new truth. The New Order which the world awaits must surely be grounded upon a truth that is already tested and known. What Hitler intended with his National Socialism had in truth a mystical seed — that ancient fraternity among mankind which values human things first. The undying flame in the spirit of man is the light by which the true is known 'and the false rejected. When with a single voice we shout the word which will unite mankind in free brotherhood the walls of Jericho will surely fall.

But even when the walls of the Nazi stronghold are down we shall not have achieved our final aim. At the moment we naturally

[1] The reader is referred to Jung's *Psychological Types*, Chapter v, for a further treatment of this theme.

think it enough to extirpate Hitlerism, root and branch, and to replace it by our own democratic philosophy. Before we shall have finished our task, however, something further will be demanded of us. The Hitler problem will not let us go until we have assimilated that quality, or value, which gave to Hitler his Messianic appeal. The savage warrior who is taught to eat the heart or brain of his slain enemy does something more than satisfy his aggressive instinct. In this ritual feast — as becomes truly manifest in the sacrament of Holy Communion — there is a deep core of primitive mysticism. In partaking of a ritual feast there is always the idea of assimilating the essential character of the victim. Primitive piety rests upon a profound sense of the inherent continuity of life. Nothing can come to an abrupt end. Essential quality, or spirit, survives. Hence, in overcoming an enemy, it behoves one to take over his best qualities. In doing so, continuity is preserved and one's own life enriched.

If Hitlerism were wholly evil it could not be human, because nothing human is wholly evil. To be magnanimous in victory is one of Mr. Churchill's great qualities. But even more than that will be needed if we are to exorcize the evil spirit which possesses Germany. We must honour with a fair appraisal that living hope which inspired the workers throughout the length and breadth of Germany to give their faith to Hitler. He promised them production and through production, prosperity. The humble but essential needs of human nature demand a new social covenant. This hope, which Hitler quickened, he betrayed. Our victory will be won on the spiritual field, when we have taken over Hitler's debt to mankind and given it a full and generous realization. It may help to overcome a natural repugnance to the idea of eating Hitlerism when we understand that a psychical assimilation of the vanquished by the victor is an inevitable natural process. In that respect we cannot choose. But the very angels must surely hold their breath when it is being decided what part or aspect of Hitlerism shall be assimilated. The soul of modern man finds neither truth nor safety in deified conceptions of State, Empire or Nation. This negative realization is already evident in the widespread apathy of the German people. But a similar detachment might appear in this country if we do not invoke the essential human principle from which the hope of the German renascence originally sprang. The invisible church which already unites mankind with a secret longing is not based on power-politics, but upon the essential significance of man as the living vessel of God. In order to heal the world-sickness we do not need more and vaster machines, but a fuller flame of individual consciousness. When darkness covers the earth, the passionate individual flame provides the source of the new light.

INDEX

INDEX

Hitler as shaman or medium, 34ff., 38, 101ff., 130, 267
Hitler Speaks, Rauschning's, 34ff., 41, 49ff.
Hitler's ambition, 52ff.
Hitler's anti-Semitism, 27, 29, 30, 47, 48
Hitler's criminality, 104ff., 111
Hitler's emotional technique, 210
Hitler's horoscope, 218
Hitler's origins, 25, 28, 29, 31, 194, 216
Hitler's paranoia, 132ff., 259
Hitler's personal myth, 26
Hitler's sayings, 267ff.
Hitler's two fathers, 27, 29, 30
Holy Roman Empire, 66, 75ff.
Hudson, W. H., 58
Hypnotism, 138, 188

IDEA AS RULER OF GERMANY, 150
Individuality and collectivity, 44
Inferiority, German, 278, 284ff., 291
Inflation, danger of, 133
Initiation, two types of, 44
Insanity, nature of, 39
Integration of the Personality (Jung), 68
Intoxication, German, 28, 38, 103
Introverted intellectual type, 277ff.
Invasion machine, dream of, 258ff.

JANET, 187
Jekyll and Hyde, 109, 209
Jesus and the Messiah myth, 28, 146
Jews and the problem of inferiority, 290
Jung, 22, 40, 51, 52, 54, 58, 65, 68, 78ff., 116, 119ff., 207, 251, 270, 300
Jung's prediction, 62, 65, 66, 73, 75

KANT, 22, 63, 64, 213
Kant's definition of understanding, 22
Kataleptike fantasia, 235
Killinger, von, 178
Kingdom of Heaven, 96, 97, 237
Knickerbocker, H. R., 51
Kundalini tantra, 69
Kundry, 193ff., 232ff.

LAWRENCE, D. H., 111, 170, 176-7, 187
Leonardo da Vinci, 58
Letter from Germany (Lawrence), 170ff.
Lévy-Bruhl, 99
Levy, Oscar, 96
Lilith, 232
Ludecke, K. G. W., 50, 53

MACDONALD, GEORGE, 232
Machiavelli, 43, 212
Machine versus man, 247
Magna Carta, 288

Magna Mater, 297
Mass, docility of the, 279
Mecklenberg legend, 80
Medicine-man, power of, 101
Medium, psychology of, 23, 24, 38, 113, 188ff., 227
Megalomania, 223
Mein Kampf, 26, 29, 32, 34, 108, 162, 198, 226, 291
Mesozoic reptiles, 137, 258
Mikhailowsky, V. M., 36, 37
Moby Dick (Melville), 184
Moses's leadership, 131, 231
Mussolini, 51-2, 117, 125, 131, 134, 135, 185, 256, 260
Mystery cults of antiquity, 40
Myth as psychological hypothesis, 28
Mythology of the Soul, 65

NEBUCHADNEZZAR'S DREAM, 182ff.
Newbolt, Henry, 84
Newman, Ernest, 202
New Order, 285, 300
Nietzsche, 65, 91ff., 158, 184, 203, 208, 213
Nietzsche and Zarathustra, 158, 184, 194, 196, 203
Nothung, 31, 84, 159, 216

OESTERREICH, T. K., 36
Original sin, 239
Oxford Group Movement, 285, 294

PAGAN-CHRISTIAN CONFLICT, 62ff., 75
Paranoidal tendency of German policy, 132
Parsifal, 59, 190ff., 194, 233
Pathological aspect of Hitler's psychology, 49ff., 55ff.
Peer Gynt, 82
Personification of unconscious, 251
Phallic symbolism, 260
Pharisaic mentality, 147, 237ff.
Philosophers of Nature, 63
Poelzl, Klara, 25
Political maturity, 279ff.
Possession, state of, 23, 38, 39, 263
Primordial image, 123, 146
Prussian spirit, 92, 98
Pueblo Indians, 129
Punch cartoon, 209

QUIMBY, 188

RACIAL SUPERIORITY, THEORY OF, 285ff.
Radloff, W., 37
Radowitz, 274-5

INDEX

Printed in Great Britain
by Amazon

42698637R00175